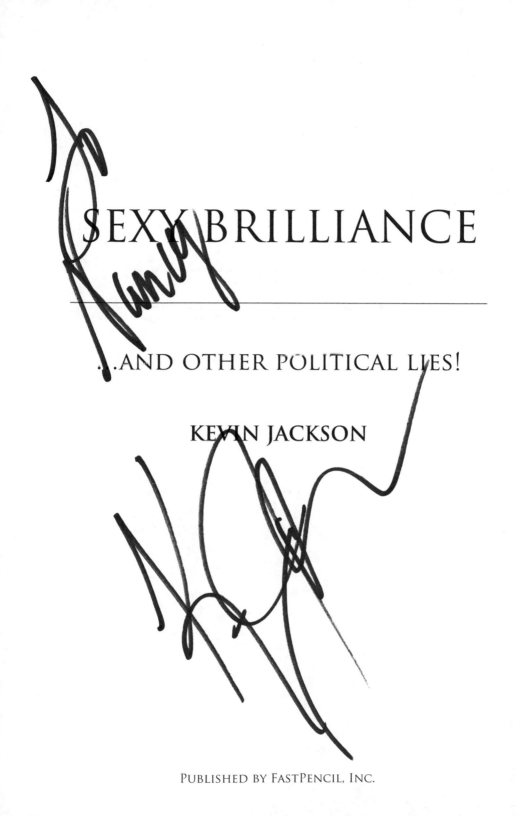

SEXY BRILLIANCE

...AND OTHER POLITICAL LIES!

KEVIN JACKSON

PUBLISHED BY FASTPENCIL, INC.

I dedicate this book to my grandmother who raised me, Adeliade Thompson. God called her home in 2010, and I truly lost my best friend. There are no words that can convey my loss or represent the impact she had in my life. As with Christ and my mother, my grandmother is with me always.

🙠

Acknowledgements

I thank my Lord and Savior Jesus Christ for his blessings, and for giving me the ability to write this book, and giving you the impetus to buy it!

I thank my four sons, Ethan, Rian, Corey, and Collier for being part of my legacy. I am comfortable with the men my older sons have become and for the man Collier will become.

Thanks to Jeannie D'Angelis who writes an amazing blog in a very unique voice. I anxiously await her first book, as Jeannie is a superb writer, and she provided indefatigable help in this effort.

Rachael Williams is one of the most gifted writers and thinkers I have had the pleasure of knowing. I am grateful for her research, ideas, as well as her writing support.

I thank my friends Brad Thomas and Dale Cole for reminding me of whom I am in their own ways. Thanks for showing me that true friendship has no statute of limitations.

I'd like to thank The Black Sphere team of Dave Perkins, Jeremy Buff, Tom Schlegel, Rick Perry, Brandon Vanderford, Marc Reece, Robbin Frazho, Essie Grant, Stacey Carbonel, KJ Adan, Jamie Treadwell, Cynthia Mooney, and many others who have contributed in so many ways.

CONTENTS

Introduction

If you're going to tell people the truth, you better make them laugh; otherwise they'll kill you. – George Bernard Shaw

***

When I think of Obama I ask myself, *"Does this budget make America's butt look big?"* I see a man completely out of touch with the average American, performing an all out assault on achievement. Worse, Obama treats America, not like he's her leader, but more like he's her savior or master.

Professor and political pundit Michael Eric Dyson said that Obama brought "sexy brilliance to the White House." I couldn't help but wonder if Obama had a pet named "Sexy Brilliance," because surely Dyson wasn't referring to Barack?!

Forget political labels for a moment and ask yourself if you're tired of being used by politicians of whatever party. It seems that the government is constantly looking for ways to get something from us, and they have boundless creativity in getting what they want—even when it's not what We The People want. Politicians are about getting our money and keeping their power, and the Obama administration has accomplished this better than all other administrations combined.

Fighting the system is like trying to put a g-string on an alligator, and it seems at times that there is no way to end the nonsense. When did we stop seeing government as a necessary nuisance, as opposed to the cure for all our ills? Perhaps a better question is how have we allowed the Left to infect us with this pathology?

Sexy Brilliance is not another historical narrative, but more of an observational journey; an attempt to widen your perspective, and show what is happening today to continue steal your imagination, dreams, and ambitions.

It's an interesting time to be a black Conservative in America. Black Conservatives may be the only group in America who have Liberals shaking like a Chihuahua pooping peach pits. Black Conservatives get to say what others believe they can't say, or at least that's what non-black Conservatives tell me.

I was discussing my work with a well-known political pundit, and he said to me, "*Kevin if I say what you say, I'd get burned at the stake.*" I found it amazing that a person who has the bully pulpit still feels hesitant to tackle controversial issues. In a *Bizarro World* scenario of the 1960's Civil Rights Era, we find today it is the black Conservative marching hand in hand with oppressed whites in order to get Civil Rights for *all* Americans.

Sexy Brilliance says what is being thought, but not said. This book explores many fallacies of Liberalism, and points the finger at politics as usual. My objective is to teach people how to look for the inconsistencies, the ironies, and of course the hypocrisies of politics; but more importantly, I want to strengthen people's resolve to confront these issues, armed with even more information and the knowledge of what they can do to undo the Change™ that America has been given.

Conservatives are constantly telling me that they are "hiding" in their jobs, afraid to speak out. How many conversations go unchallenged, as Liberals impose their distorted views, based on idiotic logic? Every time that happens, a battle is lost. And after decades of losing small battles, Conservatives have managed to lose the war. *Sexy Brilliance* speaks to Conservatives and non-political people with common sense enough to know that they are being robbed of their rights.

We are at a point in America, where Conservatives need lots of voices. Conservatives need a modern-day version of the Civil Rights movement. Liberals have owned the narrative for decades, not afraid to speak on any subject, and with no retribution. Ask yourself when Liberals have felt afraid to speak up? {crickets}

In a country where the First Amendment of our Constitution guarantees free speech, few Conservatives have the guts to exercise that right. Conservatives act much like the slaves of the past, those who would not dare speak against the Masters. Our Master has become our government.

You can't be against illegal immigration or you're heartless. *Sexy Brilliance* shows you that the Left wants illegal immigration, and not always for the reasons you think. If you don't want ObamaCare somehow you are heartless and racist. *Not so fast.* You can't be against radical Islam or you're an Islamophobe. Find out the underlying reasons why the Left sides with Islam over Judeo-Christian. *Sexy Brilliance* proves how quickly the Left can become Conservative, when homosexuality hits home, for example.

The Left has an exhaustive list of "phobias" for Conservatives and I debunk many of them. *Sexy Brilliance* examines government, the media, Hollywood and all other shrines to the Left in all their colors, religions, sexual nuances, and so on, and holds a magnifying glass of truth for the reader.

One would think that the election of a black president would be vindication of America's ability to overcome whatever horrible past of which the Left is responsible. It hasn't, because the Left loves using all their "isms" to keep Conservatives backing up.

Because it was the left who proffered America's first half-black president, any criticism of him is immediately labeled racist. An intriguing concept, when you consider that the Left got what they wanted, yet America has worsened racially... and in about every other way.

Sexy Brilliance offers real solutions for Republicans and Conservatives, while also being a self-help reference for recovering Liberals. *Sexy Brilliance* enhances what my book *The BIG Black Lie* did: Empower Conservatives[1] to embrace their political identity.

Will Republicans seize the day and capitalize on the failures of the Obama administration? Will Republicans continue to ride the momentum of the Tea Party movement and the November 2010 election and find their way back? Will Republicans embrace the mantra of the grass roots, represent the people, and more importantly follow the Constitution? Will Republicans get serious about attracting youth and minorities?

What will the Tea Party movement look like in the near future? Will the Tea Party morph? Will a leader emerge or perhaps leaders? Or will the Left continue to win the narrative?

Sexy Brilliance will make you laugh at politicians on the Left, but it skewers the Right where appropriate. Parts of the book will have you rolling on the floor with laughter at the insanity of our elected leaders, but the book never forgets to educate.

I hope you enjoy my take on what politicians serve up routinely, as well as the lunacy that brought America *Sexy Brilliance*.

***

[1] It just needs to empower a lot more Conservatives, say 250,000?

1

THE WORST KIND OF CRIMINAL

Paul is an acquaintance of mine and a native of Chicago—the South Side of Chicago; where Bad Bad Leroy Brown got into a ruckus and ended up looking like a jigsaw puzzle with a couple of pieces gone. That was the South Side back in the '70's. It's much worse now.

I enjoy my conversations with Paul. He lives a life that I could have lived as I discussed in my first book. God saw to it that I avoided that life. Paul was not as fortunate, however. The streets got him, and eventually so did the criminal justice system.

Paul reminds me of my Uncle Ray who did time in the joint as well. I have to admit I have a fascination with the lives Paul and my Uncle Ray led. Make no mistake about it, I'm happy I avoided the penitentiary; but there are very few black kids who don't have some level of intimacy with prison; too many second-hand and way too many more first-hand. That closeness to prison life may be part of the allure for young black men.

Paul brings to our talks both street wisdom and the wisdom that comes with Paul having made lots of mistakes. It's difficult to describe, but he brings a rawness that makes our talks fresh every time.

One day Paul and I were discussing his conversion from being a lifelong Democrat to becoming an Independent, and he said to me,

"You know Kev, when I was in the joint, I had a cellie[1] who was a serial rapist. The dude told me that he was the worst kind of criminal, because he would rape a woman, and then convince her that it was her fault."

I said to Paul, "I believe the worst kind of criminal is the guy who rapes a woman, and makes her believe that somebody else did it."

***

It's not whether you win or lose; it's where you place the blame.

I won't belabor the point that slavery was the beginning of black victimization[2], because that's obvious. For almost a century Democrats raped blacks literally and figuratively.

However, there was a time around the 1950's when the Democrats were losing the battle to control black people. Black people were building and growing businesses. We had strong families, and education and character were stressed.

Democrats did all they could to demoralize blacks, with all sorts of onerous rules and laws, even corralling black people into certain urban areas, in an attempt to demoralize us. It didn't work. Back then, black people were strong of body and mind, as fit as Navy SEALs. We relied on our belief in God, and that right would conquer might. We believed in excellence.

Democrats found out that the black "cities within cities" were thriving.[3] Business was booming, as blacks had to be self-sufficient. Some people say this was the unexpected benefit of Jim Crow.

Black kids today might find it hard to believe that there was a time when blacks owned the businesses in the neighborhoods where we lived, which at the time were called "the black side of town." Today the black sides of towns are entire cities like Detroit, Compton, Philadelphia, and Newark.[4]

This independence that was happening in the black community had to be derailed. The policies were in place, like welfare, and so on, however that was not enough. Blacks needed more dependence on government, to see government as their best, if not only alternative to a good life. All that was left for the Democrats to acquire was a boogeyman.

Around the 1960's, Democrats established the profile of the boogeyman. He was that guy who was always trying to help black people by interfering with Democrat policies. Republicans were the guys shooting the rope with which Democrats were trying to hang black people.

"Hey, whatcha doin' shootin' at that Nigra man," Democrats exclaimed. "You OK boy? This hangin' thing we was about to do to you, well that was just bidness; but that Republican, well he was showly tryin' to shoot you, and for no reason!"

There you had it. The Goldwater Effect[5] Democrats began pointing the finger at Republicans as the perpetrators of all past heinous crimes against blacks, and they set the stage for the future demonization of Republicans and Conservatives of today.

***

It took almost a century for Democrats to get all their ducks in a row. It began with Democrats deconstructing Reconstruction.[6] I don't think most people really understand Reconstruction and its impact on the white community, past and present. You read that right, I did say that Reconstruction had a major impact on whites.

Imagine a group of people who had been treated like animals for decades finally getting a seat at the table. Black people literally went from the fields as slaves to Congress in a few short years. There were 21 black congressmen and two senators during the Reconstruction era—all were Republicans. Can you even imagine the discipline that people who were slaves brought to the white community?

And like a man being released from prison because of new DNA evidence, blacks had little animosity about slavery. They were just glad to experience freedom. Because of strong belief systems, black had toughened in all those years of adversity, discipline taught by slavery. Long days with no pay, but actually accomplishing something.

If Reconstruction had lasted longer[7] and the work ethic of blacks had been allowed to permeate Congress, just imagine what the production of Congress would be today. We certainly wouldn't have a group of people who believe they deserve salaries that make them "rich", along with multiple paid vacations, fat pensions, limos, taxpayer funded private jets, federally funded staffers,[8] and war chests that allow them to repeat the process.

Blacks were in Congress to teach whites what it was like to do an honest day's work with little or no compensation, and for the good of the Republic. Democrats weren't about to let blacks ruin the cash cow. Democrats got very crafty and implemented all kinds of legislation to stop hardworking blacks from showing up the white workers. This brings me to a discussion of unions.

***

The growth of labor unions in the US really hit stride just after the end of Reconstruction, because America had a huge labor force, black people, former slaves who had no idea how to price their work. The timing couldn't be worse for the unions with this harder working, less needy labor force hitting the scene.

Unions were fighting for better working conditions, and rightfully so for the time. Issues like limited work days, short work breaks, and certain job protections. Nevertheless, conditions for white workers were nothing in comparison to working conditions blacks had endured for decades. The black worker could potentially set the labor unions back to the mid-1850's. It's easy to see why white folks were unnerved, because many blacks were willing to work under much worse conditions than the unions were under at that time; and they worked like they could be fired at any time.

So whites formed unions that had very discriminatory practices. These unions made sure that the good jobs went to whites, while the "jobs nobody else wanted to do" went to blacks, jobs like cooks and waiters.

Unions continued to discriminate against blacks for some time, until the light came on for John L. Lewis of the United Mine Workers. Lewis understood that in the event the UMW wanted to strike they would have little leverage if a company decided to use this pool of very capable, hard-working blacks.

Union leaders, including John L. Lewis, Walter Reuther, and Sidney Hillman, head of the garment workers union eventually withdrew from the AFL and formed the Committee for Industrial Organization,[9] or the CIO for self-preservation.

Unions formed not to help black people, but to exploit them.

Now Liberals will make the same argument for unions that they have for the racist past of Democrats, which is, "That's all in the past." *Not true.* In spite of the damages that unions have done to black workers, unions take their loyalty for granted. The unions don't even bother trying to keep their manipulation of the black community a secret anymore.

Senior VP of SEIU Gerry Hudson in arguing for the unions support of granting amnesty to illegal immigrants, admits there is a reasonable groundswell against illegal immigration, and he offers this advice to the union leadership in how to deal with problem union members both black and white.

"It doesn't take a whole lot to argue African Americans, at least to another place... not a whole lot. And I've spent not a lot of time doing it, but I've had some success. I think we need to spend more time doing it, trying to find out what's the best ways to get the work done... I think on white workers, I think we've got some real problems. I've spent a lot of time in Wisconsin and places like that where I have heard some of the most anti-immigrant sentiments around. It's also, and this is where you get the black workers first... it's so f*cking rabidly racist... 'til black people get scared."

Where else but the Democratic Party can you insult the people you need so badly and have them keep returning to you? Black Democrats have Battered Woman Syndrome, and their black leaders remind me of Ike Turner smacking up Tina, then asking, *"Why ya make me do dis to ya, Baby?!"*

Hudson was saying that he has black union members in check; however he still had work to do in order to get his white union members to get with the program. The white union members are smart enough to realize the ruse of allowing illegal immigration, and they will have to be dealt with.

Hudson's way of dealing with his white union members is the way Liberals deal with all things: Call them racists.

That's why Hudson was hired into union leadership. Hudson must keep his blacks in check, or else, and he has the added ability to intimidate white union rank and file with proper use of the race card. Hudson was the union's very own Jesse Jackson or Al Sharpton of the SEIU. Hudson's job to point the finger of racism towards anybody who would go against the union, even if that finger points at white union members.

The ultimate goal of SEIU is to grow their membership and income by having a whole new crop of people to take advantage of, in this case mainly illegal immigrants from Mexico. The unions need Latinos, because as Hudson informed, the unions already control blacks.

With Democrats getting 96 percent of the black vote, blacks are now in maintenance mode. The union's strategy must shift, if they don't want to see the continual decline that has been happening in their membership since the '80's. The unions needed a scapegoat.

Niger Innis wrote in Big Journalism that on an NAACP teleconference, Larry Cohen of the Communications Workers of America (CWA) attacked the Tea Party movement, saying the movement advocates slavery, and "*We don't need 19th Century capitalism.*"

Dana Milbank of the Washington Post wrote about the conference call:

Communications Workers of America President Larry Cohentried to make the case that the Tea Party's economic policies, too, are evidence of "hate" in the ranks. "It's an economic agenda that is hateful against workers," he reasoned. "Most of the proponents that we're talking about in this report also renounce things like minimum wage and collective bargaining rights.... Whether it's glorifying slaveryor glorifying a managerial system where workers have no voice, the Tea Party is a throwback."

Leave it to a union Democrat to use slavery as an example given the unions' support of the institution of slavery. Today's union won't admit to condoning slavery, but they do want to take away one of workers most precious rights: The right to vote on unionization. It should be inconceivable to think that unions want to remove the very same right that blacks and women fought to get. Unions want to find a host in every company, then spawn automatically once there.[10]

Along with workers losing their right to vote on unionization, if the unions get their way, workers will be locked into contracts with no ability to vote or retain their right to strike. Workers are currently forced to pay dues or be fired. The union apparently believes that all its workers are rich, because the union has threatened and fined members for exercising their freedom to continue to work during strikes. Maybe they expect Obama to pay their workers' mortgages and car notes.

And like the slave owners of the past, if a "worker" doesn't want to follow the rules, beatings can occur. There is plenty of historical evidence of union thuggery against people crossing picket lines, and against workers brought in to replace striking union workers, both groups just trying to earn a living. Yet it is the unions who act as if they are innocent victims of oppressive capitalist companies.

I suggest that Larry Cohen put down the rocks and put on a robe, because we can all see that he lives in a glass house. Whether it's SEIU or CWA, the truth about unions is they are about union leadership gathering enough people together to become a force for enriching *unionleadership*. The common thread with Liberal coalitions is to pretend that your membership is of one mind, when in fact that is a farce. The objective of the coalitions is to create group-think, even if they have to beat it out of you.

Ken Gladney learned about SEIU beatings first-hand. His union crime? Being black and Conservative.

Unbeknownst to Gladney, he was a union member of Black Liberal Local 13. While vending Gadsden flags at a townhall meeting, Gladney was singled out by two SEIU thugs for not recognizing that Gladney was black, and therefore obligated to be union-backing Democrat. His punishment was an SEIU-style beatdown.

The two SEIU thugs, one black and one white could not have been a better metaphorical representation of the new thug in the White House. It was as if Obama wasn't sure which part of his ethnicity to dispatch to kick Gladney's butt on behalf of the unions. The Gladney beatdown was a warning to all black Conservatives to know their place, particularly since Gladney was the only black at the event.

But the unions have recognized that they can't win this battle with just "blue collar" workers, so their new recruits are now the government workers themselves, as Tim Pawlenty, Governor of Minnesota points out:

Much has changed. The majority of union members today no longer work in construction, manufacturing or "strong back" jobs. They work for government, which, thanks to President Obama , has become the only booming "industry" left in our economy. Since January 2008 the private sector has lost nearly eight million jobs while local, state and federal governments added 590,000.

Federal employees receive an average of $123,049 annually in pay and benefits, twice the average of the private sector. And across the country, at every level of government, the pattern is the same: Unionized public employees are making more money, receiving more generous benefits, and enjoying greater job security than the working families forced to pay for it with ever-higher taxes, deficits and debt.

How did this happen? Very quietly. The rise of government unions has been like a silent coup, an inside job engineered by self-interested politicians and fueled by campaign contributions.

Public employee unions contribute mightily to the campaigns of liberal politicians ($91 million in the midterm elections alone) who vote to increase government pay and workers. As more government employees join the unions and pay dues, the union bosses pour ever more money and energy into liberal campaigns. The result is that certain states are now approaching default. Decades of over-promising and fiscal malpractice by state and local officials have created unfunded public employee benefit liabilities of more than $3 trillion.

Over the last eight years in Minnesota, we have taken decisive action to prevent our problems from becoming a state crisis . Public employee unions fought us virtually every step of the way. Mass transit employees, for example, went on strike for 44 days in 2005—because we refused to grant them lifetime healthcare benefits after working just 15 years."

Sounds like a good trade to me; work 15 years and get health care for life. Many unions get their members a paycheck for life, along with all other benefits, like pensions, profit-sharing and so on. This is like a farmer who doesn't plant a crop expecting to get paid with nothing to harvest. Who wouldn't want that deal? It's the ability to manipulate the system for personal gain, no matter the outcome, like the union's actions during the East-coast blizzard at the end of 2010.

In deadly blizzard conditions, Union workers deliberately slacked off so they could work longer hours and get more overtime pay. A New York City councilman confirmed that the workers responsible for clearing the roads drove with their blades pulled up high, to necessitate repeated plowing of the same areas. In addition to the cost to taxpayers—both in undue wages and lost work for the New Yorkers not lucky enough to work for the city—their selfishness also cost at least one life. The snow forced one Brooklyn mom to deliver her baby in a building lobby, where she waited for nine hours for an ambulance before her baby died. Somebody in the union should go to prison for this fiasco.

Contrast that with the mean private sector that sent people and equipment to Chile to save otherwise doomed Chilean miners? Given the choice on whom I'd depend, unless U.S. Special Forces are involved, give me the private sector.

We have been trained to believe that corporations are cruel and make profits by denying workers basic safety on the job, better working conditions, and so on. In order to stop this capitalist oppression, workers needed solidarity. Once the union served its purpose of getting workers rights, their work was essentially done, so the game needed to change. Recall when companies were offering all types of incentives to attract the best employees? Unions decided that it was not enough to simply have the opportunity for a safe, stable job, but it would get workers a piece of the action. They got corporations to offer sweetened stock incentives, as well as benefits packages, and salaries exploded. The best companies offered child care, telecommuting, flexible hours, and eventually profit-sharing.

It was in labor's interest to be a "good parasite," so the host had to be kept alive and healthy. On management's side, it had to balance the company's financial health against the happiness of the worker. Give them too much, and the future of the company was threatened by the ongoing expense; too little, and workers may strike. Both parties had the company's financial health in mind, as neither would benefit from the death of the source of the money, which is the business itself.

The union was done. Corporate America was onboard, and began sweetening the pot themselves. The private sector offered the union little growth opportunity. The only frontier left unexplored was the public workers' unions.

For many generations the obvious conflicts of interest inherent in such a system made public workers' unions impossible to legalize. Even now they are not legal in about half the states, existing mainly in heavily Democrat-controlled states, such as Illinois, California, Michigan, New York, New Jersey, to name a few. But the conflict is obvious.

In public employees' unions, there is no business to generate money for either party. Labor is government workers. Management is the government's political leadership. Who generates the money? The rube, better known as the taxpayer.

There are no "profits" to be divided up between the "company" and the workers. Therefore there is no natural interest on either side to be economically prudent or practical. There is no natural restraint for either side to try to preserve financial health, as there is no company to keep alive. The taxpayers are just there, helpless cows to be milked, a seemingly endless supply of money which only requires a bit of rhetorical persuasion and the keeping of some secrets in order to access it.

As Jason Ivey[11] points out,

"When the price of a postage stamp goes up, are you getting more for your money? No. If anything, the price of a stamp should go down because we're all corresponding with each other electronically these days... It would be understandable, perhaps, for package and freight rates to rise depending on certain external factors, like gas prices, volume, and other things. But a stamp always rises in price, because efficiency [by the postal service] is not even an objective."

In other words why does the postal service need to look for ways to cut back? They are going to get their money regardless, and there is no competition for sending letters. The cost of sending packages and overnight postage by the government has suffered, because of Fed-Ex, UPS and DHL, who offer competition. The Postal Service has responded with more competitive rates, though most people still prefer private sector alternatives.

Fed-Ex, UPS, and DHL remain the lower cost package transporters, so why can't Fed-Ex, UPS, or DHL carry our letters?

The Fed would tell you it's a matter of national security. The mail could contain "stuff." Well can't overnight packages contain the same "stuff"? The fact is there is no reason for the Fed to be in the business of delivering letters. Fed-Ex, UPS, or DHL would be monumentally more efficient in delivering regular mail, as they essentially do it every day in the form of larger mail called packages. But the postal *union* would have a conniption.
Management is normally an adversary of labor at the negotiating table, again trying to preserve financial health and maximize profits for stakeholders. However this is not the case with government unions. Management is actually invested solely in the happiness of the workers, making them both complicit in milking the rube.

In America, the Democrats are embraced and supported by the unions. Public employee unions make huge donations to Democrat candidates, perform get-out-the-vote work for them, and work hand in hand to get Democrats elected at all levels, city, state and federal. Once elected, these Democrat office-holders are then expected to sit down and represent the taxpayer in negotiations against the unions for pay and benefits? It's pretty antithetical to think politicians would bite the hand that is now feeding them.

Teachers' unions collect union dues that they funnel to Democrat candidates who then insure that teachers get whatever they want in terms of benefits. So today teachers in primary and secondary schools get tenure within two years in some cases. Teachers are not responsible for social security. Teachers generally get the entire summer off. They complain about the pay, but there are many teachers who make well into the $80,000 plus per year range.

The funds for education are earmarked almost 100 percent for public sector education. Private sector education is funded by parents or private benefactors, for the most part. Homeschooled kids receive nothing, and faith-based schools get little to no public funding. Ironically it is the private sector that produces the best students. Meanwhile the worst schools get all the money.
Jon Corzine former Democrat Governor of New Jersey gave a speech once where he exhorted his audience that he would be out there plugging for

them, fighting for their interests, doing everything he could do in his capacity as governor of New Jersey. The bad news is that his audience was not the majority of his constituents, but was New Jersey public employee union members. Not only was the governor not representing the majority of his constituents and the actual employers of the union, but Corzine was actually agitating the union against its employer.

This happens on every level, every day, all across America. Our elected leaders collude with union leaders and happily agree on more increases in the amount of our money these people will get. The unions finally found a self-healing host in the government. Unfortunately they may have milked the cows to exhaustion.

*****

Unions in place and blacks in check, the Democrats dropped the next bread crumb on the trail to socialism, the next crisis—the Great Depression. The Great Depression allowed FDR to sell "new deals," in order to keep America working, but it also solidified the caste system that was in place.

Admittedly there were good things that came from some of FDR's policies, like federally insured banking deposits, the building of dams and hydro-electric plants, and so on. However many of the policies implemented during that time started benign, but have grown into malignant cancers, like the federal Ponzi scheme of social security.

America would be better served if the government opened a casino, gave black folks our Social Securitymoney and allowed us to gamble our 'benefits' in that casino. At least we'd have some fun and we'd have astronomically better odds of getting paid. – Kevin Jackson

The sell of social security was that it would provide a great retirement, and protect the nation's truly downtrodden, specifically children who lost a parent and the disabled. Believe it or not, at the time the Social Security Act was being debated, one reason given not to pass this legislation was that too many old people might retire in order to get the benefits. Now *that's* funny!

When social security began, it was voluntary. Yes, the same thing that is now being demonized—opting out or 'privatizing' social security—began as a promise. You no longer have that option, because the government recognized how good it was to just force you into the system, then change all the rules.

By "investing" in social security, you are in effect making the government a loan at an amazing rate[12] for a lot of years. Your reward is you will get a small payout on the back end, should you live long enough. The actuaries factor those rates into the retirement age, which the government can arbitrarily move.

Social Security was tax deductable on the onset. The Clinton-Gore administration took care of that, removing the deduction for social security. Democrat president LBJ moved social security from the "trust" fund to the general fund, thus eliminating the ability to track the funds. Imagine if a bank moved your money into a big unfunded black hole, and just promised you that the money was there.

Are you beginning to follow the bread crumbs on how the government has been slowly stealing the white man's rights?[13] Yep, the program is racist!

When social security started, most women and minorities were excluded from the benefits of unemployment insurance and old age pensions. Employment definitions reflected typical white male categories and patterns. Job categories that were dominated by women and minorities were not covered by the act. These included workers in agricultural labor, domestic service, government employees, and many teachers, nurses, hospital employees, librarians, and social workers. The act also denied coverage to individuals who worked intermittently.

In 1940 women made up 90 percent of domestic labor, and two-thirds of all employed black women were in domestic service. Exclusions exempted nearly half of the working population. Nearly two-thirds of all African Americans in the labor force, 70 to 80 percent in some areas in the South, and just over half of all women employed were not covered by Social Security.

At the time, the NAACP protested the Social Security Act, describing it as *"a sieve with holes just big enough for the majority of Negroes to fall through."* [14]

When my mother died, my brother and I received social security. It was a pittance in comparison to what it took to raise two fast growing boys. But because my mother worked, we got the benefits until we were each eighteen years old.

Today, though the aforementioned inequities have been remedied, the social security program remains racist, as most black men will never get their benefits.

Many black men don't have jobs and those that do on average do not reach the age of retirement to receive benefits. I'd say it's a blessing that half the black men are unemployed, so we are not forced to donate money to a program that will never pay us back, but it doesn't pay our kids either when we die. The same is true to many black women, who instead of working for a living, rely on government welfare programs. In the event of death, their children don't get the measly social security, and certainly get nothing else, something that is now true for far too many other races as well.

So most of black folks social security money goes to other causes like believe it or not, illegal immigrants. America has Jimmy Carter to thank for providing social security for illegal immigrants, likely just looking for a new group to oppress.

Give a Liberal something easy to exploit, and they strike. *Hey little girl, wanna buy some candy?*

***

Liberals' new victims are illegal immigrants. And the indoctrination has begun. Liberals tell illegal immigrants,

"You are in this situation because of the Republicans. Republicans don't want you here, trying to earn a living, so you can support people back in your country. Republicans are the reason you live life in the shadows, and can't openly contribute to the country you illegally entered."

No, Republicans are the people who want America's immigration laws enforced, as these laws are enforced in all other countries. Republicans see that rewarding illegal immigrants with social security encourages more illegal immigration, and will eventually bankrupt the country. Liberals see enforcing immigration laws as preventing Liberals from having new victims. So Republicans must be stopped, no matter the cost.

To accomplish this, Liberals bring out the big guns, the Sharptons, Jacksons, and the Gerry Hudsons, all vying for the position of HNIC[15] for leading black folks over the cliff. These pimps want those slots, because it pays well.

Sharpton was summoned to visit Arizona to demagogue the law Arizona passed to start enforcing the state and Federal laws against illegal immigration. Sharpton was happy to get the call. *Put me in the game Coach!*

I can only suspect that Al Sharpton sees himself as the modern day "Sojourner *Verdad*",[16] leading Mexicans to freedom via *el ferrocarril subterráneo* –that's "the underground railroad" for you Americans too lazy to have learned Spanish, our soon-to-be official language.

As if Sharpton hasn't done enough damage in the black community, he now desires to spread the cancer of Liberalism to more Hispanics. After all, Mexicans only vote about 68 percent Democrat.

Let's revisit what the pimping of black America by Sharpton, Jackson, Gerry Hudson, and others of that ilk has accomplished for the black community: Per capita, lowest home ownership, business ownership, high school graduation rates, college entrance and graduation rates.

But there is good news as blacks do lead in a few areas, like number of single parent homes, teenage pregnancy rates, abortion rates, unemployment, and blacks in prison, which coincidentally is *not* per capita.

As Thomas Sowell wrote:

The black ghettos of America, and especially their housing projects, are other enclaves of people largely abandoned to their own lawless and violent lives, their children warehoused in schools where they are allowed to run wild, with education being more or less optional.

Only in the minds of Liberals is it appropriate for a man who has accomplished nothing of note in the *black* community to be dispatched to 'help' Mexicans in Arizona.

Who was Sharpton helping? The rancher who was shot by an illegal immigrant? Was Sharpton helping the couple who were beaten and robbed by illegal aliens trespassing on that couple's property? It seems Sharpton was there to help everybody but *American* citizens. I say to the Mexicans, *"With friends like Sharpton, is there a word for sodomize in Spanish!"*

Sharpton was in Arizona to help *criminals*—people who have illegally entered our country and the political criminals who need those other criminals to vote. But for Liberals, like Clinton going to North Korea to free those two female journalists, or Jesse Jackson going to Libya to free hostages, Sharpton is another on the long list of Liberal humanitarians. Forget the 1.2M people who wait every year to enter the US legally. *How stupid arethey!*

My history may be a bit foggy on this, but I do not recall Mexicans being forced to come to the U.S., like say...the African slaves? However, during Sharpton's visit to Arizona, straight from the Liberal's racist playbook, Sharpton hearkened back to the days of civil rights for blacks, saying at the time:

"The Arizona Immigration Bill is an affront to the civil rights of all Americans and an attempt to legalize racial profiling...I am calling for a coalition of civil rights organizations to work with those in Arizona to resist and overturn this state law that violates the rights of Americans in that state."

Prior to going to Arizona, Sharpton compared Arizona's law again to Jim Crow laws of the South, apartheid in South Africa, and Nazi Germany. Sharpton conveniently overlooked the fact that his constant references to the violation of civil rights of blacks, Jim Crow laws, and so on are a reflection of the racist policies of the *Democrat* Party.

Forget that Arizona was merely enforcing the state and Federal laws—laws the Federal government was unwilling to enforce, laws already on the books. According to Sharpton, asking for proper identification by law enforcement when confronting a person accused of violating a traffic law is now considered "racial profiling." Given that America is the melting pot, aren't we all being racially profiled if pulled over for a traffic stop?

Sharpton's beef with Arizona was that it has the *nerve* to enforce its laws? I was certainly confused. There was no logical reason for Sharpton to make a pilgrimage to Arizona, except for Liberals to make something racial out of something obviously non-racial.

Sharpton had no business in Arizona to advocate allowing millions of illegal immigrants to become legal in America, thereby taking jobs from Americans. With reported unemployment in the black community at 31per-cent,[17] allowing millions of illegal immigrants to take jobs from Americans should have been sacrilegious.

If Sharpton's track record of achievement in the black community is any indication, I suggest the Mexicans call the references on Sharpton's credentials, because everything Sharpton touches turns to *ghetto*.

For those who are circumspect, you have to be wondering who is pulling Sharpton's strings. I suspect Sharpton's actions in Arizona were the work of high-level, white Democrat operatives, the Liberal Illuminati. Though Sharpton is not the sharpest tool in the shed, I can't believe he would want for Mexicans what he has helped achieve for blacks.

All that said, there is somebody worse than Sharpton, and that person is Obama. His administration is the one suing Arizona, as we have shut down sovereign US territory, ceding part of Arizona to the Mexican cartels. Is there anybody in America who wants us to become like Mexico? If not, then why do you think Liberals are so accommodating to have the Mexican influx, some say as many as 4000 per day?

"We are not without accomplishment. We have managed to distribute poverty equally."
- Vietnamese foreign minister Nguyen Thatch

***

Social Security isn't the only Ponzi scheme where Americans get the shaft in favor of illegal immigrants. In the state of CA alone, anchor babies cost taxpayers $7.7B per year—just for education. The children of illegals make up 15 percent of the K-12 population—one of the many benefits to being the second largest state as well as the plethora of sanctuary cities that share a border with Mexico. Is it any wonder America's schools have become little more than failure factories.

I first heard the term 'failure factories' used to describe America's public school system when watching the movie, *Waiting for Superman*. The movie explained what we have all witnessed, that over the past few decades our educational system has deteriorated to almost Third World status. It's no wonder given the pressures to teach a very diverse group of people, which now includes illegals. But that's exactly what the Liberals want. U.S. schools are not education factories, but are indeed failure factories. We can't allow "shamnesty" voters to form opinions on their own, so the American educational system creates Liberal group-think. *Drones.*

Liberals owning the educational system didn't happen overnight. It took baby steps. Yet again, we find that the real culprit was Jimmy Carter, the guy who started the Department of Indoctrination, or as it is formally known, the Department of Education.

There are a host of reasons given; however as this report from Freeman documents, these are nothing but excuses for the money grab.

"Many so-called education experts believe that class size—the ratio of students to teacher—must be reduced to improve learning. We've already tried it. From 1955 to 1991, the average pupil-teacher ratio in U.S. public schools dropped by 40 percent.

These experts also proclaim that lack of funding hamstrings reform, and that the 1980s were a particularly bad time for school finances. Wrong again. Annual expenditures per pupil in U.S. public schools exploded by about 350 percent in real dollars from 1950 ($1,189) to 1991 ($5,237). In only two years during this 40-year period did spending fall: 1980 and 1981. Spending grew by about a third in real terms from 1981 to 1991.

The average salary of public school teachers rose 45 percent in real terms from 1960 (the first year data are available) to 1991. This increase masks a more variable trend. Real salaries rose until 1974, when they began to level off and even decline. The average salary reached a trough of $27,436 in 1982, after which it rose to an all-time high of $33,015 in 1991. Instructional staff in public *schools generally saw their earnings increase faster than the average full-time employee—from 1950 to 1989 the ratio of instructional-staff salary to the average full-time salary in the U.S. increased by 22 percent (although it sank from 1972 to 1980). Student performance has hardly kept pace with the dramatic increases in resources devoted to public education. While the percentage of students aged 17 at the beginning of the school year who graduated from high school rose 30 percent from 1950 to 1964, it has leveled off since then. In fact, the 1991 percentage is lower than the 1969 peak of 77.1 percent.*

Evidence from the National Assessment of Educational Progress and other performance measures shows how poorly served America's public school students really are. Just five percent of 17-year-old high school students in 1988 could read well enough to understand and use information found in technical materials, literary essays, historical documents, and college-level texts. This percentage has been falling since 1971.

Average Scholastic Aptitude Test scores fell 41 points between 1972 and 1991. Apologists for public education argue that such factors as the percentage of minority students taking the SAT can explain this drop. Not true. Scores for whites have dropped. And the number of kids scoring over 600 on the verbal part of the SAT has fallen by 37 percent since 1972, so the overall decline can't be blamed merely on mediocre students "watering down" the results.

Only six percent of 11th graders in 1986 could solve multi-step math problems and use basic algebra. Sixty percent did not know whyThe Federalistwas written, 75 percent didn't know when Lincoln was president, and one in five knew what Reconstructionwas."

Simply put, Americans are paying more to get dumber kids. PISA results reinforce that America is losing ground in education despite throwing billions of dollars at the issue.Between what kids are taught in school and what they grow up watching on TV, it's a wonder anyone grows up with any Conservative values. In Sparta kids were 7 before being sent away to be beaten down in training. Liberals begin our kids' indoctrination a full year or more earlier, and by one of the most corrupt groups in the entire country, our teachers' unions.

Instead of training them to love and fight for one's country like Spartans, our kids are being taught that our Founding Fathers were just a bunch of old white guys who owned slaves.

But if you happen to survive the gauntlet of primary and secondary education, the next step is the scam of "Lower Education". There are over 18 million students enrolled at the nearly 5,000 colleges and universities currently in operation across the United States, and most of these bastions of lower education should give rebates to their graduates.

There are some great colleges in the U.S., and I believe that the top students still are products of the American education system. A college education can be worth pursuing for those in highly technical or scientific fields, or for those wanting to enter one of the very few fields that is still very financially lucrative, like Medicine, Engineering, Law, and Business. But for nearly everyone else, the college experience is just one big money-making scam for Academia, sanctioned by the government.

College is being sold as a must have, when in fact it is a 'good education' that one must have. How one acquires a good education is a whole other issue. If academics were to tell you the truth, it is your paper trail that is most important, not necessarily what you learned. If you don't believe me, just look at the sexy brilliance Harvard gave to America.

Most kids aren't even ready for college when they get there, particularly those who are products of government schools. As Freeman reports,

"Another measure of the failure of public education is that almost all institutions of higher education now provide remedial instruction to some of their students. The Southern Regional Education Board surveyed its members in 1986 and found that 60 percent said at least a third of their students needed remedial help. Surveying this evidence of failure among college-bound students, former Reagan administration official Chester E. Finn, Jr., wrote that "surely college ought to transport one's intellect well beyond factual knowledge and cultural literacy. But it's hard to add a second story to a house that lacks a solid foundation."

Yet kids buy into the system. The better perceived the college, the more they can charge. Harvard is therefore better than community college we are told, because community college students don't usually end up with debt. The more debt you graduate with, the more the government owns you. You must become an immediate producer. You are *trapped* into the American Dream. The American Dream has now morphed into the American Nightmare, graduates finding that they are now being pimped by the Federal government.

Ironically, kids are forced to become who the government punishes most —the overachiever. Because the kids now need money, and the pimp is going to get his money. The graduates get trapped into productivity, in order to get those loans paid off. But when the loans are done, don't think the kids are off the track.[18] All that education and hard work just got them off the streets and waiting for the phone to ring.

The call comes when the kids prove that they can produce, and they are assigned wards. One may acquire the shiftless and lazy dude with six kids he won't take care of, as well as the family of illegals who needs an earner. The government will monitor progress, and assign more wards as the graduates continue trying to get ahead.

The system needs them. College is good, but not necessarily for the students and future taxpayers. The concept of college is not to create thinkers, just earners for the government aristocracy.

There is good news though. Students won't have to pay for it all. That $50K a year they will pay for their educations will be offset by financial aid.

U.S. Secretary of Education Arne Duncan visited students at T.C. Williams High School in Alexandria, Virginia and encouraged them to load up on college loans. He told kids that there is [pp] *"lots of money out there for you. Be sure to pick the best college, because the best colleges offer the best potential for your future.*

We have built a system where Americans now owe more than $875 billion on student loans, which is more than they owe on their credit cards. Yet Obama regulated the banking industry. It hasn't gone unnoticed on me that Obama hasn't decided to make burgers from the sacred cow called 'education.'

Since 1982, the cost of medical care in the United States has gone up over 200 percent, while the cost of college tuition which has gone up by more than 400 percent. Is it any wonder that Obama decided to make the rising cost of healthcare a priority over the rising cost of education?

Approximately two-thirds of all college students graduate with student loans, and the Project on Student Debt estimates that 206,000 Americans graduated from college with more than $40,000 in student loan debt during 2008.

After graduation, these students will be greeted with the most anemic economy in their lives, with unemployment in the stratosphere. It is estimated that there are two million recent college graduates who are currently unemployed. In 1992, America had 5.1 million "underemployed" college graduates. By 2008, there were 17 million "underemployed" college graduates in America.

Perhaps America's under-employed graduates represent the 317,000 waiters and waitresses who have college degrees. Or perhaps they are part of the nearly 25 percent of retail salespersons who have college degrees? Let's hope that there is some double-dipping and some of these waitresses and retail persons are part of the 365,000 cashiers who have college degrees. Unfortunately, it is pretty unlikely that there is any overlap with the over 18,000 parking lot attendants with college degrees.

CNN references a survey where a staggering 85 percent of college seniors planned to move back home after graduation last May. Many of these soon-to-be graduates are the kids who voted for "sexy brilliance" in 2008.

I argued with a Liberal who informed me that Obama had created jobs during his tenure, and at the time the number of jobs created was argued to be around 508,000 jobs.[19] What my antagonist didn't realize is the jobs Obama created had average salaries of $9 an hour. It's no wonder that starting salaries for college graduates across the United States are down in 2010.

Don't expect Liberals to inform you that there is now a 100 percent online university which costs substantially less, where teachers have to earn their pay and are not eligible for tenure. As the LA Times reported:

"Undergraduate students pay $2,800 per semester. That pays for as many or as few units as they can manage to take. The average graduate pays less than $15,000 for a four-year degree."

That inexpensive degree may not guarantee that a graduate will have a job waiting after graduation, but she would have just as good an education, a lot less debt, and no pimp.

***

Liberals are fishers of men. They are constantly testing baits. Take Obama's proposed middle-class tax cut. Obama could care less about cutting taxes for the middle-class; it makes for a nice sound bite though.

Obama, like all good Liberals wants *much* more taxation of the middle-class than he will admit. Obama's program is very simply a fishing expedition for the price it will take to buy the middle-class, while simultaneously redefining what middle-class really is. Redefining the middle-class is an absolute necessity, because expectations much be lowered.

Let me explain. $250K is now considered rich, and that's for two people. So really $125K is considered rich for a single person, but not really. For some reason, the government takes an additional $10K off the definition of single and rich, reducing it to $115K. Don't bother asking why. But as long as you stay below $115K, the government will allow you to keep most of your earnings.

What is sexy brilliant about Obama's tax plan is it relied on the middle-class not recognizing that it's their money Obama used as an inducement. According to this report from ABC news, one of the incentives Obama offered was a tax incentive on child care.

In a day when the average "working American" works through August for the government,[20] the least the government could do is take care of our kids. How else can we produce, if we can't get somebody to care for our kids?

This tax incentive essentially would rebate part of your money to allow you to continue to work without the hindrance of your children. The incentive would be limited to people who make less than $115,000. $115K may be rich in Afghanistan; but in America, $115K won't pay Paris Hilton's monthly wardrobe budget.

Another "incentive" in Obama's middle-class fishing trip was a $500 tax credit to match your 401(K) savings. What money is Obama planning to use to match your savings? *Your money*!

This strategy isn't even the slightest bit clever. Government doesn't *create* any money, though they can inflate it by printing more, something Obama has already done multiple times. Think about this in terms of your bank. Imagine the president of Bank of America sending you a note that says:

"Dear Patron, I would like to offer you this new fantastic incentive. If you save $1000, I will give you a credit of $500... using your own money! When you reach the age when you can withdraw your money, I'm going to keep a good portion. Have a nice day!"

A bank CEO would be embarrassed to offer such an "incentive", but the Boy Wonder had no shame, and was actually proud of his new program. Obama felt like he was truly giving back. And most people took it that way. But getting your own money back, and having the government define your "class," makes you a mark.[21]

The "good" that was to come from Obama's incentive was for people to save. If saving is good for ordinary people, shouldn't it work for the government? I did not attend Harvard, and my *alma mater*[22] didn't offer a class in *"Stupid Theoretical Ivy-League Economics 101."* But this does sound like something the government should be doing, saving that is. Put another way, the government should not be spending, particularly when we are broke.

The question the America middle-class should ask is, *"Am I am bass, a crappie, a perch, or acatfish?"* Or perhaps you consider yourself a big fish, a saltwater variety, perhaps a Marlin? Whatever; because a fish is still a fish.

Obama has chartered the boat, has all the gear, and all the *bait*. The bait is our own money. All he needs to do now is find out the threshold for most people to buy into his vision of communism. Unfortunately for him, due the election of November 2010, the price of communism in America has gone up.

Liberals know the cost of the poor, and they have purchased them, though Liberals continue to sweeten the deal. But the middle-class knows not to take the first offer. I expect Obama to do a bait change, look for new incentives. He will go from the spinner lure to blood-bait.

Because of the Tea Party movement, I predict that Obama doesn't have enough bait to make this work. With the national debt cresting $13 trillion, the bait keeps getting smaller and smaller. However, when you consider how Republicans fight however, Liberals may still be planning on fish for dinner.

***

[1]Term used by prisoners in referring to their cell mates

[2]Slavery was also the beginning of the victimization of,

[3]Unlike the ghettos of today which represent most black communities.

[4]The idea that America still thinks in terms of "black side of town" speaks to problem of politics. Black corralled into areas where we can be manipulated.

[5]Goldwater was demonized as racist for not supporting the Civil Rights Act of 1964 on its Constitutionality.

[6]Reconstruction is the period where the US was being pieced back together after the Civil War. It could be called the period of a Black Renaissance, because blacks experienced profound gains during this period, much to the chagrin of Democrats.

[7]Reconstruction lasted from 1865-1877

[8]Harry Reid is said to have close to 100 staffers

[9]Later it changed its name to Congress of Industrial Organizations.

[10]Unions want to pass Card Check, disallowing secret ballots in voting for unionization.

[11]Jason Ivey is a friend of mine who works in TV productions.

[12]For the government

[13]I wrote "stealing white man's rights," because social security has always been stealing from blacks, that is when it wasn't excluding us completely.

[14]As you can see, there was a time when the NAACP actually did good work

[15]Head Negro In Charge

[16]Verdad is Spanish for "truth."

[17]Unemployment in the black community is theorized to be as high as 50 percent.

[18]No longer working a street corner.

[19]The Liberal of course didn't want to discuss the job losses that Obama had.

[20]In order to pay your annual tax debt, you must work through August.

[21]Forget the conspiracy theory that Obama is truly a Kenyan, as I have my own theory. I'm beginning to suspect that Obama may be Nigerian instead, and the kingpin behind those email banking scams.

[22]Southern Methodist University

2

OBAMA BRINGS SEXY BRILLIANCE

Democrats must have worn beer goggles that allow them to imagine charisma in people where it doesn't actually exist. It would certainly explain why Bill Maher and Sean Penn are considered sex symbols for the Left. In the case of Obama, perhaps it was the 2004 DNC speech or two memoirs[1] that had the Liberals dry-humping one another in excitement over the guy. Democrats it seems were looking for someone, anyone, who could epitomize the "anti-Bush." Hillary represented that, and she is equally as incompetent as Obama. Yet Hillary got run over by a Mack truck, because Obama "gave good speech."

Liberals apparently just wanted a snobby, light-skinned black man who could read a teleprompter, head askew.[2] Obama could have stood on stage and read the assembly instructions for an Ikea entertainment center, and the Left would have swooned. They were begging for someone with superficial glitz and glamour to showcase to the world, even if everything underneath screamed worthless. It turns out Liberals' sparkly diamond is just a Swarvoski crystal, as I have seen nothing resembling sexy brilliance from Obama; unless you believe it's a good idea to swat flies with a hammer.[3] Obama made generic promises that were as impossible to define as they were to oppose. After all, who can argue against "hope and change?"

Obama has crushed businesses through over-regulation, yet neither he nor most of his high-level administration appointees have ever run businesses. They have watched as jobs moved offshore because of unions, yet they cater to the union leadership. America has been living in the biggest debt bubble in the history of the world and now that bubble is starting to pop, Obama is spending money like a lottery winner.[4] We are in the longest period of unemployment in the United States since the Great Depression, and Obama's policies actually *encourage* unemployment.

America's Community Organizer in Chief has given us terms like "quantitative easing,"[5] and considers over-taxation of Americans "investments." Would you invest in the current U.S. government? If I were insane enough to invest in the Fed, the only department I'd invest in is the revenue department, aka the Internal Revenue Service. Because they are the "baddest mother shut-yo-mouths" in America.

I would attend every stockholder meeting with my list of scoundrels I want extorted to get my money back. People like Maxine Waters, Jesse Jackson, Charlie Rangel, Barney Frank, Nancy Pelosi, GM, Chrysler, AIG, SEIU, ACORN, Michael Moore, Matt Damon, frankly too many to mention.

Outside of the IRS however, I wouldn't invest a nickel in the Fed. Medicare is broke, Social Security is broke, the Education Department has 50 percent fallout, the Department of Energy is circa '70's, and the military has gone gay!

Things have only gotten worse in America, since we were blessed with what Dyson declares is sexy brilliance. Obama was considered magical for Democrats and for America, so much so that James Carville predicted the demise of the Republicans for decades. Barack's act was just too mesmerizing.

Not any more apparently. Hermene Hartman of the Huffington Post laments in her article titled, *"The Barack Magic is Over and the White House is out of Touch,"*where the title about sums it up.

Conservatives saw the levitation wires and something up his sleeve, so nobody on the Right was fooled. However, Hartman offers this blame for Obama's letdown of the Left:

...the handlers have been successful in turning the first Black president of the United States into a White, male[6], elitist.

Blame whatever side of Obama's ethnicity you want, Obama has *always* thought of himself as an elitist. He finagled his way as president of Harvard Law Review based only on the potential to be the "first" black president of Law Review and not on being the best law student.

Obama's elite status also got him a residence in a posh area of Chicago due to shady "insider" land deal. Michelle got a cushy six-figure "do nothing, except run bureaucratic interference" job on the board of a hospital due to Barack's elitist status as a Senator. How many of us can get a home significantly under market value and our spouse a $300K+ job to do nothing?[7]

Obama campaigned with rolled up sleeves to imply that he was hard working. He talked in nebulous terms, all just to go on vacations and shopping sprees. Eventually even the common man wants to see something tangible accomplished; something that affects him positively. *Don't Ask Don't Tell* (DADT) may satisfy the LGBT[8] crowd, but it doesn't create jobs. DADT does accomplish that campaign promise to demoralize the military. Obama wanted a weakened military that he could eventually replace with a bureaucrat-heavy equivalent civilian "farce." So far, the plan is working.

Obama wanted no war(s), yet American remains in Afghanistan and Iraq. Obama said of America's exit strategy from Iraq, *"There will still be killings, bombings, disruptions... But it's time to leave."* Ironically, we remain there in much the same status as during the Bush years.

If Obama is able to wind down the wars, like our soldiers returning from Vietnam, war veterans from Iraq and Afghanistan will return home only to be heckled by an anemic economy:

HA! You don't actually think you're getting a job, do ya, baby killer!" – The Economy

There are no jobs for our returning heroes. Treasury Secretary Geithner warned that unemployment will go up, before it goes down. Well at least something was going up, because prosperity and morale certainly hasn't.

Obama finally acknowledged that there is a war on terror, but ceased allowing the term to be used. Obama also stopped acknowledging "jihadists", claiming that suicide bombers and the like are not jihadists, because jihad is a legit "holy struggle for a moral goal". Neither Obama's magic words nor his mere presence was going to stop terrorists from wanting to accomplish their "moral goal;"[9] however at least America was free again to call terrorists "terrorists."

As contradiction would have it, in a sexy brilliant move Obama wants to try a terrorist mastermind in civilian court, giving the terrorist all the rights of a US citizen. Obama encouraged the potential building of a mosque near the tomb of 3000 Americans, and called the country that has thousands of shrines to Islam, *intolerant* to Islam.

If Obama possessed any magic, why hasn't he made racism disappear? Gates-gate, where white cops performing their duty are bad guys and racist black professors acting like kindergarteners are good guys; the New Black Panthers case, where white Republican voters are the bad guys, menacing black men curtailing civil rights are the good guys. *Sexy brilliant leadership?*

***

To have enough time to evaluate legislation for its impact on one's life would be a good thing. That's what Obama promised, which is why we ended up with Pelosi famous quip, *"Let's pass the legislation, so we can see what's in it."*

I have one: *Let's elect this knucklehead, then we can see who he really is.*

The Democrats have mastered the art of drive-by legislation. For all of Obama's talk about debates being aired on C-SPAN and the public having five days to review all new bills online before he signed them, the only thing transparent about his agenda is the duplicity.

The guy who said there would be no lobbyists in his administration has emboldened lobbyists so much that they stated openly that there would be *"workarounds"* to the new system. And just like the changes in the tax law every year, the lobbyists are hard at work figuring out how to pilfer the maximum amount of our tax dollars from our pockets and into their clients', our Congressmen's projects.

Liberals decided to have government fix the best health care system in the world transparently by passing the bill so we can then see what's in it. The only thing wrong with our health care system is the government's intrusive involvement. The part of healthcare that the government controls is bankrupt. If Medicare/Medicaid were a private company, it would have folded decades ago. But the government has learned nothing from the failures of Medicare, and in fact has its fingerprints all over the failing parts of private health care.

The fraud that occurs in health care is ridiculous, and not just from $12 aspirins or $6 band-aids. It is the fraud that comes from lobbyists and the politicians they pay off. So insurance is not competitive nationwide, due to insurance monopolies sanctioned by politicians. The government won't allow for tort reform against outrageous jury verdicts either.

The government is the reason we have a broken system, and they are also the thugs running it. In their minds this certainly qualifies them to run another nationalized healthcare debacle.

Instead of telling America the truth about their incompetence and inability to run anything right, Liberals tell us, *"If you don't pass national healthcare, then you are a heartless racist."*

That argument could be impactful when not actually discussed beyond the soundbite. It might be difficult to debate, if you buy into the idea that only minorities get sick and that government runs anything efficiently or effectively. If you believe that, why not let Lindsay Lohan be your designated driver.

Liberals are excellent salespeople, as the cover of every edition of O magazine suggests. I'm not surprised that the Left sells hard. They have passion for their side, wrong though it may be. Being a fighter, I respect a fighter willing to mix it up.

There are many parts to a fight, beginning with the matchup. That matchup is followed by pre-fight hoopla, the time when the back scene negotiations occur. Once the match is made, the promoters start with press conferences, and the hype begins.

"All civilized nations have nationalized healthcare, except America," say Liberals.

Mind Play 101 implies that if America doesn't do what other civilized nations are doing, America could lose it status as "civilized." Thus, those against nationalized healthcare are Barbarians.

The other side counters with, *"Healthcare in America is broken, but I'll be damn if the government can fix it."*

More press conferences, and CNN does a "Healthcare Battle 24/7," as Vegas begins taking odds on the fight.

Ultimately the talking is done in the ring. Or as Obama said, *"That's what elections are for."*

If that's what elections are for, then the nationwide cheering for Scott "41" Brown's victory should have been the death of ObamaCare. Brown should have been sworn in holding a wooden stake, and ceremoniously driven it through the middle of that 2000 page ObamaCare bill, a bill that made *War and Peace* look like a postcard from Rome.

That didn't happen, because the Left doesn't settle fights in the ring; they go one step further. They hedge their bets. They find out who the judges are for the fight and bribe them. The Left had this battle fought and won, before a punch was thrown.

Obama only believes in elections when he can claim that they've given him a "mandate". He likes to remind McCain that he won and that the election's over. Someone needs to remind him that his ego's writing checks that his approval ratings can't cash.

***

If a leader can be measured by the people with whom he surrounds himself and his ability to take their counsel, Obama is as effective as Michael Moore's fitness trainer. Obama's much maligned cabinet is under constant fire, so much so that there are conspiracy theorists who say that his destruction of America is intentional. They say that Obama is simply following *Rules for Radical* doctrine, with Alinksy's rule for most effectively marketing revolution: Pursue an ideology of change.

I would agree that there is some legitimacy to this point, if you agree that Obama's ideology of change is replacing *competent* people with complete *incompetents*. Most of Obama's cabinet picks are either political payback or radicals with whom Obama knew from his past. Therein lies the problem quite frankly. Obama just doesn't have a good pool of resources from which to pick.

The outcome has brought a hodgepodge of throwback radicals, many of whom were Communists closeted since the McCarthy era. Ideologies born of their '60's radical sensibilities, which only recently have they felt free enough to showcase their true nature.

Their incompetence might not be so heinous, if it were limited to four years and could be contained from the rest of the world. However, when the top three people who represent the rest of us to the world have the leader-ship experience of a troop of Brownies, you can see that America is in trouble; big trouble.

Hillary Clinton, Liberal women's icon for achievement has achieved *nothing*. Her resume is laughable on its own merits, and certainly in compar-ison to that of her predecessor, Condoleeza Rice. I challenge anyone to debate me on this. Much like Obama, Hillary's resume is almost complete fluff, and an attempt to create gravitas where none exists.

Hillary Clinton is an embarrassment to America in her foreign policy, so much so that one has to question if any country takes her seriously. Her trip to China had her scolding a Chinese student who struggled with English, because he asked a question about her husband. Her Middle-East jaunt was scarier than Joan Rivers' facelift. And who can forget the "reset" button she gave to the Russians? Evidently throwing a pantsuit over hairy legs doesn't negate the pot-smoking hippie lurking underneath. The sad part is that as incompetent as SoS Clinton is, Biden and Obama are far worse.

As much as we lampoon Biden here in the U.S., he is that much more laughable overseas. Friendly descriptors for Biden are "pompous," and "blowhard," and the British labeled him a useful idiot when he told Israel to "get use to Iran's nuclear weapons." Biden is a veritable endless supply of gaffes, usually outing some Leftist secret, and occasionally showcasing his own "stylings," of which I have chronicled.

However, as much as Biden has been derided by me and others as the village idiot, neither he nor Clinton hold a candle to the foreign policy incompetence of "the smartest guy in the room," the guy many Liberals believe is "sexy brilliant."

Barack Hussein Obama began his series of foreign policy snafus by bowing to the Emperor of Japan. It's ok to perform a subtle bow, while shaking hands, as it shows mutual respect for both countries' traditions. However, a deep subservient bow says, "*kick me here*," and appears to be the message taken by the Saudis and the rest of the Muslim world...ok the entire world.

If Obama's perpetual need to "show his butt" were the only cross America had to bear, then perhaps bowing could be overlooked. However it seems that every time Obama is overseas America *loses* status. This is not because world leaders are conspiring to make Obama look stupid, as one might expect. Unfortunately Obama manages to look like an idiot as a solo act.

He accepted a book from Chavez on the virtues of socialism and which chastised America for being a capitalist nation and the most exceptional country in the world. If the trampling of the U.S. Constitution wasn't enough, Obama joined the likes of Chavez in an attempt to thwart the will of the people of Honduras, as well as their laws in their ousting of their president due to term limits; a likely prelude to what Obama may possibly try in America.

Until Obama turned the lectern over the Bill Clinton in pushing for unemployment extensions at the end of 2010, I would not have believed it possible for a world leader to look more amateurish, than when Obama resided over the United Nations reading the minutes of a meeting. His appearance with other world leaders literally looked like "*bring your kid to work day*" for the United States.

Though I admittedly have chuckled openly at many of Obama's gaffes, I love it most when Obama gets *tough*. It reminds me of how comedian Daman Wayans described what "tough" would be like if you were Mike

Tyson's cellmate in prison, and Mike threatens to "take your manhood." Wayans joked, "*About the toughest thing you could say is* 'For how long?!'"

Obama talked tough with Israel on building settlements, and Israel rightfully and disrespectfully took Obama's manhood by building new settlements. The Iranians were so afraid of Obama's tough talk that they exposed their previously super-secret nuclear facility, daring Obama to do something, which he promptly did, and gave up his manhood.

I can't imagine America seeing Obama's visits abroad as little more than taxpayer-funded boondoggles; a way for Obama to see the world for free without enlisting in the military. *Be all that you can be, Barry.*

Obama's foreign policy mistake was in believing that people in other countries would fall for his rhetoric. However, the world has long been over any hypnotic trance that the election of the first black American president created, as well as his incessant diarrhea of the mouth. They are seeing Obama for what he is, "big hat, no cattle." And despite what the world may think of America, a weak American economy affects the world *negatively*.

The world is finally realizing that the destruction of America is more than teaching just Americans a lesson. As America goes, so goes the rest of the world, only faster. Who else will be there to bail them out, or pay the freight for them in some disaster, economic or otherwise? Who will be their peacekeepers, their bankers, or their largest trading partner?

This time in America requires real leadership, and not somebody who can't choose good people with whom to surround himself.

***

When Obama was campaigning, Democrats were certain that the rest of the world was going to be as helpless to his charm as they were. They bought his promises of ending the wars, closing Gitmo and putting a pot of gold at the end of every. Every peacenik bumper sticker slogan echoed throughout his campaign, "I'm a lover, not a fighter." The Left wanted to "make love, not war" to Obama, so he played on their wants. Then he nuked the daylights out of them.

That is not to say that Obama likes the American military. He sees the military as a necessary and temporary evil, and something that should be scaled back eventually to, well his own private army.

Military people are for the most part black and white in their thinking. Thus Obama believes they won't understand the nuances that are Obama. It is for this reason that Liberals don't get the military vote. Because the military understands that when battling terrorists for example, there is no gray area.

McCain beat out Obama on military votes and on campaign donations, but by a much slimmer margin than Bush had over Kerry in 2004. This may be a sign that the military is beginning to become infiltrated with Liberals.

Most military personnel would have seen right through Obama, but the 2008 version might have figured that even if they were getting a president who wasn't one of them, his push for peace would make their own lives a bit easier. *Makes sense.* And their new Commander in Chief obliged making it easier on them, as most now qualify a lot easier for welfare.

2011, the 10th solid year of war, will give our troops a raise of 1.4%—the lowest in half a century. This according to Obama is on par with average cost-of-living increases in the private sector, as if that were a good thing. This certainly is not the case with public sector non-military jobs which are outpacing their civilian counterparts by leaps and bounds, because the private sector is getting pink slips in droves.

Government union employees got 4% annual raises, almost 300% higher than the military. Maybe if the military unionizes, they'd get a little recognition from the Democrats? I can see it now,

"Sarge, they're shooting at us!"

"Private, do not return fire, that's the infantry's job! You shoot, and we'll be hearing from a union representative about this!"

The military might actually get their votes counted too, if they opt to unionize. The MOVE Act, which was designed to protect the right to vote of servicemen and their families stationed or deployed overseas, was violated in seven states in the 2010 election.

The Department of Justice kept true to their word of only wanting to pursue "traditional" civil rights violations and let the issue drag on well beyond the 45 days prior to election day by which ballots must be mailed, so that tens of thousands of the people fighting to defend our Constitution were denied their Constitutional right to vote.

Convicts on the other hand didn't have to worry about their rights, as ballots were hand-delivered to Illinois prisons. You can't really blame them for it, though. Gotta send a shout out to the Chicago criminals who *didn't* make the big time in DC.

The military however gets put on watch lists, prosecuted for war crimes, and return home to no jobs. Don't feel too bad, because once our fighting men and women retire, they get the right to vote.

***

When black people go on vacation, we usually just take "off." When you take off work, that means you stay around the house and catch up on chores, maybe do a few things for fun in the town where you live, or do like my family did when I was child, visit family.

When blacks don't just take off and actually get a real vacation, it's really not much of a vacation. I mean most blacks consider a vacation going to Vegas for a few days, staying a couple of nights in a hotel. The hotel is important, and it doesn't matter about the quality necessarily. Being somewhere else and somebody else doing something for you is a real treat.

We usually have to leave the kids, though if the vacation is to Disneyworld, then we'd figure out a way for the kids to go, usually driving, regardless of the number of kids Sad to say, but most black folks try to vacation not only from work, but many times from the kids too.

Most of my white friends take real vacations, where they truly get away and for more than a few days. They go to Europe or China, and many take the whole family. White folks don't mind taking the kids because they generally have help with the kids during the year. Both sets of grandparents, uncles and aunts, so white folks don't feel like they must escape their children, as well as their jobs.

That said, black or white, I know of no working person who has taken eight vacations in two years. When you take that many vacations, vacationing *is* your job! But that's how many vacations the Obamas have taken.

Could you start a job and take eight vacations within two year? Apparently Obama had the union negotiate his vacation package. He is living a dream built on the false premise of racism in America. He used blacks to get into the White House, and now he and Michelle act like black royalty. Correction: they act like white royalty.

***

With his new found riches, it's no wonder Obama believes you can spend your way out of debt. He is doing everything he can to prove out the concept. Just don't you to try it. There's nothing sexy about going bankrupt. You'd think the government would realize that if something works poorly in the microcosm (your household budget), then it's usually bad in the macrocosm, (the Federal budget).

When it comes to Liberals nonsense makes sense. Like the election of Barack Obama, where farce met reality. For Liberals, Obama was validation that they were right, and not the "oops we were just joking" that Obama's nomination should have been.

"*See,*" they celebrated! Here is a guy who thinks like us, and he is now the HNIC, as it was important that the Liberals get a black president. Anything less would and it would not be Utopia. Race had to play a part, as guilt could finally be allayed for all Liberals, and the race card could be played even more effectively with a black leader of Utopia.

It didn't take Obama long to showcase sexy brilliance, and the lunacy of the Left. The fact is the Left has been cooking up kooky ideas for decades. Absent McCarthy to keep them in check, they got overly confident. All the signs were there to show that Obama was little more than a bad street magician, but Liberals were happy to pretend not to see where the pea was in Obama's shell game.

Fiction is obliged to stick to possibilities. Truth isn't.– Mark Twain

Obama began his presidency by letting America know the game plan. Spend your way out of debt. So the government set out on a plan that would have landed any of its citizenry in jail had we tried it. Not in office 30 days and Obama had already more than doubled our money supply.

To a Liberal, having twice as much money with the same level of productivity does not dilute the value of money by half. Liberals believe that printing more money just gives you more money. With new found money, it was time for Barack to take Liberals on a shopping spree.

As a black man, what bothers me about Obama is that we finally got a black president[10], and the first thing he did was ruin America's credit. Obama's policies have cost more money than all the white guys before him, and America has nothing to show for it.[11] Don't feel bad if you're thinking, *"There goes the neighborhood."* Or in this case—the country.

Obama can out-shop a rich man's mistress. He bought entire industries: Banking, Auto, and *Poverty*. He had just enough left over to buy the New Black Panther Party and a significant chunk of Mexico.

The Chinese were very publicly agitated at Obama's handling of the American economy,[12] or more to the point—for printing so much new currency, therefore devaluing their investment. Eventually America had to make some tough choices, and thus GM sold Hummer to the Chinese.

Why *not* give Hummers, I mean *sell Hummer* to the Chinese? They *remain* America's largest foreign creditor. I'm fairly certain the Chinese demanded collateral from America, now that Obama has taken our credit score into the low 500s.

"No moah credi fo you, Obama. We need corraterah. You a no a goo invesamen no moah! You maka e rough fo nessa bracka man!"[13]

In the spirit of having 'the most transparent administration in the history of America,' the details of the sale were not disclosed. Who were we to want to know the details of what we were getting for our 60-70 percent ownership in the new Government Motors?

GM had a CEO at the time who had nothing to do with this decision. No, this decision was made by Obama himself. And what did Obama get for the hardworking American taxpayer by *"turning out"* one of the crown jewels of Lady Liberty? The figure being bandied about at the time was $100M. That kind of money is "lip service" –pardon the pun—on the *billions* GM still owed the American taxpayer; it didn't cover the interest on the $50B+ GM owed us. No problem for Obama, however.

Obama spends $100B or so on saving the unions. Then he got the American taxpayer a *rebate* of 1% back—because Obama knows that people like rebates. We like *specials*, real bargain hunters.

Next, Obama cut 121 government programs—note the "bigness" of the number of programs, saving the taxpayers a whopping $17B. This is less than *half* of *one* percent of Obama's gut-busting budget. In case you missed the magic, Obama spent $100B to save $17B.

Here were a few suggestions from Obama for us to cut back and do our part:

"Air up your tires, get a tune up, take stuff out of your trunk, and we can save 15B gallons of fuel in twenty years. Turn down your thermostat (in winter), put on a sweater. Turn up your thermostat (in summer) and wear breathable clothes. And skip a meal every now and then you self-indulgent capitalist infidels. Live like my homies in Kenya, and we can get through this crisis."

The prostituting of GM is subterfuge to get your mind off the money he has squandered on " ... *the industry too big to fail—but did.*"

You'd think that after giving the Chinese Hummers, we could at least keep manufacturing in the US? Just one more roll in the hay for old time's sake? 'Fraid not. Manufacturing for the Hummer will now all be completely in China.

Reuters reports, *"The deal marks the first time that a Chinesebuyer has acquired a brand from one of the struggling U.S. automakers."*

This is the interracial marriage of GM to a Chinese company. Or it could be an African tradition, and we just gave away our daughter? Either way, it's another first for the Obama administration, and further confirmation that we are in the *Era of Brown Underwear*.

Liberals didn't mind much when Clinton got a few hummers, but if Government Motors is going to start selling off American auto designs to the Chinese, it sounds like the taxpayers are the ones on our knees.

Maybe Karl Marx was right? Communism really *is* Utopia. Because the capitalist American taxpayers are getting screwed—and not in that good way. Meanwhile, America's biggest creditor, communist China is the only one getting Hummers these days.

***

Given that type of economic prowess by Obama is it any wonder our money supply is lower than the teets on a pregnant weenie dog? The economy is so bad in fact that not long ago somebody stole the sprayer nozzle off my water hose. I know the thief was a crackhead, likely a former taxpaying American driven to drugs to get relief from this economy.

Obama has created a mutant strain of crackheads. These new and improved crackheads have been nuked by the new Obama economy. What next, will one of them break into my 1970 Ford Fairmont to steal the AM radio?

Obama bragged about the U.S. having a five year low in illegal immigration. It's obvious that Obama doesn't realize that he was bragging on the fact that he has created an economy so bad that people who live on $3.50[14] a day no longer see America as the land of opportunity. How bad can things be, when illegal immigrants are weighing whether to immigrate to Somalia as a possible alternative to America?

Africans are saying, "*No sense going dare; America has bean ruined!*"

Wasn't stimulus supposed to help us prevent this pathetic economy? Yet as soon as the stimulus was passed, Democrats were already out doing *pre-emptive* damage control. Think about that. The Democrats were trying to get ahead of the bad news of what a trillion dollars would *not* do to help the American economy. We were prepared to spend almost enough money to buy Italy, and the White House said that this massive stimulus plan will offer "*no quick fix for the economy.*"

The definition of stimulus is immediate, a jolt, a boost! Yet, over two years later, there is still nothing *stimulating* about the stimulus. The only jolt felt by the American taxpayer was a bump from behind by an assailant that law enforcement is still investigating. All they know is his name is Barry and he loves to vacation. All the Obama stimulus plan had to offer was "size". In the end America has been left unsatisfied and *sore*.

Biden said at the time the stimulus passed, *"We're off and running, but it's going to get worse before it gets better…"*

We were off and running like a herd of turtles. The idea that we could spend a trillion dollars and have nothing *immediate* to show for it is incomprehensible, unless you're a Liberal and resident of Utopia. Utopians are very use to spending money, getting nothing in return, then voting their politicians back into office.

You do have to give this administration credit in their strategy of "Go big and hype it." Then just before approval, start letting the air out of the balloon. I think Obama may have said it best on *Ignoration Day*, when he said that we needed to "lower expectations."

Obama and I agreed for the first time. I already had lowered my expectations on Nov 4, 2008 and again on Jan 20, 2009. My expectations just couldn't go any lower, though my outrage found new depths *daily*, and still does.

Shortly after stimulus was passed, Treasury Secretary Geithner wanted to "move fast" to get his nanny and tax issues behind, and prove to America that he was the right choice for the role. This should have scared us all. When did you ever make a fast financial decision that worked? Snake oil salesmen thrive on you making fast decisions.

I would think something like the American economy would require quite the opposite of moving fast, something more like careful deliberation. Maybe I'm just a stickler, but how about a review of what works, and what doesn't. Not the case in America under ObamaNation; because we were in a *crisis*.

Geithner's apparently couldn't wait to get his hands on Obama's large package, even though Biden foretold that the stimulus wouldn't kick in for quite some time.

Larry Summers, a top economic advisor to Obama offered nothing more than empty rhetoric, when he said:

"So even as we move to be as rapid as we can in jolting the economy and giving it the push forward it needs, we also have to be mindful of having the right kind of plan that will carry us forward over time."

Crisis management is the Liberal's way of "jolting" America into allowing them to pick our pockets. We had been led to believe that they must have the stimulus package in place or America would fail. The Liberals believed so much in their plan, they were actually selling it on the concept that it won't actually do what they say it *should* do. It was really a no lose situation for them. Democrats got what they wanted, and America didn't even get a lousy dinner out of it.

***

Don't think that just because stimulus was a bust, that the job of selling America on Obama sexy brilliance was over. In January of '10, the man who has not had a *real* job in his life and couldn't run a bake sale with "donated cakes" for profit was going to provide ideas on promoting new jobs.

Obama scoured the country asking anybody and everybody for ideas on how to create jobs. No idea was too silly. Just think, *your* idea could have been the one that Obama himself deemed worthy of further consideration, dare I say *implementation*. How did America survive prior to such sexy brilliance?

Our reward for our patience with Obama's ineptness was his commandeering a month of Tuesdays during prime time, so that he could sell us on just how sexy, his sexy brilliance was.

In one such update Obama reported that unemployment had "inched down," I suggest that "millimetered down" described the situation better. And as I wrote in my blog on *Obama's Labor Numbers*, all jobs figures from this administration are suspect at best.

It seemed that every time this administration makes a "bad news" jobs report, the report is later debunked, and we get the "oops now here's the really bad news" jobs report *update* about a week later.

I must give Obama credit, however as he *did* help the economy, particularly small businesses. He took *big* businesses and turned them into *small* businesses. Obama's business-destroying technique gave lots of people the chance to play CEO, as there seemed to be a revolving door of CEOs stepping down from government-run firms. The most recent exit at that time was the CEO of Government Motors, Ed Whitacre.

Apparently the stress of losing $1.2B while simultaneously reporting that GM will pay back $8.1B was as unbelievable as Whitacre's commercials, where he stated that GM was making better cars than Toyota. I'm no Ivy Leaguer, but I find it difficult, dare I say impossible to pay money back, when you are in debt up to your flabby butt cheeks.

The good news about the departure of the CEO of GM was I got the chance to apply Liberal math: Obama *saved* 112,000 jobs at GM. He also created one job, a by-product of Barack and Joe's Most Excellent Adventure, because the plan hadn't even been implemented yet. Let's investigate the *actual* plan, as it debuted at the time.

Obama's plan provided tax incentives for people to fix up their homes; sexy brilliance right out of the broken light-bulb box. Consider that Americans are surviving on financial fumes, and Obama wanted us to go to Home Depot to spend money, so that we can get a very small *fraction* of our money back on taxes.

How is it that America was so blessed to have a man with such keen insight on creating *and* saving new jobs?

I tested Obama suggestion in theory imagining a factory in my backyard. I would need workers and since charity begins at home, my employees would be my family, including two gassy pit-bull pound pups who can give Al Gore a run for his flatulence-flipping money. So we would begin my "not-so-clean, but green energy," environmentally-friendly, methane-producing home business. Think Congress, without the "environmentally-friendly."

All kidding aside, I like the idea of putting up some weather-stripping, insulation, and such, as my house is old and some areas feel like wind-tunnels. However, I just don't see the massive "jobs creation" that will occur from this move. Frankly, Obama's first choice out of the box to help with creating jobs left me scratching my well-scarred head. Did he even read the memo on ClimateGate?[15]

America needs high-tech manufacturing jobs. Obama has no incentives to produce those types of jobs, as the world has jumped ahead of us in manufacturing technology and education. There is nothing happening policy-wise to change this, so nothing sexy there.

***

Obama's economic delusion didn't end with "Green" energy initiatives. His next act of sheer brilliance was to bail out financially strapped states, essentially rewarding incompetence.

I'm from the school of rewarding those who are doing well; however Liberals' War on Achievement prevents this, as they seem to enjoy rewarding poor performers. Liberal states have shown that they have not one ounce of fiscal responsibility, nor the male genitalia to address their real issues, like the drain of illegal immigration on their economies, excessive taxes, excessive entitlements to those who don't deserve them, and so on.

Many of these underperforming states have lotteries, casino gambling, and the highest tax rates in the country, yet they still can't pay their bills. Obama's solution is to give states more money, allowing them to procrastinate further on finding *real* solutions.

Weatherproofing our homes is a good idea; however it doesn't create an industry. Giving money to bankrupt states is not the answer, and I suggest giving money to crackheads would be equally effective. Obama may be the Left's definition of brilliance, but in truth he's a maladroit.

Who asks anybody and everybody their ideas for how to create jobs or for anything? Obama was "hired" to be presidential. He went to Harvard, so isn't he supposed to have the biggest brain and the best ideas? *Exactly*!

What about his Columbia and Harvard friends, all those academics, theoreticians? Where were their Ivy League ideas? Based on execution, one thing we know for sure is either an Ivy Leaguer or a Chicago idiot won the suggestion contest; there is no wrong answer here.

Obama's approach of asking anybody and everybody for potential answers doesn't surprise me. Why should he have to work, when there are other people willing to do it for him? Obama has been carried his whole life, so why can't he just have a suggestion contest? That certainly beats having to understand how to connect the dots of how jobs get created and what policies kill jobs.

Did anybody suggest to Obama that perhaps he should get government out of the way of businesses, and stop over-regulating companies into oblivion? Sure they did, but Obama ignored those suggestions. Government must be involved in Obama's world.

Additionally, how about providing incentives for small businesses to hire, like lowering their taxes, and establishing less restrictive microloans? Maybe Obama could set up incubators that truly help small businesses with real issues like preparing financials and possibly with consulting?

Anybody think Obama will challenge the unions? *Not!*

But Obama asks crackheads and winos to help him make a decision on what to do. Sexy brilliance would be better described as "Junior stole the car and the credit cards, and was headed to Vegas" brilliance.

Oh who to blame? Where is the scapegoat when you need one? I know. It's the Tea Party's fault.

***

Before Obama decided to ask anybody and everybody how to create jobs, he campaigned on the idea that he would *create* or *save* 4.1M jobs. Government doesn't create jobs, as government exists by the good graces of the people or more specifically, our money. And even Alvin Greene[16] knows that if you can't create a job, you certainly can't save one.

Nevertheless, Obama believes that he can create or save, because what government can do is make legislation that causes businesses to jump through hoops in order to serve government. To Obama, *regulations* create or save jobs.

So when Obama began his "green" initiative, and he began visiting companies extolling the virtues of stimulus, he showcased Namaste Solar—a company that created 18 jobs at a cost of millions to the tax payers.

Have you considered what the jobless rate needs to be before you can't get enough money from the taxpayers to pay for the unemployed? Well if you have, you can stop. We've arrived at Obama's destination.

It was calculated recently that if the government taxed the top 5 percent —Obama's target tax audience—100 percent, America could not pay the debt that we have already incurred. Yet Obama continues to spend. Obama may be getting his historical evidence for spending one's way out of debt from Banana Republics with inflation rates in the thousands of percent to support his insanity. Even socialist nations now know that the real solution to economic recovery is to trim the fat, lower the tax rates, and get government out of the way, as I said earlier.

We can't blame all of this on Obama, however. Though we do have two years and counting of *failed Obamapolicies,* prior to Obama's election however, we had two years of a Democrat-controlled Congress who contributed greatly.

At the time of Obama's election *about 1.5 million Americans were getting benefits under an extended unemployment pay program approved by Congress last year.* That would be during Pelosi and Reid controlled Congress.

At the end of 2010 we found ourselves battling over an additional extension of 56 weeks, in a negotiation to maintain the Bush tax cuts. Republicans negotiated to keep what we already have by extending unemployment an additional year and change.

Unemployment benefits began at just 26 weeks. Pre-Obama, Pelosi and Reid you didn't need much longer than that to find a new job. Nowadays, you may indeed need an unlimited timeframe to be unemployed, or as Pelosi would have you believe, *stimulated.*

Steve Kroft suggested in an interview of Obama on *60 Minutes,* that Obama was "punch drunk," implying that Obama was showing no prowess in *any* area of government. There was not one successful area of government that the Obama team can claim, and at the end of 2010 Obama still hadn't fielded an entire team. *When that happens, doesn't the team have to forfeit?*

America's beacon of light from Heaven was just Liberals looking up at the light emitting from the belly of a lightning bug. Even Hugo Chavez recognized Obama's incompetence and called him ignorant. There are a few people from whom you should take no "guff", and a guy named Hugo is one of them. But Obama had to grin and bear it, because what Hugo said was true.

For you Everclear-spiked-kool-aid-drinking, Obama-worshipping, "it's ok to touch my binky", drunk-uncle Democrat racists who voted for Obama, I ask you, *"How many promises does he need to break for you to admit you're a pinhead*?" Obama hasn't saved or created 4.1M jobs. Obama's job creation and saving is so dismal, he now needs to *create* over 10M jobs to get things back to *"mess that I inherited."*[17] Obama's only real jobs plan is for him to keep his.

***

Ronald Reagan, the greatest president in modern times, perhaps history is lampooned by the Left, even though his legacy of his achievement helped Bill Clinton's[18] hillbilly butt become iconic to the Left. Reagan's policies continued into the H.W. years. According to the Left, George W. Bush was just plain dumb, and they had the nerve to compare Bush's grades to Gore's. As it turned out, Bush's grades were better than Gore's, and Bush was smart enough to speak Spanish fluently.

Meanwhile Obama, the man who is said to have brought "sexy brilliance" to the White House won't let you even peek at his elementary school grades. What could be so bad that you won't let me people see grades from elementary school? Even if he had flunked out of his madrassa,[19]

What about his high school grades? There would be no controversy, as we all believe Obama went to school in Hawaii. What could Obama possibly want sealed about that? Needless to say, there are major questions about Obama's records for college. Yet we are just supposed to accept Obama's superior intelligence, because h went to Harvard?

I paraphrase my friend Dave Perkins[20] in explaining intelligence is not an indicator of superior morality. Intellect is a morally neutral tool, able to be used for good or evil. Often the most intelligent people are the most morally misaligned or even the most corrupt people. The Left puts much stock in their mythical intellect, even in their recent campaigns. How many times did John Kerry, Hillary Clinton or Obama say, *"We'll do it smarter"*? Well they haven't.

Liberals believe that Harvard guarantees intelligence, but community college apparently has no guarantees. If this is the case, why are all companies run by Harvard grads? Why are successful companies run by people other than those with Ivy League degrees? Why do so many Ivy Leaguers work for so many graduates not from Ivy League schools, even community college, or how about working for those who have no college at all?

The hypocrisy of Liberalism is so obvious, that you have to wonder why more people don't see it. Conservatives often miss it too. Unfortunately when Conservatives don't miss it, they refuse to rub it in the faces of Liberals.

Just think, sexy brilliance got us Joe Biden as Vice President. That alone should have had Liberal intelligentsia pumping the brakes.[21] Obama's sexy brilliance had him pronouncing "corpsmen," with the 'p.' Maybe Obama should have a "sychologist" study Obama's brain? Or perhaps Obama should have been a pathologist, where they study "corpses?"

We've learned from Obama that you can spend your way out of debt too, and he suggested that "Austrian" is a language. After saying that America should learn Spanish, Obama would later quip that it was "Cinco de Quattro" (The 5th of 4th?) while celebrating *Cinco de Mayo* with a group of students on the fourth of May…*Quattro* de Mayo. George Bush wou not have screwed up that quip, and could have understood the entire event had it been in English or Spanish.

Obama fumbled the ball with this statement, *"On this Memorial Day, as our nation honors its unbroken line of fallen heroes — and I see many of them in the audience here today — our sense of patriotism is particularly strong, "* a comment rivaled only by Joe Biden asking wheelchair bound Chuck to *"stand up."*

The people who got "sexy brilliance" elected are less smart than Obama. MSNBC resident Liberal Chris Matthews *"forgot he was stupid"* when he said, *"I forgot [Obama] was black,"* in referring to what Matthews thought was a transcendental speech by Obama. I guess Matthews didn't believe that black people can give good speeches? Maybe he forgot that the white half side of Obama might have given that great speech?

How elitist and racist was Matthews' comment, and it just goes to show that Liberals are continually looking at color. Would a speech make Matthews forget somebody was white?

Let's pretend for a moment that Obama is actually as brilliant as Obama would have you believe. The reason he got that education was on the backs of Republicans. But don't expect Obama or black Liberals to thank Republicans any time soon. Nor should you expect Obama or other Liberals to attempt to close the racial divide. There's just too much in it for their side for them to do it.

How brilliant is it that Obama has done more to polarize America along racial lines than Democrat racist icon Woodrow Wilson—the Progressive who reinstituted segregation both back into the White House and America? This is extremely shrewd if your plan is to use race as a polarizing weapon. And that is exactly what Obama does. When he's not exonerating Black Panthers who were clearly in violation of others' civil rights laws as the New Black Panthers attempted to beat back the very voters who freed black people in the first place, he's pandering to Latinos, like when Obama turned his henchmen on Arizona for enforcing laws against illegal immigration. It was said that Arizona was racially profiling Mexicans during traffic stops with the upped enforcement. Given the ethnic makeup of Arizona, if the highway patrol stopped pulling over Latinos, there would be nobody left to pull over except non-Latinos passing through.

But don't expect Republicans to begin fighting against Obama by drawing attention to his early onset of dementia. That's just not how Republicans battle. They prefer to let people come to their own conclusions. Why bother establishing the Republican narrative, providing alternative food for thought for America.

Obama is about as smart as Rosie O'Donnell is thin. But the Republicans will continue to let America believe that Obama has sexy brilliance. How smart does that make them?

***

[1] Both of Obama's books were written by Bill Ayers. If Obama's so brilliant, why can't he write his own books?

[2] Obama was said to have been coached to tilt his head upward as he does. It demonstrates power it is said.

[3] There is no reference to Obama swatting flies with a hammer, although Obama did make a big deal about killing a fly once.

[4] Like lottery winners after a few years, America is headed towards bankruptcy.

[5] Quantitative Easing is a euphemism for printing more money. Politicians use these clever terms so you don't realize they are doing things in government that would get your arrested if you tried it as a private citizen.

[6]

[7] In full disclosure, I'd certainly accept it, if anybody wants to give me one to offer.

[8] Lesbian-Gay-BiSexual-Transgender

[9] Jihadists like killing infidels, aka Americans

[10] Obama is technically "halfrican," half-African. Dwight Eisenhower was 25% black, thus could easily qualify as a black president. There were other presidents with sufficient black blood to be considered black presidents as well. Obama is however, the president with the most blood of African descent.

[11] Pardon the pun. We have Obama to show for it… get it?

[12] Private memos show that the Chinese were mad at the purchase of the New Black Panther Party. They felt that America has spent enough on blacks.

[13] No more credit for you, Obama. We need collateral. You are not a good investment no more. You are making it rough for the next black man!

[14] It is estimated that ½ the world's population lives on less than $3.50 per day.

[15] ClimateGate was the name given to the discovering of emails by Liberal climate scientists admitting that manmade global climate change was a farce. They were found to be modifying the data to fit their narrative.

[16] Alvin Greene is the mentally-challenged Democrat Senate candidate

[17] Obama constant reference to the good old days of 'The Bush Years.'

[18] Notice that the Left never credits Reagan when giving accolades to Bill Clinton, yet Obama's issues were "all Bush's fault."

[19] Islamic religious school

[20] Dave wears many hats for me, mentor, radio producer, and cheerleader (he wears what he wants for that role)

[21] Pump the brakes: Term meaning to slow down or rethink things.

3

OBAMA TRIES RECOVERY

Unfortunately for America Obama won't check himself into an institution to treat his disease of Liberalism, though his policies certainly warrant an intervention. Another possibility is Obama is back on drugs; he is an admitted user. I'm not a professional psychiatrist, but I have slept at Holiday Inn Express before.

The reason I have diagnosed Obama as a sufferer of a brain malady is despite what can only be described as the most dismal period in America's history since Jimmy Carter, "Sexy Brilliance" deemed the Summer of 2010, *Recovery Summer.*

The real name for Recover Summer should have been, *"I'm In Way Over My Head Summer" perhaps, or "Above My Pay-Grade Summer."*

I'm not sure what Obama was thinking at the time. However in a Liberal's *vida loca*, record unemployment, record deficits, and the inability to create jobs certainly qualify for celebration. As Harry Reid proclaimed, *"It could be worse."* Harry was suggesting that had we not spent $1T on stimulus, who knows where we would be? Dare I suggest that we would be $1T less in debt?

The Recovery Summer party atmosphere was enhanced, if you considered the threat of a nuclear Iran, the growing threat of radical Islam, the assault on our borders, the looming tax on air through Cap and Trade, and the then promise of DeathCare. As the Chairman on *Iron Chef* would have shouted [pp]: *"Let the recovery begin!"*

Recovery Summer could not have come at a better time, as morale in America during the Summer of 2010 was lower than a homeless man's bank account. Along with all the ills of the economy and the worldwide embarrassment of his administration, Obama gave us Oilbama—the Gulf Coast blackening of the beaches.

To hedge the impending economic disaster along America's southeast coastal communities, Obama suggested that Americans get in their cars and vacation on those oil soaked beaches, likely reminding Obama of Hana's black sand beaches. That will be good for everybody. A little oil never hurt anybody. Swimming in oil would provide a better workout, perhaps negating the need for that more expensive tan.[1]

In spite of all the stolen taxpayer money Obama has tossed into the black hole formerly known as America's economy, the money has done nothing for "working Americans." The man who ran on the *stolen* mantra of hope[2], appears to have robbed many Americans of the very same.

The good news about Recovery Summer is there is always suicide to help you get through it. And what should not come as shocking news, people are enjoying that option, as in *The Time of O*, suicides are up.

Obama may have inherited the worst economy since the Great Depression,[3] however only he can take credit for the dramatic rise in suicide rates —the highest since the Great Depression. During Recovery Summer Americans were offing themselves in record numbers. Thankfully the oil crisis remained the #1 issue of the day or we might actually have delved into why people were giving up on hope and change, and not recognizing all that sexy brilliance.

***

Obviously Congressman Emanuel Cleaver (D-MO) remained high from the toxic fumes of hope and change, as he still believed that Obama could create jobs for black folks in Kansas City after meeting with sexy brilliance. Obama couldn't create jobs for white folks, so how on Gore's green earth would Obama create jobs for black folks? Maybe Cleaver expected stimulus checks for bail bondsmen, "pharmaceutical" salesmen, or barber and beauty shops? He certainly wanted stimulus for a black Democrat politician from Kansas City.[4]

Though unemployment in the state of Missouri was at 9.9 percent at the time, unemployment for blacks in Kansas City, specifically part of the district represented by Cleaver was estimated to be around double the national average, or roughly 20 percent. In fact there is hardly a major metropolitan area in the US where black unemployment does not exceed the national average by *double*. The common denominator for all these cities is they are run by *Democrats*.

Lucky for Pastor Cleaver he was in a congressional district that all but guaranteed he would get re-elected in 2010 and he did. This and other districts like it all over America were gerrymandered when Democrats were in office in order to implement The Negro Project—the project that put prominent pastors in charge of black folks, with the intent of limiting the economic rise of the black population.

Pastor Cleaver returned to Kansas City after his meeting with Obama, as if he were a conquering hero. Upon his arrival, he imparted these words of wisdom about Obama's job creation strategy:

"He [Obama] obviously couldn't guarantee that it would happen, he only guaranteed that he would try to make it happen."

Black people of Kansas City rejoice. Cleaver got Obama to commit to *try. Hallelujah.* That's all that matters to Cleaver and frankly all black Democrats was that Obama *tried.* After all, Obama is a Nobel Peace Prize winner. Though Obama has accomplished *nothing* to earn this prize, at least he *tried.*

In his meeting with Obama, Cleaver obviously bet more on "hope" than "change." Anybody willing to bet on how that strategy of hope pays off for black people wanting jobs in Kansas City?

It just goes to show how useless the Congressional Black Caucus is in really solving the issues plaguing the black community. They are not looking for *results*, just *"trying." Everybody gets a trophy.*

Trying won't pay the bills, and trying without a real hope for success is a fool's folly. Black people need a lot less *trying* and a lot more *"resulting!"*

Cleaver's discussion with Obama on black unemployment in KC was fruitful, however. In order to solve the unemployment issue in black America, these two geniuses decided to *try* to provide *temporary* jobs for black *youths*. It is truly the moronic leading the deaf and dumb.

Cleaver believed that black kids will take $7 an hour jobs, when they can sit at home playing video games and have sex on the public dole? Because those *are* the choices that Democrats have given them. Most can make more money thwarting the system, than these "temporary jobs" would provide.

Cleaver and the rest of the Congressional Democrat Black Caucus act as if the issue of black unemployment is a new thing; like it just sneaked up on them. Well it didn't. They've known about it for years. But these so-called black leaders have passed and continue to pass the buck, as Cleaver explained:

African-Americans and Hispanics missed out on the Industrial Revolution because of race ," said Cleaver, who chairs the Congressional Black Caucus's jobs task force. "We should not miss out on the Green (Jobs) Revolution.

Essentially what Cleaver was saying is, "*It's not* my *fault. It's the fault of white men from the past.*"

I'm inclined to agree. It was the fault of white men from the past. But Cleaver doesn't even have the courage to tell you the Democrats at fault, icons like FDR with The Raw Deal, LBJ with The InGrate Society, and Jimmy Carter with his peanut-brain mentality assuaging his racist guilt. Those three racist Democrat icons are the *real* architects of the demise of the black community.

Cleaver goes on to take a shot at Americans who are tired of carrying the freight for the lazy and those who finance his incompetence, saying this:

People who are looking for jobs aren't going to have boisterous town hall meetings," Cleaver said. "They're out looking for jobs.

Those politically astute townhallers (Tea Partiers) are the real culprits here. Damn them for educating themselves on the issues and stopping the gravy train that has created an entitlement mentality in able-bodied black Democrats.

One of Cleaver's constituents, 20-year old Ronisha Rogers complains that, she *"lacks transportation and child care options to be able to work jobs in much of the metro area."*

Perhaps Ronisha expects America to buy her a car and provide a baby-sitter? Better yet, how about we get her a chauffeur-driven limo and a freakin' nanny?

Cleaver and his ilk are all too ready to pass the problems plaguing the black community on to the taxpayers of America, leaving personal responsibility in the dust. Allow me to suggest this to people in Roneisha's circumstance. Before you get pregnant by some ne'er-do-well, you ascertain if he will be a good father and mate, in it for the long haul. The potential for two incomes gives you a better shot at success in America, than reliance on a government that treats you like its ghetto mistress.

Next, change your circumstances. If you can't get childcare, then rely on family and friends and do what millions of other Americans do in similar circumstances...make it happen. America owes you *nothing*. Believe it or not, there are people who do walk to work or take public transportation, move in with family, and the myriad of other options available to you.

Democrats have destroyed blacks' ability to see a way out, a way to overcome. Democrats did this when they destroyed the family. Democrats replaced the nuclear black family with some government-run ugly hybrid of family that does not work.

Today, black Liberals for the most part live like herds of elephants, the matriarch in place generation after generation, and some rogue male elephant coming along every now and then to fertilize the herd. The good matriarchs keep dying off, leaving a weaker and weaker group of females to lead. And the rogues who are impregnating the herd are more abundant and lazier than ever.

Cleaver needs to stop passing the buck on what has been his responsibility for over 20 years as a politician in Kansas City, and is the problem plaguing almost every major city in American and almost every district represented by a member of the CBC.

Further, Cleaver has been complicit with the rest of the Congressional Black Caucus shirking his national responsibility to help blacks, since getting elected to Congress in 2005. He and the rest of the Congressional Black Caucus should be ridden out one a rail, butt naked and on a razor sharp rail. They have been wholly ineffective, and it's time black people and "Guilters" stop rewarding this type of gross incompetence.

Detractors will ignore their lying eyes, as they drive through major metropolitan areas in their oversized luxury SUV, navigation set on "Urban Black Area Avoidance." Maybe it's time for Conservatives to step up and look for real solutions in black and other minority neighborhoods.

***

In case you didn't realize that we are stupid[5], we have John Kerry to remind us that we are. Kerry suggested that most Americans are incapable of understanding the facts and truth of politics if it's phrased any more complicatedly than "simple slogans".

C'mon, we can't be that stupid—we didn't elect Kerry as president now did we? Since Kerry likes slogans, I thought of one:

"John Kerry: Less electable than the black dude with no job experience!"

John Kerry seems to be condemning an institution that has been owned by Liberals for decades. Further, he is exposing America's educational caste system.

There are two classes in the education caste system. The elites have their schools and the rest of us have ours. Kerry being a member of the elites explained in his statement that there is a group of intelligentsia who are the intellects of America, and the rest of us can't rub two brain cells together. We are too stupid to understand just how fantastic our elites like Kerry, Obama, Pelosi, *et al* are. Biden said the same thing a while back. *"Barack is just too smart."* Barack is indeed too smart…*for his own good!*

Obama pegged my BS meter in a discussion on education, as he attempted to straddle both sides of the issue while being interviewed on *Good Morning America*. In responding to the question of why his daughters are in private school in DC versus public schools, Obama offered this excuse:

There are some terrific individual schools in the D.C. system. And that's true, by the way, in every city across the country. In my hometown of Chicago there are some great public schools that are on par with any private school in the country.

Obama admitted that DC schools are struggling. Yet he took no responsibility for the struggle. Recall that Obama cancelled the Bush DC voucher program—a program that had a proven track record of success in DC for minority students. You can draw your own conclusions on whether Obama felt the children of DC were more important than his promises to the teachers' unions.

Obama knows that public schools in DC[6] are pathetic, which is why his daughters attend private school. And it's not Malia's and Sasha's first foray into *école privée*! They attended private school in Chicago as well.

As for "school choice" in DC, Obama came clean about *his* daughters' school choice in answering a question about sending them to private school:

I'll be very honest with you: Given my position, if I wanted to find a great public school for Malia and Sasha to be in, we could probably maneuver to do it.

That's how an elitist answers a question. Elitist tell you the problem they have avoided in their own lives, but you can't. Obama could have *maneuvered* Malia and Sasha into the top public schools. Sure, and his daughters would be the groupies in a rap video within two years, or pole dancing within five years.

America's government schools fail as many as 50 percent of our children, yet Obama and other Liberals do nothing except provide platitudes for the peons. His daughters get superior educations, avoiding the gang-infested, crime-infested, drug-infested gauntlet of the inferior government schools—the schools where our kids are relegated to attend.

To put education in America in real life terms, consider that a school is in the business of producing scholars; in other words, manufacturing good students.

In the case of our manufacturing analogy, the schools acquires product in the form of students. Think of each grade (grades 1-12) as a stage in a twelve step manufacturing process. You get the raw materials in good shape for the most part, as even children in bad circumstances are redeemable.

It is around the 4th grade when the manufacturing process begins to break down. By the 8th grade or middle-school, the product has begun to become defective. About half the kids are not prepared to continue their education at this point. In other words, our manufacturing plant is losing 50 percent of its product.

Our public schools manufacturing plant could care less. They continue to operate inefficiently and ineffectively, yet they continue to ask for more money. The American public, the taxpayer is the stockholder of the public school system, but has very little voice in it. When the corporation known as the public school system wants more money to run one of the worst businesses in the world, they simply *confiscate* more funding with the help of politicians and the teachers' unions.

Unlike a good manufacturing facility, public schools offer no statistical process controls, nor do they employ manufacturing experts to improve production. They remain content with 50 percent fallout, and continue for the most part to operate in a "business as usual" mode.

I argued this point with a professor at a major university, because he asked me why I blame Liberalism for the destruction of the black community. It was evident that he had never thought about education in terms of the real world, because he had no real frame of reference. In fact he had never worked outside of academia.

In the real world of manufacturing, if you have 3 percent fallout, there would be company-wide panic. Executive would call meetings with quality engineers, manufacturing engineers, plant managers, and they would not rest until they could get to 99+ percent throughput. In the real world, it would not take decades to solve this problem. This is because in the real world, their livelihoods would depend on solving the problems. Not the case in academia. Incompetence and conformity is built into the system.

Teachers can get tenure in as few as two years. Once a teacher gets tenure, it is practically impossible to fire one.

To be clear, almost all public schools are struggling, which is why Obama is saying that public schools are for "other people's 'chirrens'," not the Obama's. It's not like they didn't have enough taxpayer-funded flunkies to help find that "great public school" for Malia and Sasha, or were Michele's 32 suck-ups[7] conveniently unavailable?

Barack Obama has no intention of actually addressing the fundamentally flawed educational system. In education, the teachers' union—the very union who has failed America's children—is owed favors by Obama and all other Liberal politicians, so the system is safe. The teachers' union is free to continue its incompetence.

All systems in America are about Liberal elites providing less for the populace than they demand for themselves. It's no different in healthcare, housing, or whatever. The rules are for paupers, not the princes.

Obama opined:

> *But the broader problem is, for a mom or a dad who is [sic] working hard but who don't have a bunch of connections, don't have a lot of choice in terms of where they live, they should be getting the same quality education for their kids as anybody else, and we don't have that yet.*

And this is not just Obama's issue. The Kennedy's kids don't go to public schools, nor do most of other politician's children. If public schools are so good, then why are there waiting lists at these elitist private schools? Liberals have baked in elitism into the educational system, then they pretend it doesn't exist. They decry Republicans as elitist, as they manufacture a continual batch of their own Biffs and Buffys.

If you read between the lines of Obama's comment, he was saying that America's kids should be going to private schools, just like Malia and Sasha. If only all Americans could be elites, we might not be fat, dumb, and unhappy, and can be sexy brilliant like him.

***

Thankfully religion doesn't have a caste system, or Obama, the Great Uniter might put Islam ahead of Judeo-Christian values. He might imply that Christianity is subservient to the religion of Islam, and also intolerant because we didn't want to build a mosque near the site where 3000 Americans died at the hands of radical Muslims.

You can call me a bigot for opposing the Ground Zero mosque, I don't mind—I've already been branded a racist, tea-bagger for opposing Obama's far-left agenda. It seems that there are many racist, teabagging, Islamophobic bigots out there hiding amongst us, since *Time* cited polls at that time showing that 70 percent of Americans feel the Ground Zero mosque is *"an insult to the victims of 9/11"*.

If Park 51[8] is genuine in their desire to build bridges between Muslims and non-Islamic society, they need to just buy the world a Coke and call it a day, because the mosque isn't going to help matters.

The pacifists on the left are cowering behind freedom of religion as a reason to allow a mosque to be built as a trophy for the greatest achievement of radical Islam on American soil. Liberals only like the Constitution when bastardizing it allows them get away with something that is ethically incorrect. Unfortunately for them, there is already a Supreme Court precedent that would allow us to prevent this martyr shrine from being built.

In 2004, the Supreme Court upheld a 50 year-old ban on cross burning, but only when there is intent of racial intimidation. Without evidence of intent to intimidate, it is still Constitutionally protected free speech under the First Amendment. I imagine Justice Clarence Thomas threw the rest of the justices a major side-eye glance before writing the dissenting opinion, which was pretty much called BS to the notion that burning a cross could be done as a "symbol of group solidarity lacking intent to intimidate."

An argument regarding freedom of speech or freedom of religion is not about common sense and a literal interpretation of the Constitution. In the Kagan-era Supreme Court, it's all about precedent—and in the case of the Ground Zero mosque, the intent to intimidate seems pretty clear.

Everything about this mosque is an in-your-face attempt to raise a memorial and shrine not to the 3,000 Americans who lost their lives on 9/11, but to the murderous martyrs who killed them. Even the originally planned name, "Cordoba House" reveals the mentality behind its construction.

Cordoba is a reference to the city in Spain where in the eighth century Islam dominated what had previously been a peaceful society with a mix of Muslims, Jews, and Christians. Non-Muslims were treated as second class citizens and forced to convert to Islam. Those who refused to denounce their faith died as martyrs, with several religious leaders boldly proclaiming with their last breaths:

"We abide by the same confession, O magistrate, that our most holy brothers Isaac and Sanctius professed. Now hand down the sentence, multiply your cruelty, be kindled with complete fury in vengeance for your prophet. We profess Christ to be truly Godand your prophet to be a precursor of Antichrist and an author of profane doctrine."

The building was to be named after a multi-generational attempt to establish Islam as the only remaining religion by way of forced conversions and genocide, and yet the left still insists that the building of the mosque is protected by the Constitution.

If you think this is really about freedom of religion, I've got a certified copy of Obama's birth certificate to sell you. Apparently, there are a few supporters of the Ground Zero mosque who know that the freedom of religion argument is a losing one. The liberal rag Huffington Post featured an op-ed claiming that the Ground Zero mosque isn't a mosque at all, because the building will feature a culinary school, basketball courts,[9] and a pool, it's an "Islamic Community Center".

Even if we pretend that there is some dramatic difference between a mosque and a community center, the fact remains that there is a Supreme Court precedent to deny the existence of a religiously-oriented structure, if the intent is intimidation.

There's no grey area here. The plan to build a mosque here—especially when there are nearly a hundred mosques in NYC, 20 of them in Manhattan alone—is so incredulous that non-American Muslims don't actually believe that Muslims are behind Park 51.

Prominent Sunni leader Al Masry Al Youm spoke of the "devious mentality" that could drive one to do such a thing, when clearly it will do tremendous damage to interfaith relations. He speculated that the mosque was part of a "Zionist conspiracy" to "confirm a [fictitious] clear connection between the strikes of September [11] and Islam."

While the "Jews did it!" meme doesn't seem to be widespread, the international Muslim opposition to Park 51 is. The Middle East Media Research Institute featured an article explaining that the majority of Muslims don't want or need a mosque near Ground Zero. The Al-Arabiya Director was quoted as saying *"The last thing Muslims want today is to build a religious center that provokes others, or a symbolic mosque that people will visit as a [kind of] museum next to a cemetery."*

While American liberals are busy claiming the mosque must be built not in spite of such opposition but "precisely because of" it, the rest of the world sees that argument for the charade that it is. Even Howard Dean agrees that the 70 percent of Americans who oppose Park 51 aren't Islamophobes or bigots, and have Constitutional precedent on their side in keeping the mosque from being built.

The majority of the world's Muslims who actually do want to practice their religion peacefully and sincerely desire to build bridges do not want a Ground Zero mosque built. If the mosque issue really centers around religious freedom, aren't they the ones we should be listening to?

Then there is simply believing what you see.

In most Muslim countries, Christianity can only be practiced behind closed doors, if at all. Muslim countries allow no religious symbols from other religions, so no Bibles, no crucifixes, no pictures of Jesus, and no Virgin Marys on the dashboard of your hoop-t.

If you are caught practicing "other religions" then you might be treated like Prabhu Issac, where in 2001 Saudi police raided his home after hearing that he might be practicing Christianity. *The* horror!

"The Muttawa [Saudi police] confiscated Prabhu's computer, photo albums, Bibles, songbooks, and all his audio cassettes and videotapes. Fellow Christiansare concerned that the personal files on Prabhu's computer may have contained the names and addresses of other Christianswho often would meet

together in each others' homes to sing and study the Bible. In Saudi Arabia, it is illegal for Christiansto gather together to practice their faith… The Muttawa are constantly on the lookout for foreigners who are openly practicing their faith, including gathering together for religious purposes other than observing Islam."

Imagine if in America there were a crackdown on people practicing Islam, and police raided Muslim homes in America. Nevertheless to hear Barack Obama speak on religion, *America* is the intolerant nation.

The fact that America actually respects the memory of the 3000 people killed on Sept 11 by Muslim radicals, and prefers that Muslims add their one more mosque to the community elsewhere is considered intolerant.

Obama later retracted that statement, essentially saying that he was only speaking about Muslims' *legal* right to put the mosque at Ground Zero, and he wasn't necessarily saying that he was for or against the mosque. That's confusing, so let me put it this way: Obama voted "present."

It may surprise most Americans to learn that Christianity can be practiced in some Muslim countries. In fact, they are so tolerant, in Qatar there is actually one Christian church. There actually may be two Christian churches…if you count all of Arabia. There have been negotiations between the Pope and the king of Saudi Arabia to allow a Catholic church to be built in "The Kingdom."

Based on the Muslims' rules for Christianity, I suspect that church will have an outward appearance more of a US Government "black ops" buildings, with not a clue that the building is a Christian church.

Outside of catering to the infidels who are absolutely necessary to service them, Muslims consider the practice of other religions punishable by *death*. Could it be that allowing these churches to be built is just a way for the Muslims to know where all the Christians are, when the time comes for jihad?

In both Obama's comments and his clarification statement, he failed to mention all the calls to worship for Muslims heard throughout the communities of New York, and other cities, so much so that some American cities more resemble [*insert American-hating, Christian-executing Muslimcountry here*], than they do former American cities.

In Manhattan alone, there are approximately 20 mosques and growing. In Detroit, it's over 300 and counting. But hey, Christians do have one overtly Christian church in all of Arabia, with the *possibility* of one more.

Islam is practiced openly in America, and we allow their Qur'an and other religious artifacts without prejudice. But in Muslim countries, Christianity must be practiced in private, or face penalty of death. Yet it is America who needs to show religious tolerance, according to Barack Obama.

America is going to find itself moving from the cry of racism to the cry of religious tolerance (with a racism chaser) as the major topic of discussion. And we are going to lose this battle, because the Muslims know how to use our laws, the media, and Liberalism against us.

Muslims are students of Liberalism, sitting at the head of the class and going for extra credit. So as they build thousands of mosques, cultural centers, and enclaves in America, they give us a token gesture of one church, or just enough to show their "tolerance." Their laws forbid the spread of other religions, yet we usher in their radicalism at every turn.

History proves that Muslims build shrines as monuments of their conquests. Let us not forget that the "religion of peace" was successful in their destruction of Capitalism represented by the Twin Towers and the lives of 3000 people.

Obama never fully explains his obvious preference of Muslims over Jews and Christians, however others on the Left are happy to explain it to us.

PBS talk show host Tavis Smiley on May 25, 2010 was interviewing author Ayaan Hirsi Ali, a bold critic of radical Muslims and at the risk of a fatwa having been issued against her own life since 2004. Ali was explaining that jihadists *"got into their minds that to kill other people is a great thing to do and that they would be rewarded in the hereafter."*
Smiley shot back: *"But Christiansdo that every single day in this country."*
Ali questioned, *"Do they [Christians] blow people up every day?"*
Smiley's responded, *"Yes. Oh, Christians, every day, people walk into post offices, they walk into schools, that's what Columbine is — I could do this all day long... Here are folk in the Tea Party, for example, every day who are being recently arrested for making threats against elected officials, for calling people 'nigger' as they walk into Capitol Hill, for spitting on people."*

Life as we knew it in America changed forever on 9/11. Some will even argue that it is Muslims who gave America "change we can't believe in." But there is no argument that Liberals did.

But enough is enough. No token gestures of Christianity by Obama will do anything to change the war against Christianity (and Jews). It's past time that we allow anybody to attack Christianity, all for the sake of being tolerant. The religious right is both religious and right.

***

While negotiating deals with those who wish us dead, Obama assured us that he would do *whatever* it takes to protect America. Just don't ask him to torture anybody.

Protecting America and torturing those intent on destroying America are not mutually exclusive. If you won't torture, then you won't do *whatever* it takes to protect America. Such is the contradictory nature of Obama and the Liberals who support him.

Most second-graders know that terrorists will not admit to *anything* without some potential bad outcome? Imagine being caught planning to destroy America with a nuclear or biological attack, and getting harsh interrogation with *words*. Worse yet, even *words* are limited—as the *words* you chose can even be considered torture by Obama. That's right you "sons of motherless goats." You could go to Leavenworth for using harsh words to interrogate someone fanatical about destroying our country.

About the toughest thing with which we will be able to torture people hell bent on the destruction of the United States will be to use Liberal women—a homely bunch for sure—to handle the interrogations. Even with a bad breathed Janet Reno "hoffing" in the face of a captured terrorist, I just don't see him giving up the goods. It's just not the same as getting the crap kicked out of you until you talk. If a terrorist intends to destroy America and doesn't mind dying, then what makes you think you will *coax* the location of his dirty-bomb out of him with a halal Happy Meal and a coke?

It has been discussed that if indeed we could not *coax* the information out of a terrorist who had knowledge of something potentially devastating to America, then the president *could* authorize the use of torture. However a high placed source in the Pentagon said that it's not that easy—nobody wants to be hung out to dry by ObamaNation later for torture, even if it could save millions of American lives.[10] Who could blame a member of the CIA, NSA, the military, or anybody for not sticking his neck out based on Obama's *word*?

Liberals say that torture lowers America's status in the eyes of the world. The idea that protecting our citizens through any means necessary diminishes our standing in the world community is completely ridiculous—superseded only by idea that we should care at all what the world thinks about how we protect ourselves. Is there any discussion here in America about how Germany protects itself? France? Spain? Do I even need to discuss how Muslim nations handle interrogations of those trying to harm them?[11]

Ask a parent what he or she is willing to do to protect their child, and see what answer you get. I will state this for the record, if you were to kidnap one of my sons and I get ahold of you, death would be a reprieve from my torture. I believe most Americans feel identically as I. Sarah Palin named her organization Mama Grizzlies for a reason. Mama grizzlies don't negotiate to save their cubs, not even against papa grizzlies. If you sneak up on a mama grizzly with her cubs, she may not kill you, but you may wish you were dead when she's done with you—no *words* needed.

Left to Obama, we would still be using our tough words with the four Somali pirates who kidnapped a freighter. Thankfully one of America's fighting men, a Navy commander understood that actions speak louder than words. In the tradition of a true military man, he was prepared for the fallout of an unsuccessful outcome. *America 4, Somali pirates 0.*

There is torture happening in *The Era of Brown Underwear*. Unfortunately it is not terrorists being tortured, but American citizens and our sensibilities. Americans are being shown that we no longer matter. That the *world's* view is more important, than how we feel about ourselves—about *America*. We are just part of the collective.

With the torture initiative Obama was promoting the idea that America needs to regain some moral high ground, as if protecting America is an immoral ideal. The fact is America has never lost the high ground. America does not want to destroy the Muslim world, as they do us. So this is yet another example of Obama attempting to reshape something that doesn't need reshaping; he's meddling. Creating activity where none needs to exist. This is what people like him do. They want their hands in everything, yet contribute nothing at the end of the day. Obama has an image of an America that most reasonable people see as foolish.

It took the people torturing Obama in the November 2010 mid-terms for the country to get some sanity back. Obama still hasn't learned anything however, so we will get to waterboard him and his crew again in 2012. The bad news is that we must endure through 2012, and who knows what catastrophes await?

When something drastic does happen, sleep well knowing that Obama *might* give the word to torture the person(s) responsible. Or he might not. For the Left, either way Obama decides to handle it will be considered sexy brilliant.

***

I am asked often by Liberals, "*What good has George Bush accomplished*? I guess the fact that since 9/11 there have been no terrorist attacks on American soil doesn't count for anything with the Left. Many people are quick to say that the US shouldn't be fighting wars in Afghanistan or Iraq, though that argument no longer resonates since Obama is fighting the same two wars.

What about President Bush's policy for Africa? You'd think that Liberal blacks or certainly Hollyweirdos who act as if they care about world affairs would have some interest in African policy...the *Motherland*? Because if blacks and other Liberals did look at Bush's policies in Africa, one major policy initiative being PEPFAR, The "President's Emergency Plan For Aids Relief", they could come to but one conclusion: Bush has done more for Africa, than any other U.S. president in history.

Conversely, Clinton had one of the *worst* policies for Africa. He actually appointed Jesse Jackson ambassador to Africa, which was a dismal failure. Recall that Clinton gave this assignment to Jackson during "The Lewinsky Affair",[12] so Slick was a bit distracted. The 300,000+ African deaths for which the Clinton/Jackson team was responsible rates pretty low, given the larger issue of trying to put the protein-stained, blue-dress wearing genie back in the bottle.

The media was quick to showcase Darfur, Zimbabwe, the Sudan, or Somalia, when mentioning the Bush administration. In other words, pick your African country *failure* then blame Bush, as if he himself is there creating civil wars or captaining Somali hijackers' vessels. But like most Liberals, even when it's proven that a Conservative has done the right thing, they can't give credit without an 'escape clause'.

Said Melvin Foote, president and CEO of Constituency for Africa, a coalition of groups that work to improve conditions on the continent:

"The Bush administration has broadened and deepened U.S. policy towards Africa... I don't know if it got involved for all the right reasons, but once it got involved it realized this was a good thing to do."

What Foote is referring to is the Bush administration's efforts to stabilize Africa's fledgling democracies and combat its daunting health problems, specifically HIV/AIDS and malaria. Since 2003, the Bush administration has provided funding to increase the number of Africans receiving anti-retroviral drugs from 50,000 to 1.4 million, according to Jendayi Frazer, the assistant secretary of the Bureau of African Affairs. The actual number now exceeds 2M.

And for you pro-life Conservatives that felt as though Bush has done nothing for the cause, here's a morsel for you:

"It's probably true that the Bush administration has directed more resources to the African AIDSproblem than did the Clinton administration," said Nicole Lee in a grudging offer of support. But Bush's African AIDS program has been "a double-edge sword," said Lee, executive director of TransAfrica Forum, a Washington-based advocacy organization for Caribbean and African policy. It has been undermined, she said, by the "Gag Rule," a Bush administration policy that forbids foreign non-governmental organizations from receiving U.S. financial support if they offer abortionor abortion counseling."

What Ms. Lee is saying is that Bush tied *strings* to this money. The strings were that the US would not fund the programs, if the funding was used to promote abortion throughout the world.[13] Yes, Conservatives, abortion is not just a US issue, and apparently knowing when life begins was not above Bush's pay grade.

The other thing you should note about Ms. Lee's comment is how she casually mentions that Bush spent more money than Clinton in Africa. It was not that Bush just outspent Clinton, Bush's policies were *effective* in Africa, and not just a needed distraction from the Missus.

So how has The Bush Doctrine that has been so disparaged by the mainstream media benefitted Africa? Let's look at the statistics.

In 1989, there were only three countries in sub-Saharan Africa that were considered democracies by the international measures of democracy: Botswana, Mauritius, and Senegal. Today there are over twenty. These are measured by Freedom House and several other independent groups.

Ask any Liberal knowledgeable about this topic [if you can find one], and they will quietly admit that Bush's Africa policies were an overwhelming success. The real question is why don't the media report this?

The media can't have black folks rallying behind Bush or the Republican Party in *any* way. So just like the Liberals have swept the racist policies of Democrats under the rug, they are doing the same with the phenomenal work done by the Bush administration in Africa.

Most of the world has done nothing but *take* from Africa, a nation teeming in natural resources. And unlike most of the world, the U.S., specifically George Bush has shown compassion for helping Africa, taking nothing. The Liberal hypocrites in America with all their causes just aren't that interested in telling the truth about the Bush policies in Africa.

Given Obama's African background you would think that he would continue George Bush's stellar programs in Africa which have saved millions of lives. But instead of continuing those programs, in what should outrage blacks and gays (gay blacks doubly so), Obama showcased what happens when sexy brilliance gets involved.

Scott Evertz, an openly gay man began as Bush's top adviser in the White House Office of National AIDS Policy and later became senior adviser to Tommy G. Thompson who at that time was Secretary of Health and

Human Services. Evertz stirred up controversy in Bush's base by advocating the use of condoms and AIDS prevention workshops when overseeing the administration's efforts to fight AIDS globally.

Evertz' stance angered the gay rights activists, who were fighting the stigma of AIDS being a sexual disease associated with homosexuality. Bush reassigned Evertz to a position where he could continue to advance the fight in the war against AIDS. In Evertz's place at the White House Bush appointed *another* openly gay federal official and physician, Dr. Joseph O'Neill who, before moving into the White House advisory position was the "Acting Chief of the AIDS Policy Office in the Department of Health and Human Services."

Dr. O'Neill was central to Bush's PEPFAR policy that was initiated in 2003 one year after O'Neill joined the White House Office of National AIDS Policy. Dr. O'Neill assisted G.W. in the fight against AIDS, part of the team that provided medicines to about 2 million people due to his initiative."

I repeat; supposed racist homophobe Bush successfully launched a program that saved the lives of millions of AIDS victims on the African continent. Then Obama stepped in, and unceremoniously fired Dr. O'Neill. Obama then hired Jeffrey Crowley, whose responsibilities, in addition to AIDS were healthcare related and focused on "Medicaid and Medicare policy as they impact people with disabilities and chronic conditions."

Along with diluting the AIDS focus, Obama also reneged on the "sharp increase" in funding for the Global Fund to Fight AIDS, tuberculosis and malaria an organization through which the United States provides funding for the worldwide fight against AIDS. In short, Obama has not taken America's role in Africa a fraction as seriously as George W. Bush, the white guy.

Lucky for Africa, Bush was effective and didn't just rely on sexy brilliance.

***

[1] And that 10% tanning tax!

[2] Jesse Jackson was first to use "hope" as a mantra. Because Obama stole it, Jackson would later threaten to "cut his [Obama] nuts off." Speculation is Jackson eventually succeeded and either

Michelle Obama or the Clinton's are in possession of the nuts. Others speculate that Obama had no naughty bits to begin with.

[3] He inherited this economy from the Congress of Pelosi and Reid, not George Bush

[4] Cleaver requested over $4B late in 2010. Apparently Cleaver believes he is now a white Democrat politician?

[5] If you fell for Kerry's yacht tax story, then perhaps you are.

[6] Public schools in any major city are substandard, and that's being nice. Pathetic is a better descriptor.

[7] Michelle Obama has the largest staff of any FLOTUS.

[8] The group wanting to build the mosque.

[9] If successful, I bet they name the basketball court after Barack Obama.

[10] Translation: ""

[11] Hint: Don't lose your head thinking too much on this one.

[12] Bill Clinton was proven to have had "something close to sex" with Monica Lewinsky, and was later disbarred and verified as an American scoundrel, thus making him a hero to the Left.

[13] One of Obama's first acts as president rescinded this order.

4

DON'T PEEK IN A LIBERAL'S CLOSET

If you are about to open a Liberal's closet, I invoke a Joe Biden-esque warning with these two words for you: *Stand way back!*

Liberals are the most racist, sexist, homophobic, Jewophobic, Christophobic, Conservaphobic, people, and they have other phobias they dare you to discover. Liberals fight for things that will ultimately destroy their own beliefs and are full of contradictions, as I have pointed out.

This may be because, if you happen to discover their two-faced nature, Liberals simply rationalize their way out, accusing you of being what they actually are. The good ones eventually get others to believe the lies. Like the lie that anything Conservative or Republican is evil and racist, regardless of color.

How else could you hate Sarah Palin, unless you have warped sensibilities? You can disagree with Palin's politics, but to showcase the vitriol for the Sarah Palin the woman, there is no excuse. So instead of honoring a self-made woman, and a shining example of womanhood in America, Liberals make women like Hillary Clinton their standard-bearers, and lionize cheating womanizers like her husband. Why not just give them both Nobel Peace Prizes, and call it a day?

Bill Clinton cheated, lied, got caught, embarrassed his wife, his daughter, and the nation, only to get a 3rd term as president. He's already pulling a

Jimmy Carter in the Haitian Relief effort. *"Here he comes to save the day!"* An Arkansas Appalachian-American rodent declared a Liberal hero.

Bill Clinton is not the only high profile Democrat womanizer either. John Edwards cheated on his deceased wife Elizabeth, and he did it while she was dying of cancer. Edwards actually managed to make Bill Clinton look wholesome by comparison. A Republican doing anything close to this would have decency to run in front on oncoming traffic.

John Edwards on the other hand appeared on Oprah, and various other high-profile TV shows to give his side of the story. Edwards might as well had his mistress wait outside his bedroom door, while he mercifully put a pillow over his dying wife's face to speed up what Liberals would have deemed was "an inevitable outcome."

It's just a matter of time before America is subjected to Edwards' mistress Rielle Hunter, a bereaved but perfectly-coiffed Edwards together with love-child, Frances Quinn, smiling out from the cover of [insert Liberal rag here], sharing their story: Our Struggles to Hide Our Love, as The Bill Clinton Chorus sings their new hit, *"It's their private lives."*

Like Eliot Spitzer, the Democrat who humiliated his wife and family by partaking of prostitutes, maybe Edwards too will get a primetime talk show with CNN?

Eventually Liberals will attempt to sell us into forgetting his little transgression, giving Edwards a "solid."[1] The evidence of his sin in the form of the "out of wedlock baby" no longer exists. Edwards just helped a needy child find a father. It's just too bad the child wasn't from the African Congo, as that would have put a nice bow on Edwards' innocent *faux pas*.

***

Congressional Black Caucus member Congresswoman Eddie Bernice Johnson (D-TX) cheated poor black kids in her district out of college funds by funneling thousands of dollars in college scholarship monies to her grandchildren, as well as the college age offspring of staffers. When found out, Johnson paid back $31,000, but maintained that she was depicted unfairly. And so was Bernie Madoff.

Johnson steals from taxpayers, enriches her family and those of her staffers, but she feels she has done nothing wrong. No, she *really* feels like she's done nothing wrong, except to get caught. Because black elitist stealing from black peons is not a crime. And this theory was validated.

No harm, no foul as Johnson was overwhelmingly re-elected to a 10th term in Congress by the same black people from whom she stole.

Johnson wasn't the only scoundrel ripping off blacks, as her entire crew was involved. The CBC raised $55M from 2004 through 2008, with less than $1M going for the money's stated purpose of helping black youth. Don't expect any investigation into that money trail, as that was the payoff from Democrat higher ups, a Pelosi-Palooza.

In the Pigford case, black "farmers" have been awarded billions of dollars for so-called discrimination by the Department of Agriculture. The problem is any black person who ever raised a potted plant could be considered a farmer. Black litigants are cheating to get something for nothing because that is the Utopian way.

Did that pathetic woman who blathered that the election of Obama meant her bills would all get paid get her mortgage paid or her gas tank filled after Obama got elected? Of course not and thankfully so. However, many people like her defined "hope and change" in that way, where they would happily take something for nothing.

Obama did nothing to counsel America that this country is not about getting something for nothing, because he is the patron saint of "getting something for nothing." Nor did he tell them that his plan was to eventually get the half of the world's population living on less than $3.50 a day to a new standard, using the money America's poor thought was earmarked for them.

Obama perpetrates the lie of Liberalism for political expediency. Obama essentially said to that exuberant young black lady, "*Sure Loser, the government will take care of you. You can quit trying, as I will do all the trying for you,*" just like Obama agreed to "try" to get jobs for the black people of Kansas City.

Black people keep waiting on these so called leaders to get them their fix. Blacks keep voting for them, and black politicians continue to steal. But there is always "hope" for black Liberal rubes.

***

Does the CBC have the backs of their black constituents or what? When I first began investigating the Congressional Black Caucus (CBC), I was focused on the congressional districts they represent, and how those neighborhoods are usually the worst in the country. Crime infested, drug infested neighborhoods, with most of the occupants unemployed, on welfare, and by and large wards of the government.

Liberal policies are killing most of America's cities, and millions of American dreams. Liberals are at fault for trying to socially engineer whole ethnic communities, though certainly not for good the constituents. Liberals rationalize their meddling and social engineering guising it as humanitarian.

There are no earthquakes or floods in black communities that have required the amount of intrusion in the black community, yet Liberals are there, experimenting on blacks like Josef Mengele[2] did the Jews in Nazi Germany. As surely as eugenicist Margaret Sanger strategized the demise of blacks, Liberal puppet masters found their black pied pipers in the form of the CBC. And those *faux* black leaders have been leading black people over the cliff for decades. All the puppet masters needed was the system to gerrymander the districts, insuring long, uncontested tenures in Congress, thus keeping these black terrorists in power.

The CBC wields racism so recklessly that it has become more destructive than an atomic bomb. The cry of racism has destroyed whole cities, as it has Detroit. The once proud jewel of Michigan now looks like the epicenter of Hiroshima circa 1945. Detroit has become a perennial hell hole, its future certain, its fate sealed.

As one Detroit denizen put it:

Tons of money and resources were poured into the downtown area, while the neighborhoods of Detroit continued to fester under the contagions of drugs, murder, poverty, homelessness, and hopelessness. Crooked mayors like Coleman A. Young and Kwame Kilpatrick continued to put their own personal profit ahead of the good of the city.

To kill a big city, all you need is a large Liberal black population, a Liberal mayor (ethnicity doesn't matter), and a member of the CBC. Detroit has had it all for decades.

The CBC representative in Detroit is Carolyn Cheeks Kilpatrick. If the name Kilpatrick rings a bell, it is likely because Carolyn is the mother of the aforementioned Kwame Kilpatrick—one of Detroit's scandalous ex-Mayor.

Carolyn's political career began in education. Two years after getting her Master's degree, she would abandon teaching to become a member of the Michigan House of Representatives. She served in the Michigan House from 1979 to 1996.

In 1996 both Kwame and Carolyn would get promotions, as Kwame assumed his mother's Michigan House seat, and mom would go big time, getting "selected" to the US House of Representatives. Carolyn was now a member of the black elite.

Kwame was being groomed for the Detroit mayor role, ultimately achieving that distinction in 2001—the youngest mayor in the city's history, and unarguably one of the worst. Had it not been for his troubles as mayor, Kwame's DNA would have qualified him as the next crooked member of the CBC representing Michigan.

Over the next few years, mom and son would be integral components of the Michigan political machine, Kwame's mom attempting to do what Jackson, Sr. had done for Jackson Jr. in IL. In the end, it is easy to see how this system has crippled Detroit.

$200M+ in debt, 67 school closings since 2005, less than 25 percent graduation rate, an estimated 60,000 vacant dwellings, and Detroit sold one of those vacant houses for $1. One Detroit woman has birthed 24 children at taxpayers' expense. Such is the outcome of almost all the cities the CBC represents.

You might think that members of the CBC come from poor backgrounds, thus their illness of Liberalism was acquired. Wrong; it is innate and part of their DNA.

CBC members rarely moved from the private sector to public office. Most of their adult lives thus far have been spent in some sort of public office, campaign/community organizer role, or they had strong union ties, like Carolyn Kilpatrick.

The most striking irony in my research on the CBC is that many of them had succeeded so brilliantly in America. Like many of their non-black Congressional peers, a great number of the CBC have law degrees, and generally come from wealthy or "privileged" families. Or as described earlier with the Kilpatrick's, many even had parents who were politicians.

Andre Carson (D-IN) is another good example of this, as he fuels the perception that he is a former cop from a tough Indianapolis neighborhood. As it turns out, Carson was raised by his politician grandmother. As a "cop," Carson enforced sales tax collection from local retailers, or what is known as an "excise officer." *Not exactly patrolling the mean streets of Indiana.*

The CBC thrives on convincing Liberal black Americans that they are being held down by somebody who "doesn't look black." But it's not white men ruining black neighborhoods; it's black hoods. Liberal blacks appear to be fine with about anybody representing them, as long as the antagonist is another Liberal black person.

Marion Barry was a crackhead. William Jefferson put his stolen booty on ice. Maxine Waters stole money from the taxpayers, and gave it to her husband's bank. Charles Rangel is a slum lord in NYC, Eddie Bernice Johnson steals black kids college funds. Black Democrats would be better off having Crips and Bloods represent them, because it doesn't take a psychic to know what will be said about your city if you elect a black Liberal politician to run it.

***

Powerful examples of white Democrats like Bill Clinton and Nancy Pelosi directing' blacks to the back of the bus to make room for whites exist, but are rarely examined. Kendrick Meek (D-FL) and Jim Clyburn (D-SC) were cajoled and bribed respectively by their white Liberal mentors and handlers to step aside to benefit white men, yet this is not the way the black community hears it.

Clyburn was offered the newly fashioned, "3rd from the top" leadership position by Nancy Pelosi. All Clyburn had to do to get an extra ration of pig's feet[3] was to agree to step aside, thus ending his bid for the position of minority whip, so Democrat, Steny Hoyer (D-MD) could assume the position of minority whip, the No. 2 Democrat behind Pelosi in the House.

For agreeing to loosen his grip on the minority whip, Pelosi and other liberal leaders threw black man Clyburn a bone—which lodged itself nicely through his nose. The good news is the bone matches Clyburn's well-worn leash.

The simple truth is the left wing of the Democrat Party was in dire need of black support in order to maintain the House majority, as moderates and Independents were fading away like James Carville's hairline. The new token role Clyburn assumed actually made it easier for Pelosi to control the CBC. Instead of having to deal with 40 black Democrats whining three-year-olds, the former Speaker only had to crack the whip on Clyburn's readily accessible back. Clyburn's charge was to keep black folks in check, "by whatever means necessary." Bring the black votes!

How good a fall guy was Meek, the black senate candidate who got whacked Mafioso style...by a {clear throat} friend. It was the first black president Bill Clinton who arranged 'the meet.'[4]

Clinton pressured Meek to drop out of the Florida Senate race on behalf of a white guy named Charlie Crist. Just so you fully understand the significance of this, let me explain it this way. Bill Clinton extorted a black man, Meek, to drop out of the Senate race in favor of a white man and former Republican Charlie Crist, so the white man might defeat the Latino man, Marco Rubio. *How Progressive is that!*

That Bill Clinton is one mean-spirited Cracker, when it comes to oppressing minorities. Black folks won't hear the story told like this on BET, and Latinos won't hear the story explained that way on Telemundo.

The Liberal spin for that situation is, *"Just because you feel a probe in your anus, and my two hands are on your shoulders doesn't mean I don't have your back."*

***

Meet another black victim of America's oppressive society – LeBron James. Asked recently why his Q-Score, a measure of popularity had him dropping from one of the most popular sports figures to sixth from the bottom, Lebron had this to say to CNN:

"I think so at times. It's always, you know, a racefactor," said James.

If you're imagining how one of America's young, black multi-millionaires manages to think of himself as a victim, you only need to look at his influences.

Jesse Jackson informs us that America's potential next black billionaire sports figure is not immune to America's racist policies. Jackson said of a statement made by James' employer, Cleveland Cavaliers' owner Dan Gilbert that Gilbert's *"feelings of betrayal personify a slave master mentality."*

Gilbert's crime was describing LeBron as "narcissistic" and displaying "cowardly behavior," when LeBron very ceremoniously dissed the city of Cleveland in his departure from the team. I don't know if I agree with Gilbert that LeBron displayed cowardly behavior; however there is little doubt that LeBron displayed narcissist behavior.

Anybody witnessing the hoopla surrounding "Decision Day" certainly witnessed LeBron's ego in the display case—likely where he has pictured that "pending" NBA Championship trophy. I know as I watched some of the theatrics around "Decision Day," I couldn't help but find myself hoping Miami would not win a championship during The LeBron Era. After all, LeBron was not demonstrating a real champion's character.

The good citizens of Cleveland didn't deserve to have their town and team torn down in the process of LeBron declaring himself Superman. Championships are won on the court, not on paper or in the minds of precocious twenty-something soon-to-be-billionaires with all the common sense of a person featured on *Jackass*.

There is at least one person who wanted a championship more than LeBron. His name is Dan Gilbert. Gilbert is the person investing his money and passion into what is more than just a paycheck or a trophy. People like Gilbert put their money where their mouths are, and not just for profit, but for the pride of the community.

Winning is a metaphor for people like Gilbert. It's their identity. It defines them. Frankly, it's the air that they breathe. The winner's mentality also defines the American spirit. The idea of taking a lackluster franchise to the pinnacle of success is what guys like Gilbert live for.

That is why Gilbert makes the perfect target for Jesse Jackson. Gilbert is a successful capitalist, and white (bonus). Gilbert is a man who has actually worked for a living, and not relied on the charity of others. Jackson and Gilbert couldn't be more diametrically opposed.

Gilbert credentials: He grew Rock Financial—a company he co-founded in 1985—into one of the largest independent mortgage companies in the country. The company went public in May of 1998. Just over a year later Intuit purchased Rock Financial, and the operation became what is now Quicken Loans. In 2002, Gilbert bought his company back from Intuit, and he continues to serve as CEO.

Jesse Jackson's credentials? Race-baiting for decades.

When Cleveland selected state basketball hero LeBron James in the 2003 lottery, as far as the city of Cleveland was concerned the basketball gods had smiled on the franchise. Ohio's native son re-awakened the American spirit in Cleveland. And in only a few short years, the Cavs made it to the Finals. It was only a matter of time until like the Chicago Bulls, Cleveland would have won that coveted championship; that is if LeBron had thought more like Michael Jordan, than "Mookie" Jordan.

Michael Jordan waited on the missing piece of the puzzle, Scottie Pippen. Six NBA championships later, Jordan remains a household word, long after his departure from the NBA. He will remain a basketball icon and legend decades from now.

Last time I checked victims don't make $14.1M a year—not that LeBron needed a salary since he had received a $90M contract with Nike before he ever played an NBA game. And if LeBron's salary was slave wages, then can I be Gilbert's next slave? It certainly pays better than being a ward of the government, the plight of many of LeBron's black male contemporaries.

Gone are the days when sports franchises picked their players to be part of the community practically for life. Think Kareem, Magic, Bird, Russell. Almost anybody knows the teams for which these icons played.

These days, it's inevitable that you will eventually boo the guy you currently cheer loudly for, because he will be playing for your nemesis. That's sports in the 21st Century. But what has not changed are the fans.

Winning LeBron in the lottery was more than just a draft pick for Cleveland; it was nostalgia. LeBron reminded people of the good ol' days, when players understood that they were more than just a tool of the NBA. Players were family.

The fans may indeed have made LeBron a victim, a victim of a bygone era. But I say, *Liberalism* made LeBron a victim…a victim of LeBron.

There are more million dollar babies that have been created by Liberals, for example the black players on the Rams who said a while back that they would not play for Rush Limbaugh, should Limbaugh purchase the team. With the Rams 0-fer record at the time, my contention was the black players were not playing for the current owner *either*.

Most black football players have no clue about the politics of their current owners, yet they are happy to accept their paychecks. I have worked for many companies, and in the interview process, I have never asked, "*Is the owner of the company a racistby chance?*"

Black football players were supposedly angry with a comment Limbaugh made about Donovan McNabb years ago, when Limbaugh implied that if McNabb were not black, there would have been little discussion of his abilities as a quarterback. Limbaugh opined that McNabb was an average quarterback, unworthy of the big deal being made about him at the time.

Nothing racist there; just an observation, and one with which I and millions of other football aficionados, black, white or otherwise agreed.

Limbaugh went on to say that the NFL needed a black quarterback darling, which is why McNabb got the press he received. This may or may not be true, and again was the *opinion* of Limbaugh. The comment was in no way racist, unless you suffer from a victim mentality, or you are by chance a race-baiting Liberal. The comment was meant to be thought-provoking, and it was. In this time of political correctness, it was an interesting point to ponder. There are no black owners in the NFL, and the NFL had just begun addressing the issue of black coaches, after years of "black coach oppression."

Prior to the coaching issues, there was the black quarterback issue. It had been a theory that the NFL did not want black quarterbacks, since the position of quarterback implied leadership of the team, *ergo* the guy running the show. The NFL back in the day said openly that there were no qualified blacks to be NFL quarterbacks. But black quarterbacks who led their college teams to national championship in college were not good enough to do so in the pros?

Limbaugh shined the light on the idea that the NFL may be practicing that age old Democrat practice of subterfuge, when he asked people to look at the bigger picture, *i.e.* McNabb being selected as the "NFL darling," as yet another apology to racism.

If Bill Clinton had said what Limbaugh said, it would have been considered astute, ground-breaking commentary, and Clinton declared a cigar-toting hero![5] A great Democrat looking out for "that colored fella," and protector the lowly Negro—just like Southern Democrats protected blacks in the past.

However, because Limbaugh said it, Liberals pulled out their race cards *en masse*, and the public lynching of Limbaugh began in earnest. Limbaugh was ceremoniously fired from Monday Night Football, and order restored to Utopia.

Black players, most of whom are from poor backgrounds wanted to suddenly take a stand on by whom they would be owned, a modern day slave revolt. Black players were content not to revolt as long as their masters were Democrats.

Limbaugh is a capitalist, because he wanted to buy the Rams, and not have the government give him the Rams in the form of a bailout, reparations, or otherwise. Limbaugh preferred to buy low and sell high, which implied *improving* the team; the product. That is the definition of capitalist. The Left hates Republican capitalists.

A man who has built an empire, arguably the most successful radio talk show ever shows interest in an under-performing team, and the black players painted him as a racist—as if they could actually *spot* one.

Limbaugh is a winner, pure and simple, and an old school winner at that. Limbaugh has more in common with those black athletes than any owner for which they have played or the white racist Democrats who are always so ready to speak on behalf of blacks. Limbaugh knows the value of training and preparation, so that you are ready for the game.

The black players in the league should have taken a page from The Dixie Chicks, and just *shut up and play.*

***

America's victims are not limited to our precocious black millionaires. Victimization by America is a global issue it would seem. Liberals believe you can enter our country illegally, then expect us to write laws to protect you. *Son usted estupido, hombre*?![6]

The irony that illegal immigrants can march against America, *in* America is a great reminder of American exceptionalism. America is so great a country that immigrants are willing to leave their homes to get here. It's tough to get me to leave my home to go to a movie, much less to another country. Think about what it would take for you to abandon all your possessions, your way of life, your family and friends, to go to another country to live.

In the old days, immigrants were escaping oppressive governments in order to get to the U.S. to find the American Dream, for *opportunity and mostlylegally*. More recently however many immigrants now come to America for the *opportunity* to drain our system. And they are being *invited* to do so by the Left.

Mexicans are flooding into America, because their country can't provide opportunity. Why remain in Mexico *working* for a living, when you can come to the U.S. and get exponentially more for free. Free housing, free food, free cell phone, free car, and have access to the best medical system in the world...for free!

Would anybody in their right mind want to immigrate to Mexico for their definition of "opportunity?" Mexico has no jobs, abject poverty, drug lords, and a government more corrupt than our own Congressional Black Caucus. No wonder Mexican citizens are saying "*Hasta la vista, Baby!*" And so is about every other immigrant population.

Mexicans could head south into South and Central America for their opportunity. But they don't. They immigrate north to America, where opportunity exists. South and Central Americans march right through Mexico to immigrate, usually illegally into the U.S. You'd think that a few of them would stop along the way and say, "*You know, I think I will stay in*

Mexico City or Acapulco... it's not so bad here!" But they do not. They continue marching towards the "tyranny of the U.S."

It is this illegal influx that has caused American citizens to say enough is enough. This issue is about enforcing America's laws, and not allowing the false issue of "foreigners doing jobs Americans don't want" rule the day.

At present unemployment rates, Americans are certainly more willing than in the past to consider any job. There are many examples of ICE raids that have occurred where illegal immigrants were deported, and the next day American citizens were lined up to accept these so-called "jobs Americans don't want." A convenient excuse for the Left to use to allow approximately 20M illegal residents the opportunity to vote Democrat.

Adding insult to insanity, Al *"Where's the Camera"* Sharpton compares America's lack of enforcement of our laws to Apartheid in South Africa.

Sharpton wants you to believe that a group of non-Africans, the *Dutch,* oppressing the indigenous people of Africa, the *Africans* is parallel to what is happening to Mexicans who have illegally come to America?

Illegals entering out country should have no rights, except to be treated humanely and shipped back to the apparently miserable countries they left. However because of the ignorant Left in this country, illegal immigrants expect to be treated better than our citizens and ironically are.

Non-citizens of the U.S. are demanding rights that would not be availed to U.S. citizens in similar circumstances in other countries. There is never a discussion of the process of immigration into other countries by people from the U.S., when the Left is arguing shamnesty. When was the last time somebody from America entered other countries illegally? I seem to recall the two female reporters who entered North Korea and were jailed! It made worldwide news, because the journalist claimed they were not in North Korea, just near the border, and also because Americans enter countries legally for the most part.

In the case of those two female journalists, it took a former U.S. president to obtain their release. Do you think Calderon or any other presidential figure from around the world has to come to America to free their citizens from our jails from serving harsh sentences from being in or near our borders illegally?

Not that anybody would want to, but to expatriate to Mexico is both complicated and *astounding. Illegal entry into Mexico will get you two years in a Mexican prison, where I'm sure you can demand your rights. I'm sure there will be thousands of Americans illegally residing in Mexico to protest in the streets on your behalf too.*

Immigration into any country is difficult to say the least, and enforced; however Obama is upset by the enforcement of our immigration laws. The man who swore to uphold the Constitution of the U.S. publicly burns the document.

Americans for the most part seem to love living in our definition of America. I have never seen a group of Americans marching for their "rights" to reside illegally in another country. We visit, have a few lattes, then head back to our Motherland, America. We don't want to change anything, when we go to other countries. Yet when immigrants get here, they seem to want to "change" America to fit them to what they just left.

Which is it, America is exceptional and everybody wants to be here? Or America is "the bully of the world," and everybody *still* wants to be here?

I say this to all illegal immigrants in America, "If you don't like America, take your butts home!" I don't care if you *"do the jobs that Americans don't want to do"*, not that I believe that Liberal nonsense. I understand that without illegals the costs for my goods and services likely will rise, as I did see *"A Day Without a Mexican."* I'll pay more.

Ask a Liberal to name a single country that doesn't protect its borders or enforce its immigration laws, and you will get the silent treatment. But laws protecting America's borders are immoral and discriminatory?

As for Mexicans, the biggest abusers of America's porous borders, where's that Mexican pride? The idea that Mexicans seem comfortable being known as the people who take our menial jobs is pathetic. The notion that such a prideful people can't provide for themselves, and need the Mexican-hating nation of America to help them out is equally pathetic.

I know that many Mexicans have immigrated to the U.S. and gone on the find the *American Dream*—that being the *pre*-ObamaNation version, and not what we have now, *The American Nightmare.* My ex-father-in-law was one such Mexican.

He left a world of poverty in Mexico and immigrated to the U.S., legally, without a pot to pee in or a window to throw it out of. He later joined the Army and actually fought for this country. He was honorably discharged from the Army, and opened a restaurant in San Antonio that became successful in its own right. He subsequently opened a second restaurant, thereby doubling his success.

After about 20 years of being an entrepreneur, he retired from the restaurant business and had a life of leisure, though not necessarily luxurious. He died a happy man. That was *his* American Dream.

Our problem is that many of the Mexicans who are entering the U.S. are doing so illegally, and frankly just don't know how to live civilized. They are no longer bringing that strong Mexican work ethic and family tradition. They have caught on to the system, and know that they are free to be lazy in America like much of the Liberal demography.

Admit it. Our welfare system to most illegal immigrants is living the good life, compared to where they come from. America has become welfare to the world. Liberal Democrats love people who want to be part of the system. *A cog in the wheel.*

So I'd like to thank all the illegal immigrants, particularly the Mexicans for coming to America to lower our standard of living, and helping Liberal Democrats like Obama and Pelosi expand their *War on Achievement*. I doubt they have even considered where they will go after they ruin America?

When other countries begin getting the influx of illegal Americans immigrating to suck mother's milk from the breasts of their countries, then they will have the right to bash America. Until then, just send us *legally* the best and brightest keep your deadbeats.

***

Introducing the newer, hipper race-baiter Marc Lamont Hill. Associate Professor of Education at Columbia University Teachers College describes himself on his website as follows:

"Dr. Marc Lamont Hill is one of the leading hip-hop generation intellectuals in the country. His work… covers topics such as hip-hop culture, politics, sexuality, education and religion."

Hill should have also added presidential prognosticator to his resume, along with "chubby hater," because Dr. Tolerant comfortably suggested that Chris Christie (R-NJ) could not be president as Christie is "too fat."

What is it called when you don't like "chubbies," a chunk-o-phobe?

Hill did qualify his statement that Christie is "too fat," by adding: Too fat… *"for a politician."*

One thing is for sure; Christie may not be too fat to be a Columbia associate professor, but he's definitely too *smart*. Since when do politicians need the body of a Chippendale dancer to get elected? Suddenly the party of Barney Frank (D-MA) disqualifies politicians from office because of physique?

Hill inadvertently exposed the Leftist political caste system; an invisible ceiling for chubbies. Are chubbies not allowed to ascend to the ultimate political throne, to be leaders of the free world because of their weight?

The Party of Tolerance seems to be obsessed with appearances, I'd say. If Barack Obama talked like Jesse Jackson or Al Sharpton, he would *not* be president. If you don't believe me ask Harry Reid; then ask yourself why neither of those two presidential candidates ever made it to the Oval Office, but the "light-skin [guy] with no Negro dialect" did?

As for Christy, he apparently earned the scorn of Hill and other Lefty chubby haters by simply being qualified and effective. Lefties prefer ignorant, do-nothing leaders, especially black ones. It also helps to believe in things like global climate change and welfare as stimulus. In other words, be as looney as you'd like, just don't be *fat*.

Interesting that Hill is noticeably silent on what size is fitting for the position of First Lady. One would have to be blind not to see that Michelle Obama is a bit more roomy these days, despite being put in charge of thinning out the Nation's chubby children. We wouldn't want fat black kids not having their chance to become president, because of the biases they will face from Liberals like ML Hill. It's one thing to be a black president, but to be fat, well for the Left that's completely unacceptable.

For as much as the Left likes to bash Chris Christie's weight, it's his dedication to fiscal conservatism that really has them nervous. Either way you look at it, Christie is twice the man Obama is.

***

[1] A free pass or a favor.

[2] Called the Angel of Death for his torture experiment at Auschwitz, during WWII

[3] Clyburn wanted this position, because "leadership" get a car and driver.

[4] Mafioso talk for, "You're about to get whacked!"

[5] Clinton and Limbaugh are cigar aficionados, though for very different reasons.

[6] Are you stupid, man?

5

FEELING SAFE?

We've learned from Liberal Marc Lamont Hill that fat kids can't become president, and now we have Michelle Obama who wants the government to take control of fat kids' diets. We can't run the risk of having a fat president, now can we?

I know this is hard to believe, but fat kids get fat when they have too much to eat. Anybody over thirty can recall the commercials featuring Africa's poor children with their distended fat bellies. Well those kids were not fat, only their bellies were. But that was just to fake people out. Those kids could barely standing on those very skinny, frail legs, as they were suffering from malnutrition. Those poor little African kids had flies circling all around their heads, but they were too weak to even swat the flies away.

How hungry do you have to be to ignore flies landing on you? I can't stand seeing a fly in the same room as I am, so for a swarm of flies to be crawling all over my face without me swatting like a robotic "wax on, wax off," I'd have to be on death's doorstep. That's where those African kids in the commercials are: On death's doorstep.

America's kids however actually have too much food. But don't expect Michelle Obama to cut back, because that is not the Liberal way. All America's fat kids need is: *"Change in a diet they can believe in."*

That change needs to come quickly too, as there is a crisis. According to a source in the military by way of Michelle Obama, [pp] "America's fat kids are a threat to national security."

Who knew? Here I thought *terrorists* were a threat to national security. When was the last time one of America's fat kids wore exploding underwear or shoes? I couldn't find one example where fat American kid had blown up anything besides their waistlines.

Maybe it's not the idea that fat kids are suicide bombers, but instead fat kids are responsible for America's exploding national debt? It is said that exploding debt is a threat to national security. I found research on what fat kids contribute to the national debt, and it seems that fat kids are no bigger drain on the national treasure than America's skinny kids.

Maybe our fat kids are mainly Chinese? Because with a significant part of our debt being held by the Chinese, I feel a bit threatened. The Chinese are communists, mortal enemies to our Republic. They also sneaked a submarine into our sovereign waters and fired a missile off the coast of California. I guess the fact that they didn't fire a nuclear missile and actually land a bomb on a U.S. population center, proved they are not a threat, and just a bunch of fat frat boys fooling about.

Perhaps fat kids are designing weapons grade nuclear programs, though again my researcher team could not locate any such evidence. We were able to find evidence of Iran's and North Korea's malevolent nuclear programs. Perhaps the administration doesn't believe these two countries a threat to America's national security? Iran is just all talk about the destruction of Israel, and as Obama assured Americans while he campaigned, *"They're little,"* in reference to Iran.

North Korea provoking our ally and their southern neighbor is just fooling about too, right? The notion that North Korea is willing to sacrifice their own kinfolk should not concern America. That's just how North Koreans show their anger towards family. They wouldn't dare let their rage out on the rest of the world.

It's good to know that none of those other things are of concern to Obama, and that we have narrowed our national security threat theater to America's fat kids.

Michelle Obama quotes military leaders in selling us on the idea of fat kids being a national security threat. Apparently one out of four of our nation's young people would be unqualified to serve in the military, because of their weight.

I didn't attend Princeton on an affirmative action 'scholarship,' but I have surmised that four out of four of our fat kids would not be able to serve... because they are too *young*.

Is it a sign of desperation that Michelle Obama is using the military to sell the idea that government should regulate what our kids eat? This is proof that Liberals can't sell this idea even to their own. So Michelle Obama is trying to punk the Conservatives by saying, even the military agrees with this ridiculous idea.

It is mainly Liberal parents who can't or won't care for their kids, but we must all suffer. This certainly reminds me of military school, where if one person screwed up, the entire platoon had to do pushups.

I have a suggestion. How about we put give parents of obese kids 90 days to get Junior off his video-playing, Dorito-eating lazy butt, or go to jail for a few months? I bet you'd see parents interacting with their kids then. At least my idea involves parent-child interaction, unlike Michelle Obama's idea for more government control and yet another money-grab.

Liberals want a Utopia where fat people and Conservatives don't exist. Look at who's in the media, movies, television, and marketing. Liberals set the agenda for what is beautiful, healthy, or politically correct in America.

Skinny people die at the same ratio as fat people and Conservatives... 100 percent.[1]

Michelle Obama's vision for America sounds suspiciously like discrimination against the chubbies, if you ask me. It is also reminiscent of Hitlerian politics, in that she has a vision for a thin Liberal America. *No blonde hair, blue eyes either in Michelle Obama's vision of Utopia.*

The fact is we are all born with a "due date," ordained by God. And no matter what the government or anybody else does, one's date with destiny is set. You may be able to affect the quality of your life, but that should be how you define it, not the government.

I know many fat kids who have grown up to be skinny adults. One of my fat childhood friends grew up to become an Army Ranger. Fat kids grow up to become professional football players, titans of industry, even governors of states.

If somebody enjoys food, then let them enjoy it. What's wrong with junk food, if that floats your boat? Maybe junk food is what your body needs, as everybody is different. Who is the government to tell you that you must eat salads, tofu, or cyanide-laced Al Qaeda salads?

One hundred percent of skinny half-black presidents are unfit to serve in the US military .[2]

I live in America, because I want personal choice. Understanding the background of discrimination, I don't think the government should be singling out any group for experimentation. They have tried this with black people and the results are dismal.

So what if fat kids can't lose weight, does the government take them from the parents? And if the kids are under government supervision and can't lose weight, maybe they can just execute them?

I guess for now all the government will do is single them out, persecute them so they develop issues about their weight at an early age. Maybe "fat" is the new N-word.

I'm not sure how big of a national security threat fat kids may pose to American. However I am 100% sure that Liberals are a real threat to national security.

***

Regulating the food of all kids[3] is what Michelle Obama has accomplished with recent legislation signed by her husband, however the goal of Liberalism goes much deeper: Regulate the food for *all* Americans.

Having been a track and football athlete back in the day and martial artist for almost forty years, I'm all for healthful living. But can you imagine how things would be if the government regulates our food. Well you don't have to imagine it; it's happening. Let's just hope that the government doesn't manage food like they mange the postal service or we will be fasting at least one, possibly two days a week.

At one of Michelle Obama's luncheons, she served "sun gold tomatoes from the White House kitchen garden, eggs harvested minutes earlier from the farm's chickens and chicken with eggplant and ratatouille – also from the White House garden." While it is fine for Michelle Obama to have a White House vegetable garden, you can't. Apparently growing one's own food may now be a national security threat as well.

Dick Durbin (D-IL) introduced Senate Bill 510, officially known as FDA Food Safety Modernization Act, which is said will keep our food sources safe. If there was a terrorist plot to poison the food supply, would it not be better if Americans had their own gardens? So why doesn't the government want us to grow our own food or stock up on seeds? If there were a terrorist attack, wouldn't the government want us to stay put, and not have to go to the grocery store or farmer's market?

Nevertheless, SB 510 will *"require that each person (excluding farms and restaurants) who manufactures, processes, packs, distributes, receives, holds, or imports an article of food permit inspection of his or her records if the Secretary believes that there is a reasonable probability that the use of or exposure to such food will cause serious adverse health consequences or death.*

If you're a want to save money, regularly acquire food from a food coop, or just to garden you're out of luck. SB 510 bill will regulate everyone from Uncle Tony's tomato garden to the largest of farmers. If you think sending a letter is expensive, just wait until government gets even more tentacles on our food.

If you think not having food puts a wrinkle in survival, imagine what life is without water and food. The outcome of government intrusion is that in Fresno, a city of 505,000, 24.1%of Fresno's families are going hungry.[4] The irony is that Fresno is the agricultural capital of America,[5] and more food per acre in more variety can be grown in the fertile Central Valley surrounding this community than on any other land in America. Lack of water has created a veritable wasteland resembling 1930's Ukraine.

The economy in the central valley is reeling from 16.9% unemployment among the packers, cannery workers and professional agricultural fields. Other Central Valley cities such as Hanford-Corcoran, Merced, Modesto,

Stockton and Visalia-Porterville have similar jobless numbers, the highest in the country.

Costly environmental regulations and reduced water supplies were enacted to save a two-inch bait fish known as the Delta smelt. In this case, those who smelt it dealt it, as in this catastrophic move for the Central Valley of California was driven by environmental extremists, state and federal officials. Water allotments in the southwest part of the Central Valley are as low as 10% of normal, and have created a dust bowl in that region.

If you want to know the impact of state and federal regulations, note that Fresno was ranked as the worst city in America to do business, according to a 2010 MarketWatch survey, while four other Central Valley cities made the national bottom 10 — Bakersfield, Sacramento, Modesto and Stockton.

Victor Davis Hanson in commented about California's Central Valley, an area infused with illegal immigrants, "Many of the rural trailer-house compounds I saw appear to the naked eye no different from what I have seen in the Third World. There is a Caribbean look to the junked cars, electric wires crossing between various outbuildings, plastic tarps substituting for replacement shingles, lean-tos cobbled together as auxiliary housing, pit bulls unleashed, and geese, goats, and chickens roaming around the yards."

Hanson further noted as he shopped at a neighborhood grocery store that these people were paying for their groceries with government provided food cards. So they were living on the taxpayers, but driving late-model cars and had iPhones, BlackBerries and other items of what Hanson refers to as "the technological veneer of the middle class."

If the government can't control your water in order to protect a fish, there is always the risk that water poses to you. According to this report, millions of Americans are regularly drinking hexavalent chromium, the carcinogenic chemical made famous in the film "Erin Brockovich."

But why control some of the water, when you can control all of the water. That's exactly what legislation proposed by Russ Feingold would do.

Russ Feingold is the last name you should want to see on legislation. His campaign finance bill which was supposed to reign in campaign spending, making political office available to the common man has actually made pursuing political office unaffordable for 99.999 percent of Americans.

In the era of McCain/Feingold we got the most expensive presidential election in history, the combined spending of McCain and Obama exceeding $1B. With that record of accomplishment, Feingold wants the Federal government to take over of any and all bodies of water in the 50 states, and that's no exaggeration. An excerpt from the text of his new bill:

"…*all waters subject to the ebb and flow of the tide, the territorial seas, and all interstate and intrastate waters and their tributaries, including lakes, rivers, streams (including intermittent streams), mudflats, sandflats, wetlands, sloughs, prairie potholes, wet meadows, playa lakes, natural ponds, and all impoundments of the foregoing, to the fullest extent that these waters, or activities affecting them, are subject to the legislative power of Congress under the Constitution.*"

Simply put, with this legislation the Federal government would control the water in America's bathtubs and toilets. If Feingold does for water what he did for campaign finance reform, water will cost more than gold.

U.S. Senator James Inhofe (R-OK) certainly understands how egregious the Fed is being, and the blatant attempt to trump states' rights, as his comment indicates:

"*Allowing EPA and the Corps to exercise unlimited regulatory authority over all inter- and intrastate water, or virtually anything that is wet, goes too far and is certainly beyond anything intended by the Clean Water Act. But, that is what S. 787 does. It vastly expands Federal control of private property, despite assurances contained in S. 787. In fact, the very premise of the bill is to override a State's fundamental right to oversee waters within its borders and to usurp the power of land owners to manage their property as they see fit. The Constitutionnever envisioned federal jurisdiction being boundless; it carves out room for state and local governments and private property owners to manage their resources.*"

The stated intention of S.787 is to reduce pollution. I'm not sure what controlling a lake in "Inthemiddleofnowhere, MN" has to do with pollution. Usually when I go to an area where there is a lake, it's the cleanest air I have breathed in some time.

I think this type of delusion that Feingold demonstrates comes from city dwellers who believe that the air in Los Angeles is what all of America breathes. I suggest they take a drive out to the countryside and breathe some fresh air, because that DC air is choking off their sensibilities.

But if reducing pollution isn't enough, the government uses the excuse that terrorists are trying to contaminate our water supply. Fair enough. But if our government can't protect a border with Mexico, explain to me how they are going to protect hundreds of thousands of bodies of water and tens of thousands of miles of rivers?

I'm no conspiracy theorists as I know that terrorists might plot to attack our water. But that's been true for years; nothing new. What is new is the Obama's administration's ability to tip their hand and show us just how far they are willing to go to control the populace, and that they will use any means necessary to do so.

The Obama administration makes no bones about controlling our industries, our healthcare, our diets, and quite frankly all aspects of our lives. These fools truly believe that they know best, and that they are the best people to regulate our lives; they actually believe they know you better than you know yourself.

Government control of food and water reduces you to begging, regardless of how much money or gold you have. God asks you to fast occasionally; the American government may soon demand it of you.

***

[1] Research from The Black Sphere University

[2] ibid

[3] Michelle Obama's program addresses not only the 25% of children she says are the national security threat, but also the 75% who are not. Great example of the minority affecting all.

[4] National average is at 9.1%

[5] Fresno supplies about 25% of America's fruits and vegetables

6

SPENDING OTHER PEOPLE'S MONEY

Whether it's the Obamas taking a vacation every quarter or having a $100,000 taxpayer-funded date night, or Pelosi commandeering taxpayer funded jets, Liberals love spending other people's money, or more specifically *our* money.

When it comes to using their own money however, Liberals hold on to money like vice grips. Still, Jesse Jackson called Conservatives "heartless and uncaring toward the silent poor," as he consistently donates a whopping one percent of his personal income to charity each year. Jackson is a wealthy man by most people's standard. He runs a non-profit that even the IRS won't audit. Perhaps Jesse feels his charity occurred when he paid his mistress' salary; part of her out of wedlock child, demonstrating his compassion. Scratch that compassion part ... the child was his.

Another Jackson family's charitable foundation collected over $964,000, yet gave less than $50,000 to charitable causes—token gifts to two colleges. You can bet there was something reciprocal for Jackson, like $50,000 in speaking engagements {wink}. But the Jackson's did use $84,000 of foundation money to have a gala in honor of Jesse Jackson. *Gone are the days of the house party for the Jacksons.*

The Liberal mantra: *We care, Conservatives don't.* And the lie of Liberalism flourishes. But here are some truths.

Throughout the 1990's when Gore was choking up $353.00 in one year to charity, G. W. Bush silently tithed 10 percent of his income, every year.

In 2005, Cheney donated 77 percent of his income to charity, only to be criticized by [liberals] who claimed he was getting too much of a tax deduction. Liberals hated that Cheney gave away money, because Liberals like to confiscate it. In Utopia giving too much is depicted as nefarious, while not giving anything at all is completely overlooked, if not lauded.

I'm no John McCain fan, however with respect to charity, he certainly represents Conservative values. In 2006 and 2007, John McCain gave 27.3 percent and 28.6 percent of his income to charity.[1] The late Senator Ted Kennedy who ran for president in the '70s donated a scant 1% of his money to charity. Apparently Kennedy was for free healthcare for all; he just didn't want to pay for it.

Barack Obama is not much better at giving, though quick to castigate the "Republican rich." While threatening to raise taxes on the rich, because they have too much, yet give too little, Obama points the finger at himself.

How did the guy who has accomplished nothing keep the lights on, before he became Resident of the U.S.? With *book* deals.

Apparently the majority of the money that Obama earned prior to ascending the throne came from his two works of fiction, namely *Dreams of My* [Deadbeat] *Father,* and *The Audacity of a Dope.*

From a gross income of $4.2 million in 2007, then Senator Obama gave $240,000 to charity, which works out to be 5.7 percent, and that's because he was under the microscope. The 2008 Obama tax return was not much better. Out of $2.6 million Barry and Michelle gave a whopping 6.5 percent, and it took running for president for him to give that.

Maybe Obama will give more since he has a new children's book is on the horizon—fitting when you consider that America is being governed by a man with the financial intellect of a 2nd-grader.

Perhap after his first and hopefully only term as president ends, and proceeds from the children's book spent, we may get the sequel to *The Audacity of a Dope,* titled, "*Psyche ... The Audacity of Me Punking America.*" Expect this book to be printed in twenty dialects of Arabic, with free downloads to

Muslims from the Al-Jazeera website. And of course this book will be translated to Austrian.

As for Joe *"Every Family Has One"* Biden, not a bad few years for a guy who technically could be declared mentally unstable. Crazy Joe did write a book which managed to ride on the coattail of his boss' success. Joe's book sales roughly equaled his Senate salary, when you do the math. I doubt you could find anybody who will admit to buying it though.

Despite only modest success of his book, Biden will write another. Now you may be thinking that Biden's next book won't be a hit; however I beg to differ. A potential big seller might be *Biden's Biggest Blunders*, and you can certainly see the potential marketability of *The Unauthorized Autobiography of My Life* by Joe Biden.

Admittedly, I might actually buy those books as a reminder of some of the hearty laughs Joe provided during *The Era of Brown Underwear* – when lunatics ruled Amerika.

Book deals notwithstanding, Crazy Joe is indeed representative of the typical Democrat gifters. Biden lectures others about giving, but he has exempted himself from it. Joe defines cheap too, donating less than 0.5 percent of his income to charity in 2008. That same year Biden paid roughly 18 percent taxes on his income that year. I'd say Biden is not as *"patriotic,"*[2] as he wants the rest of us to be.

As Ann Coulter pointed out in an article of similar discussion, about the only two Liberal givers are Bill Gates and Warren Buffet, who seem to be single-handedly giving on behalf of most Liberals.

Liberals like to give with lots of fanfare, throwing themselves lavish parties that could feed hundreds, if not thousands. At these galas, they give a fraction of what the gala cost.

"So when you give to the needy, do not announce it with trumpets, as the hypocrites do ... But when you give to the needy, do not let your left hand know what your right hand is doing, so that your giving may be in secret. Then your Father, who sees what is done in secret, will reward you." (Matthew 6:2-4)

Instead of dance like no one's watching, sing as if no one's listening, and love like you've never been hurt, I suggest Liberals live as if there are cameras everywhere. That's about the only way to get them to not steal from the donation basket.

***

John Kerry the aristocratic nobleman and stingy senator who married money[3], in 1995 spent $500,000 to purchase *half* of a 17th century painting, but gave zilch, zero and nada to charity that year. After he married into the Heinz fortune, Kerry's philanthropy lay cloaked behind the Heinz Foundation's wall of secrecy. I guess Kerry wouldn't want people knowing just how generous he has become these days.

We can speculate however. Not long ago Kerry went as far as to park his yacht, *Isabella* in a "sanctuary state" in order to avoid Massachusetts' taxes. When caught, Kerry promptly paid his taxes, and soon you will be hard pressed to find the story on the internet.

Kerry is but another example of how cheating, lying, disingenuous Lefties roll. It is fascinating to watch how the laws of unintended circumstances catch up with them, even more entertaining than watching them try to weasel their way out.

As Jim Carrey did in *Liar Liar*, Kerry kicked his own butt by voting for the new yacht tax back in 1990. Way back then, Kerry might have pondered, "*What are the chances I will find some wealthy ketchup widow interested in a resume-padding, gold digging dude with chin like Jay Leno's?*"

Kerry indeed found his fortune, and Ms. Heinz had found her hero. And in typical Liberal omega-dog response, when first nabbed for evading yacht taxes, Kerry proffered, "*It's my wife's yacht!*"[4]

So it's Kerry's *wife* who is the tax-evading scoundrel, not John Kerry. I can certainly see why he married Teresa: Teresa is more like Mother Teresa, the bullet-blocking female flak jacket. Poor Teresa Heinz likely believed Kerry's story of bravery, when he was unwilling to "check the bump in the night[5]" on the yacht tax issue. I suggest Kerry give his wife at least one of those Purple Heart's he got for all the paper cuts he received in Nam.

Eventually Kerry rethought the "It's my wife's yacht" defense and changed tactics, proclaiming *"The yacht was 'under warranty'. It was being worked."*

Yeah, and so were we. As soon as Kerry started explaining the circumstances of why a yacht with a Latina name was hiding out in a sanctuary state. *Was Isabella doing housekeeping for the other yachts?*

Kerry wanted us to believe that a new yacht needed warranty service right out of the wrapper. Admittedly, I've never owned a yacht, so it's possible that multi-million dollar items are delivered with no quality control. Maybe all $7M boats could have "issues." I suspect however that Kerry was having gold toilets installed.

Kerry said of the "warranty" work:

"Let's get this very straight… I've said consistently that we will pay our taxes. We've always paid our taxes. It is not an issue. Period. We've always paid our taxes, we'll pay our taxes."

A bit defensive, when he had me at *"It's my wife's yacht."*

Anyway, why shouldn't Kerry's yacht *Isabelle* get all the tax-free privileges of illegal aliens? *Isabelle* was merely doing the job most American yachts were unwilling to do.

Here I thought it was rich Republicans who are supposed to have yacht and tax problems.

***

Who are the political rich and powerful? One party certainly has no providence over another in this regard, as there are rich on both sides of the aisle. However, when it comes to painting the Republicans as the evil wealthy, Democrats are loaded with Picassos.

To hear Liberals decry the rich, you'd think none of them are rich. Well the Liberals criticizing the rich the most are indeed not rich; they are filthy rich. Most of the Liberals democrats are wealthy beyond recognition.

Nancy Pelosi for example is superbly wealthy. The woman who called welfare stimulus is worth almost $125 million. Here is how Pelosi came by some of her wealth:

Nancy Pelosi 's socialist political views are exactly what have kept her elected in San Francisco, along with the flow of union campaign money. The staunch "union supporter" Pelosi has even received the Cesar Chavez Award from the United Farm Workers' Union . But her $25 million Napa vineyards and winery that she and her husband own are non-union shops.

The hypocrisy doesn't stop there. Pelosi has received more money from the Hotel Employees and Restaurant Employees unions than any other member of Congress in recent election cycles.

The multi-millionaire investors own a large stake in an exclusive resort hotel in Wine Country, the Napa Valley Auberge Du Soleil Resort. It has more than 250 employees. But none of them are in a union , according to Peter Schweizer , author of "Do As I Say, (Not As I Do) – The Hypocrisy of Democrats" and a regular contributor to the New York Times.

Pelosiis also partners in a restaurant chain called Piatti, which has 900 employees. The chain is – you might have guessed — a non-unionshop. It is a very high-end restaurant group with locations in Carmel, Sonoma and Danville to name just the locations I dined at. Hardwood-fired ovens, exhibition kitchens, Napa wines, a very nice experience. I did notice some Hispanic kitchen help and busboys. I'm wondering if they are illegal alliens? No, the Speaker of the House wouldn't hire illegals, would she?

Pelosi is apparently for unions for other companies, just not hers. And we can certainly see why Pelosi is for illegal immigration, since she may be one of California's biggest employers of illegals.

In 2003, Dianne Feinstein was ranked the fifth wealthiest senator, with an estimated net worth of $26 million. By 2005 her net worth had increased to ~$99 million, and her 347-page financial disclosure statement for that year drew clear lines between her assets and those of her husband's, with many of her assets in blind trusts. Estimates of Feinstein's worth today are anywhere between $75M to $108M. *Imagine if that blind trust could see?*

How do you go from $26M to $99M in two years, when your salary is less than $200K per year? A better question is why is Feinstein even getting a salary?

The Left is fine with rich people, as long as they don't *earn* it. That's Conservatives' problem is we work hard for our money, thus Liberals consider us rubes.

John Kerry had some wealth, but nothing like what he married. His estimated worth is about $295M, though there is no way to tell, as he has his money tied up in the Heinz Foundation making it impossible to track. Bill Clinton entered politics as a perennial ward of the government, and now has a net worth of over $100M. Not bad for a disbarred, womanizing Arkansas hick.

Elitists have no qualms about showcasing their double-standards, either.

Former middle-class maven Michelle Obama, together with her husband became multi-millionaires recently discouraged women with a median income of $38,000 a year in a county in Ohio from aspiring to high paying corporate jobs. Only six short years ago, the Obama's were paying off their student loans, and now they have people on the payroll to count the zeros after the commas on their bank statements. But no one else is allowed to fast-track their way into the American political elite.

When Ted Kennedy was stricken with a brain tumor, world champion elitist and proponent of ObamaCare promptly opted out. Do you think under ObamaCare any of us would be flown by helicopter to the finest hospital in Boston for the best health care available? Under ObamaCare you'd have to wait in line at Dr. Feelgood's Chicken Shack and Surgery Center.

America's Liberal leaders shamelessly eat what they want, while preaching healthy lifestyles and smoking 'fags.'[6] Liberal politicians push job stimulus by providing incentives for the jobless to remain unemployed; they write tax law, and conveniently forget to pay their taxes.

The Liberal upper class are egotistical elitists. They define "rich" for the rest of us, pitting rich against poor and then extracting themselves out of the discussion. What they don't tell you is that they are the powerful. And with that power comes the ability to enrich oneself beyond belief.

As witnessed throughout history the system of Liberal Progressive Socialism ultimately fails. It invariably devolves into two classes: Upper and Lower.[7] The Upper class is the powerful and frequently oppressive government class that justifies implementing socialistic policies by arguing that

for the first time they will get right what no one else has. It's time we got
took that power back.

***

[1] McCain filed separately from his wife.

[2] Biden called not paying enough in taxes, "Un-American."

[3] The least successful way that Liberals acquire their wealth. Politics, inheritance, and union
leadership are the top four.

[4] Talk about being a lady's man!

[5] Protect her

[6] Fag is a old slang term for cigarettes. However, in this case Obama may be smoking gays as
well, given his policies on AIDS.

[7] There are also the "classless," however this is mainly made up of the children of the Upper
class and most Liberals.

7

LIBERALS HAVE THEIR ISSUES

Government is so pervasive in all parts of our lives, that it is nearly impossible to find something the government doesn't touch in your life. Imagine a "thought bubble" that popped up every time the government touched something in your life. So for example when you use your phone, the bubble would show taxes like "telecom taxes, state excise tax, clean environment tax, brain cancer tax, and 'Africans don't have cell phones tax.'" Or if you watch TV, you would see all the government fees, like "Poor people need cable too" tax, or the "buy a ghetto kid an X-box" tax. And don't even think about having an alcoholic drink, or you could get hit with the "fund a crackhead" liquor tax. Death and taxes, not necessarily in that order. Wouldn't it be nice to know what your body might be worth?

According to *Wired* magazine, when broken down into fluids, tissues and germ fighting capabilities the human body is worth more than 45 million dollars. Bone marrow alone is worth more than $23 million. DNA can fetch $9.7 million, while extracting antibodies can bring $7.3 million. A lung is worth $116,400, a kidney $91,400 and a heart $57,000.

The prices are based on cost estimates taken from hospitals and insurance companies, and are based on projected prices only in the United States. So imagine what you might be worth on the world market?

Currently it's not legal to sell your body parts, notable exceptions being semen, blood, and hair. You can offer your body as a scientific guinea pig to pharmaceutical companies, and when you die, you can donate your cadaver to medical schools. Let's face it though, there is very little money in that last option for you. Your potential future earnings for the government are astronomical, when you ponder it.

So is it any wonder that Obama's Regulatory Czar, Cass Sunstein wants to control and kill you, now that we know what you are worth? Thankfully he will only do this at the appropriate time; like when you have no more usefulness to society. Sunstein thinks you can't be trusted to make your own medical decisions, or do the right thing when you are too expensive to care for.

This is why Sunstein is in the business of regulation by way of "nudging" [1] Americans toward everything Sunstein thinks we should be doing, from quitting smoking to wearing motorcycle helmets to signing over those kidneys. As for the latter, Sunstein has devised a clever method to harvest your organs.

If you're distracted at the DMV and you don't check the 'opt out from organ transport' box on the license renewal form, you have given the Fed the authority to take your organs, before the monitor flat lines.

How many Americans do you think have unknowingly allowed the Fed to have this control of their bodies? You can't sell your own body parts, but the government can take them. Maybe the Fed is a little less pro-choice, than Liberals believe.

You don't have to wonder why Congress writes bills that are 2000 pages long. You can bury lots of hidden jewels in bills that large. And as John Kerry said Americans are stupid, unable to understand anything longer than a sound bite.

The bottom line is regulatory commissions are put in place to control the brain dead (living or dead) and to stamp out capitalism and eventually individualism. Why should you have control over your body, when the government can control you from the cradle to the grave?

I imagine a people junkyard at some clandestine facility, where wealthy from all over the world shop for body parts sold by the U.S. government. Outside the building in non-descript. Inside it looks like a Chinese meat and produce market. Activity is vigorous, as the wealthy elite extend their survival age to 125, while the rest of us die at 30. A Logan's Run for the new millennium.

Look on the bright side. You can survive with one kidney and lung, part of your liver, bone marrow, blood, hair, no eyes, skin and ligament drafts, semen, and eggs, so no complaining. It could get worse.

***

Here's a reason the government may soon need to harvest organs or begin killing its citizens. According to the latest figures, the number of American households on the Supplemental Nutritional Assistance Program[2] is up to a record 40.8 million at a cost of over $72 billion a year.

This time last year, that number was 34 million households; and in less than a year the ratio has climbed from 1 in 9 families collecting food stamp benefits to greater than 1 in 8— with an average household of 2.61 people, that means a rise of over 17 million people in one year. That's more than the populations of Los Angeles, Chicago, and New York, NY combined.

Factor in the 53 million Americans collecting Social Security benefits at a cost of $675 billion last year—running the Social Security program in the red for the first time in 30 years—and the $676 billion spend on Medicare & Medicaid, and nearly half our budget is spent on entitlement programs.

The crisis, however, doesn't lie in how many are receiving benefits or even in how many qualify. Rather, the problem is that the coming economic collapse appears to be completely scripted, and the disproportionate effect in the black community appears to be entirely deliberate.

In 2008, the last year for which the statistics are available, black families were shown to be three times more likely than any other race to collect food stamps. Blacks currently have an unemployment rate that is 160 percent higher than that of whites, which hints toward a cause-effect relationship. However, the unemployment numbers don't quite explain the high participation in food stamps benefits.

The official number of unemployed persons is 14.6 million, and even if discouraged workers and the underemployed are included, that number rises only to 29 million. Essentially what I am saying is that 12 million more people are getting funding than are currently unemployed or underemployed. When you do the math, there appear to be about 106 million Americans getting SNAP funds, and 44 million of them are newbies.

Interesting statistics when you consider the passage of ObamaCare and Financial Reform, while Democrats itch to pass "shamnesty" and Cap & Trade. Certainly these crises are not a coincidence.

The Obama administration and the rest of the Democratic Party have taken Alinsky's rules to heart, and the war they wage is one against any American who stands in the way of their wish to transition America to a European socialist state. The disproportionate number of Americans dependent upon the government to sustain them serves as evidence that Alinsky tactics are working.

The Fed is doing a great job of creating the "have nots." I'm beginning to feel redundant in reporting that the people are first pitted against one another, so those in power are given free license to rebuild America in whatever image they see fit.

Many on the Right have seen the similarities between the tactics suggested in *Rules for Radicals* and those used by the Obama administration as far back as the election cycle—such as the tendency to whitewash extremist views in neutral terms like "hope" and "change."

Proof positive that Alinsky's model was being used was provided by Organizing for America, Obama's permanent campaign group, in January of this year. While recruiting at an Ohio high school, OFA listed *Rules for Radicals* as one of their "suggested readings."

Alinsky's tactics have already been given a test drive when the Cloward-Piven Strategy was used in New York in the 1960s, whereby Richard Cloward and Frances Fox Piven expanded upon Alinsky's rules and provided an actual strategy for community organizers: Overwhelm the welfare system.

They used race riots and other crises to spur populist feelings of entitlement, and in less than a decade they more than doubled the amount of single-parent households on welfare from 4.3 million to 10.8 million.

Obama has everything possible at his disposal for this plan to work on a national scale. He's admittedly spent his life working as a community organizer to help corrupt groups like SEIU and ACORN. The mainstream media is dedicated to him like a battered wife, continuing to worship him and sing praises of his policies, while their ratings dive faster than a Maltese falcon.

Militant minority groups like La Raza and the NBPP threaten violence as retaliation for perceived injustices—and just as Alinsky predicted, the cowards and panderers in DC are eager to throw more entitlements at them to keep the peace. Who needs success when you know you can just be the White House's lapdog and sit up and beg for a bailout if the need arises?

There's just one problem: The Right has finally caught on. Americans see how the entitlement-based government model turned out for Europe and Americans don't want it. The Alinsky plan depends on keeping Americans angry and ignorant, and all the Left is getting in return is a double serving of the former. If you need proof, look at the results of the last election.

***

Racial dishonesty, class dishonesty, tax evasion, and curtailing freedom are just a few things bulging the closet door of the typical Liberal. But there are more hypocrisies that leave me shaking my head in amazement.

Pop culture Liberals like to haul around their offspring like cheap bowling trophies and wear little red ribbons on lapels as self-righteous testimony to homosexual issues.

In 1992 Bill Clinton and his political wife Hillary together with daughter Chelsea Clinton were featured on the cover of *People* magazine in an exclusive entitled "*Road Warriors: At home in Arkansas, the Clintons talked about friends, family, faith – and pierced ears.*" The article was all cuddly on the surface, but for anyone aware of the Clinton's Left wing politics the double standard was obvious.

The most glaring contradiction had to do with Chelsea, who at that time was 13-years-old. The article stated that at the Clinton homestead, "*Adolescence [was] being foreshadowed by early skirmishing over pierced ears.*" Hillary said, "*We really held out against it.*" The doting mother then said, "*I feel strongly that children deserve to have some childhood and some innocence and time to accommodate to the world of adulthood."*

Now that's clean Conservative living. Hillary advocating for childhood innocence of her child. In fact, to prove devotion to childhood purity, Bill and Hillary Clinton, both of whom disavow parental notification before driving underage girls to abortion clinics, wouldn't let Chelsea pierce her ears.

Pro-choice, sex education-in-kindergarten liberals believe children should have "time to accommodate to the world of adulthood?' Teach our grade-schoolers, the kids relegated to public school how to use condoms. But don't you dare come near the Clinton's child with an ear-piercing gun.

Hypocritical liberals shield their sons and daughters from the policies they promote for America's children, those stuck in public school. Pop culture is no different.

The woman the book 'Sex' to the world and who exploited MTV as a one woman sex-ed teaching machine, teaching millions of pubescent girls to sing "Papa Don't Preach," morphed into a strict disciplinarian after having children of her own. The former Mrs. Ritchie, Madonna banned daughter Lourdes from dating until eighteen, and Madonna's children [were] forbidden to "watch TV… look at magazines" or eat ice cream.

How's this for irony. Madonna taught America's teenage girls promiscuity, as other Liberals taught them about abortion and condoms in the second grade. And now that these doped up former hippies have matured, they forbid their kids from experiencing their disingenuous Liberals former selves?

***

I bet you thought Liberals were tolerant, particularly when it comes to gay issues. Certainly that's what they would have us to believe. Yet another Liberal lie that is long overdue for exposure.

In 1998, Cherilyn Sarkisian, better known as Cher headlined the 9th Annual GLAAD Awards. The Gay and Lesbian Alliance Against Defamation Media Awards honor "positive portrayals of gays and lesbians." Cher received the "GLAAD Media Award [and] in 1999 *The Advocate* named Cher one of the '25 Coolest Women.'"

Perhaps GLAAD wasn't aware of Cher's reaction when her precious little pig-tailed girl named Chastity, transformed into a chubby, confused "man" named Chaz. Despite Cher's gay icon status and open support of the gay way of life, when Chastity "came out as a lesbian at age 18," Cher "*flipped out... ordered Chaz out of her New York apartment and told him/her to see a shrink.*"

I paraphrase the words of a famous Liberal man-of-the-cloth Reverend Jeremiah Wright when I quip, "*Cher's chicken came home to roost and the chicken was a he/she!*"

More recently Liberal activists and "champions of gay and transgender rights causes," actors Warren Beatty and Annette Bening were described as "stunned," and Warren as 'heartbroken' and 'grief-stricken' over Kathlyn's decision." The stun and heartbreak was caused when 18-year-old daughter Kathlyn renamed herself 'Stephen Ira,' and is planning to submit her femininity to the defilement of sex change surgery.

Beatty "*expressed his left-wing politics through highly successful and much acclaimed political satire 'Bulworth.' A longtime activist in various liberal political causes, Beatty has been extremely active in the Democratic Party.*"

Wasn't Beatty notorious in Hollywood for his less-than-traditional and prodigious pre-marital activity? So what's the big deal? One would think that liberal elites like Beatty-Bening would heartily applaud their eldest child's plan to transition from a girl into a boy. Isn't that what a liberal activist encourage our children to do? Wouldn't that be the tolerant thing to do?

Warren's wife and mother of his four children Annette Bening recently shared with Parade.com that "*parenthood is a bit of a mess and chaotic.*" Bening opined, "*There are so many different kinds of relationships, it's sort of difficult to define what is considered normal.*" How avant-garde, open-minded and accepting. No wonder young Kathlyn suffers from gender confusion.

Maybe Beatty's little girl is emulating Mom, who stars in the lesbian movie, *The Kids are All Right* with pro-choice activist and mom Julianne Moore. The only problem is Annette's kid isn't "all right," that is unless "heartbreaking" has become the new definition of "all right?"

During the 2008 campaign, the politically outspoken Bening did not hold back when given the opportunity to ridicule Vice Presidential candidate Sarah Palin. Bening said Hillary Clinton fans would be "bizarre" to support a candidate like the "incredibly Conservative" Palin. *Guess who's Conservative now?*

Lest we forget, the former Alaska governor actually chose to give birth to a child with Down's syndrome, and her teenage daughter Bristol decided to forego abortion and gave birth, out-of-wedlock to a baby boy named Tripp.

Given Palin's track record in playing the cards she's dealt, I suspect that if she were confronted with the issue of a transgender child, she would handle it with the same class she demonstrated in dealing with a pregnant teenage daughter, and a Down's syndrome child. *There Palin goes, clinging to her religion.*

All that Liberalism and tolerance by Beatty, Benning, and Cher couldn't protect Hollyweird from themselves. As two young women are wheeled into sexual reassignment surgery, one can't help but wonder if the Bono-Bening-Beatty trio of crushed homosexual supporting parents secretly fault the Liberal lifestyle they so clearly "tolerate" for what they believe are damaged goods?

Supposed champions of gay rights shunning their own homosexual or cross-gendered children, the purveyors of promiscuous sex and abortion outfitting their daughters with chastity belts, supposed civil rights activists serving up minorities for slaughter.

Meanwhile we homophobic Conservatives and Republicans just roll with the punches, as Dick Cheney did. Intolerant homophobe that he is...*not*... supposed Neanderthal Dick Cheney treats his Lesbian daughter with respect and acceptance.

In the 2004 Vice Presidential debate, John Edwards showed his lack of class by responding to a question about gay marriage by saying that he supported it because of wonderful people like Dick Cheney's daughter. If Edwards had hoped to embarrass Cheney or paint him into a corner, he failed. Cheney thanked him for his kind words about his daughter as his sole answer to the question.

Cheney is the perfect example of many people on the Right, who the Left likes to render anti-gay—rich, white, Conservative Republican male. We have the guts to say that we prefer out children grow up 'straight;' however if our children for some reason are gay, we deal with it, generally with class.

If we are to really pin the tail on the intolerant homophobe donkey, John Kerry makes a great ass. Like racist Democrats who exploit blacks to secure black votes, supposed pro-gay Liberals like John Kerry feel no shame when cruelly embarrassing the homosexual child of a Conservative politician as a means of gaining political points.

I've observed liberals clapping along to gay theme song YMCA while exploiting homosexuals, comparing the LGBT struggle with the civil rights struggle of blacks, all in an attempt to solidify the Democrat power base. Same tactic, different venue, and sexually brilliant.

Democrats want gays to think that there is only one party that views them as real people. Further Democrats want and get the same voter loyalty that they already get from blacks. Aside from the fact that Democrats have mischaracterized many Conservatives, they've got a bigger problem: Blacks don't like that comparison.

Ask an older black person who's been turned away from a restaurant because they don't seat Negroes, or someone who's had a cross burned in their yard, and they're not likely to say that they think Don't Ask, Don't Tell was on par with what they went through. If there was a way to stay in the "race closet" back in the day, I'm sure a lot of blacks would have been fine with a DADT policy of our own.

The LGBT community doesn't struggle with the poverty, unemployment, and outrageously high incarceration rates as blacks do. LGBT don't have the abortion problem that plagues the black community. Though if a gay gene were discovered, and there were a possibility that homosexuals could be aborted in the womb, it's quite probable that a lot more Liberals would become pro-life.

***

Planned Parenthood believes in the choice of a woman to kill an unborn child. But if that same woman chooses to know if someone plans to willfully infect her with HIV/AIDS, that's where Planned Parenthood draws the line.

International Planned Parenthood (IPPF) and UNAIDS wants "*to do away with disclosure laws which require HIVpositive individuals to inform their sex partners of their potentially deadly infection.*"

The campaign maintains that mandating HIV positive individuals disclose to sexual partners that they have a potentially deadly virus fuels "stigma against HIV persons."

To put this in perspective, these agencies prefer to protect the person who will murder you, because nobody should know the identity of the murderer. Protect the reputation of selfish, irresponsible people and while you're at it, create more potential selfish, irresponsible people.

Planned Parenthood and UNAIDS are campaigning for a practice that will most assuredly spread the disease, so the question is why?

In 2006, black men accounted for 65 percent of the new infections among all blacks. In that same year, "*the rate of new HIVinfections for black womenwas nearly 15 times as high as that of white women and… 4 times that of Hispanic/Latina women.*"

Couple those disturbing statistics with Planned Parenthood's dark, racist history and nefarious, genocidal motives could be the reason IPPF and UNAIDS are promoting such an irrational campaign.

If Planned Parenthood misses the opportunity to abort blacks before birth, changing the law so that HIV infected blacks can pass the disease back and forth to each other is a sure way for Margaret Sanger's original goal to "exterminate the Negro population" to be accomplished, to eradicate the blacks, people Sanger called: "*… human weeds, reckless breeders, spawning… human beings who never should have been born.*" What better way to accomplish that goal, than by giving HIV/AIDS carriers a green light to have sex without disclosing they could infect their partner.

Seventy-eight percent of Planned Parenthood clinics are in black neighborhoods for a reason. But regardless of ulterior motives, the Planned Parenthood and UNAIDS campaign poses a tiny bit of a dilemma to supporters of a women's right to choose. It appears that pro-choice for Liberals means that you'd better choose to wear that condom. Because your sexual partner has the pro-choice to kill or not to kill you.

***

From rappers to other forms of art, Liberals have controlled the messaging. Reality TV provided the next lesson on sexy brilliance, and how Liberals have weakened the black community. KJ Adan wrote of an experience that illustrates what happens 'once you go black.'

"Tonight on TV I watched a group of white art critics turn their noses up at a sculpture, produced for a reality show art competition. They seemed to be disgusted with their lack of disgust, as the artist had been challenged to make something shocking. He had produced three black heads, to which one critic said looked like "primitive candle art."

When the artist, a young black man, explained that the heads were like bombs waiting to go off, symbolizing the state of the young black man in urban neighborhoods, the critics slowly began to "understand" the art. The "critics" began discussing the piece amongst them, and came to find the young black man's art, "a work of genius."

This is a quirk of leftist intellectuals. Once a speech, piece of art, music, or agenda appears to reinforce their concept of a noble, struggling minority, suddenly it is utterly brilliant. When something comes from a subculture, it has a gritty urban validity that is for some reason of crucial importance to Leftists.

I've tried to sort out this "Black is Better", or rather "African-American Is Authentic" phenomenon among the white Left for a while. I thought it might be a white guilt thing, but if that were the case, wouldn't white Leftists spend more time around actual black people? Wouldn't they be tripping over themselves to buy homes in the 'hood?

I don't think it's guilt. It seems to be a reach for relevance. Having family who came over on the Mayflower is now seems snobbish and bland, and no longer enough to be the belle of the bourgeois cocktail circuit. To white folks who grew up pretty much privileged in carbon-copy suburban neighborhoods, the "black experience" is apparently quite seductive.

Black people in America are born with a meaningful background. It gives instant validity and gravitas to the person who can claim it. Even if you had a lovely family life and grew up with two cars and an Ivy League education, a black person is only a generation or two removed from tragic treatment.

That sure beats being white bread, right? There is no need for black people to claim they worked for their privilege because they are owed by the universe. Being black or communing with "black issues", excuses you from just being normal and happy, which are intellectually unchallenging or something.

The authenticity of blackness is drummed into us by our popular entertainment. As a little girl in England, I was fascinated with the American portrayal of American blacks on television. They were colorful (no pun intended), insightful, and funny. In dramas, they were frequently tied to unfair treatment wherein the bad guys (educated white businessmen, it seemed) would get what was coming to them by the closing credits.

My mum and I were always cheering for the black underdog. What I now realize is that black persons have been deified in American entertainment. Hollywoodseems to have produced a giant "We're sorry! We're just awful!" to the black population; likely as payback for all the blaxploitation films of the 1960s.

This long, sloppy and wet apology has treated black people as an exalted class in Hollywood's output. Black men overcome insurmountable obstacles; they are advisors, level-headed sidekicks, healers, and leaders. A black character endowed with anything less than godlike powers of perception, compassion, common sense, and wit would be seen as a racist caricature, that is unless the character was created by black people for black people.

There is nothing wrong with black people getting a positive spin in movies and TV, especially since some would argue that some forms of black music, such as gangsta rap, paint a negative picture. However, I do feel like we've been groomed over the years to readily accept, with giddy glee, any black leader who would come along. Guess who came along?

Allow me to answer that question: I give you "Sexy Brilliance!"

Erik Rush discussed similar concepts in his book *Negrophilia*, where the intro states simply, "Black is cool." That's certainly how Obama got elected. Even when Obama fails, there is somebody there to paint "black" his failure. Much of the time I feel like Liberal whites see black people more as their pets, rather than human and their equal.

Liberals pretend to love blacks once every two years, coincidentally around election time. Liberals scratch black people behind the ears and rub our bellies. Once black Democrats have exited the voting booth, it's back to the kennel for them.

***

It's an easily identifiable pattern. The very constituencies the Left claims to support are nothing more than 'black and gay' smokescreens behind which the Left hides their real disdain for the people they claim to represent.

The Left looks far and wide for a racist at any Tea Party gathering, yet refuse to see the ones in their midst. Whether it's Reid discussing light-skinned Negros, Biden commenting on the "cleanliness" of blacks, or Janeane Garofalo protecting lowly Negros in high places, the one common thread among Liberals is their ability to showcase their real racist feelings, in their so-called exposé of Conservatives and Republicans.

Liberal racism is not just showcased by Liberal politicians. Liberal artist are notorious as well. One such racist is John Mayer, the *chanteur* who gave us *"Waiting on the World to Change."*

In an interview in *Playboy* magazine, Mayer attempted to convince the world he is down with black people and gay people. However, what Mayer revealed was he is a racist homophobe.

During the interview, Mayer likened his penis to a white supremacist, saying he doesn't think his penis "opens himself" to black women.

Mayer (or his penis) may not like black women, but he sure likes Jimi Hendrix and has made lots of money off a son of a mother Mayer would have nothing to do with.

By now most twenty-somethings have been exposed to enough of the world to realize that color is very simply a genetic trait, a descriptor. People are people, or at least should be. Apparently this is not true for Mayer.

It's ok if Mayer *performs concerts* with blacks, *hires* blacks, *acts* like he is supportive of causes affecting blacks; however, he won't have sex with black women. Apparently that's just too nasty, thus Mayer's point of demarcation.

But Mayer wanted the readers of *Playboy* to know that he was all good with black people as he tried to intellectualize the word "nigger" by using it. *Pump your brakes, white boy!*

Mayer didn't realize that no matter how long he waits on the world to change, white folks just can't say, "nigger." Most white folks experience discomfort reading the word "nigger," which is why I have written it out quite a few times. So a white guy actually *saying* nigger is an obvious taboo, even for Liberals.

Such is the power of a word that should have as much significance as the word cracker, a word we hear all the time. When referring to whites as crackers, most people just showcase a wry smile. But don't even think using "the N-word."

To cover all his bases in the *Playboy* interview, Mayer felt the need to prove he could "out-gay" Perez Hilton, and prove that he didn't "hate fags." So Mayer opened himself up to a gay man, and gifted Hilton with a long kiss. *"I'm not a homophobe, watch me kiss a queer"*.

Sounds like Mayer should stop waiting on the world to change and perhaps begin changing himself. Stop trying to be cool and hip and all accepting of both blacks and gays and just admit to being a racist homophobe. I know that I don't have to kiss a man to prove that I'm not gay or down with white men.

It shouldn't surprise anybody to know that Mayer endorsed, liberal candidate Barack Obama. In doing so, Mayer had this to say:

"That's why hope is a worthwhile commodity...To those who question whether hope is a tangible product worth building a campaign around, I'd say take a look at despair and how powerful that has been in reshaping how people think and live."

Mayer supported a man for president whose wife, daughter, niece, sister, he wouldn't touch with a 10-foot "white supremacist" pole. So I'm a bit foggy on what hope Obama symbolized for Mayer. Perhaps the hope that Obama would help Mayer come to grips with his abhorrence of black women? I suspect that like many Guilters, Mayer felt that voting for Obama eased his racist guilt.

You may think that I'm coming down too hard on Mayer, but I'm not. If you are a single, heterosexual man unwilling to have sex with Halle Berry because her skin is caramel brown, then you are one of three things: A racist, an idiot, or a racist idiot!

And if Halle's not your type, I'm sure there is at least one 'sista' who can get Mayer's attention. Has this guy ever watched Soul Train, BET or an Ice Cube movie? Mayer should get a subscription to *Ebony,* because America has some smokin' hot black women, and Mayer is around them all the time.

I guess for Mayer *"Your [White] Body is a Wonderland."*

Mayer caught pure hell for his interview, as he should have. No cool points for using the word "nigger." He kissed a gay guy, which I think is *very* gay—I'm just sayin'. He pissed off black women all over the world, especially Africa, and he showcased just how hypocritical and ignorant the Left is.

Damage done, Mayer swore off interviewing, as if *interviewing* was his problem. Like most Liberals, John Mayer doesn't recognize that it is he who is the problem. But don't think for a second that the Left doesn't consider Mayer sexy brilliant.

***

The now very Liberal enclave known as Hollywood can discriminate based on anything. *"Sorry, but you're too black. You're good, but you're too fat. I like you, but you aren't pretty enough."* Hollywood can pick whomever they want, for whatever reason, and with no repercussions. Discrimination for the sake of art.

That's why we had movies where Charlton Heston plays a Mexican, then a Jewish-Egyptian. Hollywood has given us white guys in black face, because Hollywood can pick and choose who they want for a role. If they want a white guy to play a black guy, no problem, *"Hey black guy, you're out. We got De Niro."*

With respect to hiring people of color getting roles in Hollywood, they had a policy of *"Don't Tell, We Already Know, Negro!"* For many years, blacks were type-casted as pimps and prostitutes, or at the very least, stupid. It's slightly better today, however the major roles still go to Denzel Washington, Morgan Freeman, or Samuel L. Jackson.

Despite what Hollyweird is able to get away with, the group who allows us our freedoms, the military has to now conform to the LGBT[3] agenda. Do you think the topic of gays in the military is being discussed in China's military? What about North Korea's? Iran's? Score one for the Communist, Marxist, and other 'totalitarianists,' because they don't have to tolerate the insanity of Liberals, at least in their military organizations.

Gays in America's military say they want to be openly gay. What exactly is openly gay anyway? Do gays in the military now want to run around like Klinger from *MASH* in celebration of the repeal of DADT? If I were gay I'd be offended to be called *"openly gay."*

And if you can explain to me what it means to be openly gay, then I will certainly want to know the definition of being "openly straight," while you're at it. Are straights in the military flaunting their "open straightness?" Bravo for us; yet again we have identified an unwitting oppressor and new victims.

When I think of being 'openly anything,' I think about the black folks who say to me that I don't "act black." Sure I do. I am *openly* black. I don't act like a rapper or a street thug, if that's what they mean. I don't run around speaking in Ebonics and holding my naughty bits in public. That notwithstanding, I am still very much openly black.

However, being black doesn't define me. Being a good father, a good companion, a good friend, a Christ-follower, those things define me. I certainly would like them to. I'm cool with being openly American and openly human. I don't walk through life trying to act *black*, as some weirdos in society believe *black* to be.

I believe that most gays in the military could care less about openly exposing their sexuality and are content to just do their jobs. Unlike Hollywood where being gay or bi considered *a la mode*, the job of the military is to create military 'personnel,' regardless of sexual orientation, ethnicity, creed, or whatever. Black soldiers are not walking around saying, "I'm a black warrior." All the military cares about is the "warrior" part; truth be told, the military is more concerned with one's *competence*, and not as a gay, but as a warrior.

The same would be true of most gays, as most military men and women don't care what type of sex another soldier is having, as long as that sex doesn't infringe on them, or their ability to do their jobs.

I further suspect that the military has a much better "gaydar" than gays think. Their peers either know who is gay in the military or they have their suspicions. There are high ranking gays in the military now. The woman who filed the suit to repeal DADT is a retired Colonel. I'd be willing to bet you that most of the people who promoted her already knew the female Colonel had a penchant for the ladies. Given her rank, her gayness apparently didn't negatively affect her career. It would appear that the only person who was concerned about her gayness was her.

So what Liberals have done for the military is what they have been doing to all of America for decades; infecting the military with cancer. Soon promotions will be measured by how many "gays" we have at a certain rank, or "I didn't get this promotion or billet, because I am gay." Gays will require their own facilities, and they could end up where black people were in the '40's...segregated.

Blacks have been discriminated in the military for decades. Be it military or civilian, with rare exception,[4] people already knew who the blacks were in the military. Yet somehow in what Liberals believe is the most racist country in the world with the most heinous military, blacks managed to get a black Commander in Chief[5], and a black Chairman of the Joint Chiefs of Staff,[6] the two highest ranks in the military.

It has been argued to me that DADT is needed so that gay military personnel could invite their significant others to events. Not true. Gay military personnel could have appeared with their same sex partners, and under DADT nobody could question either of them. It was just two buddies hanging out, or "girl's night out," as far as DADT regulations were concerned.

But don't expect bases to look like the Mission District of San Francisco, because as for showing affection towards one's "partner," PDA[7] is forbidden by everybody, gay or straight. No fraternization or 'sororitization' either. Gays will likely try to change that.

I'm not sure what this new development will do to morale within the military. I do believe that there will be an "us versus them" mentality amongst homosexuals, which cannot be good for anybody, especially the military.

The military who is supposed to protect us now has become a victim of the Liberal agenda. Go ahead; declare your *open* gayness, whatever that means. But don't expect the military to act according to the gay agenda like the civilian world.

Legislating based on sexual proclivity is wrong. Few jobs require knowledge of one's sexual nature, and most that do are located in or near Hollywood or San Francisco. Repeal of DADT is just the Liberals' way of attacking an institution, an institution that was not discriminating against gays. The military is like Hollywood, in that they have a set of guidelines that make them effective. It's their effectiveness in voting to preserve the Constitutional values that they fight to protect that makes them a threat to the Left.

Turnabout is fair play, however. I say we attack Liberal and gay institutions—the media, Hollywood, Academia. Let's sue them for discriminating against Conservatives, straights, Republicans…those are creeds. Let show Liberals that we really understand… *the art of war.*

***

The Left is emboldened in their attempt to mold the military in their own vision only because they had so much success taking over another field that used to be overwhelmingly conservative: Religion. So I have decided to chastise three religious groups: Catholics, Jews, and "blacks,"[8] or more specifically the Godless Liberals hiding therein.

I don't consider any Catholic who voted for Obama to be a *practicing* Catholic. To have voted for Obama and refer to yourself as a Catholic, you are either a CINO—Catholic In Name Only—living a secular life, or you are just in a fog. Those are the *only* two choices.

Obama is for birth control, *real* Catholics are not. Obama is for partial birth abortion, *real* Catholics are not. Obama is practically a Muslim, *real* Catholics are *not.* And if Obama is not a Muslim, he is certainly not for religions that don't practice Black Liberation Theology.

These Catholic frauds should just stop fronting. They are not Catholics, nor are they religious. They don't even really give anything up for Lent, unless it's something they could easily give up without hesitation, like taking the Lexus instead of the Mercedes. No fasting in the wilderness, like the old days. They should just leave the Catholic religion and start worshipping some golden idol. I suggest a well-tanned Simon Cowell from *American Idol*, though he has left AI. Regardless, Cowell is just as Nobel worthy as these *faux* Catholics' current false idol.

I find the Jews even more perplexing than the Catholics who supposedly voted around 54 percent for Obama. The Jews supported Obama at around 78 percent, second only to black people, who were around 95 percent. Jews simply ignored the Muslim upbringing of Obama, his Black Nationalist leanings, and decided that voting "black" superseded their sanity.

Meanwhile Israel fights *daily* for its survival, constantly embroiled in a battle for their lives against Muslim enemies who surround them on three sides. My question is, "If the Muslims were to destroy Israel, do secular Jews think the Muslims will make a distinction?"

"Oh, you weren't a practicing Jew, so I won't cut off your head. Salam wa aleikum!"

Last time I checked, the Muslims want to destroy all Jews, practicing or not, and this would have included converted black Jew, Sammie Davis, Jr.[9]

I know Jews are pissed at Christians over the Jesus debate, but Christians are not trying to destroy the Jews or to cut off their heads. When perturbed, Christians won't launch rockets into the neighborhoods of Jews either.

Jews might get a few racist Democrats (*faux* Christians) who will accuse them of being money-grubbing Capitalists or not allowing Jews into one of their elitist clubs. But that's about it.

Admittedly, there is that venerable group of nostalgic Democrats[10] who might demonstrate from time to time in their white robes, hearkening back to the good old days when they were intimidating black people, occasionally getting their hands on a Jew for bonus points. But these days their numbers amount to little more than a pep rally in comparison to the Muslims—yes even moderate Muslims—who want Jews 187.[11]

As for blacks in America, "being black" has become a religion all to itself. Never in the history of American politics has a group been so targeted for monolithic thinking than blacks. For those wishing to gain 100 percent black-think, that conversion process is a *religion*.

Blacks who voted for Obama would easily pass for Conservatives in many ways, yet they have acted more Liberal than the Guilters who voted for Obama simply because he was black. Black theists exercised what I have defined as "moral relativity," which in effect makes them Liberals. They chose to disregard Obama's disdain for religion, the right to life, the sanctity of marriage, notwithstanding Obama's lack of fiscal responsibility, which has led to America getting her credit cards revoked.

Most blacks know that Obama attended church for *show*—for street cred. Street cred led to Obama gaining political clout, and Obama chose the church with the most political clout in the black community in order to *use* the black community.

Black theists proved to be equally racist, as they disregarded Obama's Godlessness in favor of "making history." Most knew Obama to be racist, with his policy of spread the wealth around and his obvious dislike of whites, as he proclaimed in both his books. Black theists chose to disregard the same racist policies of the past, in order to satisfy some cultural urge to elect a black man at any cost, even if it cost them their souls.

In fact, these black Democrats are not religious at all. Yes, they *attend* church, but that's it. They *pretend* church. It's like voting Democrat...they are programmed to do it. They may be fooling themselves, because they are *not* fooling God. These Sunday-only Christians have mastered the Democrat art of making their actions the complete opposite of their supposed beliefs.

I blame all three of these so-called religious groups for the election of Obama. Exactly what were these groups voting for? Apparently racism and Godlessness. None of them had *any* reasons to vote so overwhelmingly for Obama. Electing Obama, was essentially a slap in the face to God and a kick in the crotch to America. No one has ever answered "What Would Jesus Do?" with "vote to protect partial birth abortion" or "omit 'endowed by our Creator' from the Declaration of Independence". And yet, black Democrats convinced themselves that a vote for Obama was a vote for a good Christian black man.

We can only hope that these groups have learned their lesson. Obama has done nothing to further the cause of religion, or any of the tenets that religion speaks to, but that doesn't matter to the Liberals.

The support of Obama by people who call themselves religion is a sign of the times for America. The further slippage of America's moral values. These idol worshippers followed a false god. Obama is leading blacks (and others) to the depths of depravity, and far away from God. Obama is their god on earth. This is about as close as most Liberals will get to the *real* God.

***

Who needs the God of love, compassion, and human unity when you can have Allah—a god as hateful and hypocritical as the worst that the Left has to offer? No wonder they make an exception in their hatred of religion whenever Islam enters the equation.

The Left's disdain for Judeo-Christians is one reason they are so quick to fight for the rights of Muslims. What are Muslims, if not religious? They pray multiple times a day, and cling to their Qur'ans, yet not a peep against their religion from Liberals.

When Liberals speak of Muslims, their discussion is always centered on respecting their "religious rights," actually arguing for integration, not separation of church and state.

I certainly don't believe in much of what Islam offers, particularly in its treatment of women they deem unworthy, or "out of pocket"[12] a pimp would say. Pimps give out of pocket women beatdowns. Muslims go much farther, trumping beatdowns with burning and stoning as punishment for their 'disobedient' women.

But I do believe in their idea of a woman's purity, and how women should be treated special. My great grandfather told me that it is a man's responsibility to honor his woman.[13] Christ-followers are instructed by the Bible that "*a man is to love his wife as Christ loved the church.*"[14] I can see why Liberals are threatened by crazy talk like that.

Why is the Left so accepting of the idea of the absence of religion, but are so intolerant of those who believe in a religion or a God, except with Islam? Absent a moral authority, people can be very dangerous. Many see life as for the taking, literally. I'd prefer that a person have a moral compass. And if they happened to have a guide, say a Bible that they thump periodically, at least I can check out their instruction manual.

Telling me you're spiritual, as you rob me and try to sleep with my mate, I'm just not buying it. Atheists come with no instructions. If they wrong me, to whom do they report?

That lack of accountability is probably part of the appeal of atheism. As empty as their lives must be without the comfort of having a relationship with God, I'm sure they think it's fun to pretend that they are the Alpha and Omega and that they can literally change the world. What other group's faith (or lack thereof) can afford them the narcissism of believing that their decision to use incandescent lightbulbs or driving an SUV could cause the earth to spontaneously combust? The only person an atheist answers to is himself. Without a higher power to teach them humility, atheists have no reason to be tolerant of those who believe differently.

But that is where America finds itself, allowing the Left to openly show its disdain for Jewish and Christian religions with no repercussions, as time after time Muslims get preferential treatment. Like complaints over the word Christmas being used to describe Philadelphia's Christmas Village resulting in a name change to Holiday Village.

A small bank in Perkins, Oklahoma got a Christmas visit from the Federal Reserve examiners that cleansed the joint of Christianity in a hurry.

First to go was the Bible verse of the day. Then crosses on the teller's counter and discriminatory buttons that said, "Merry Christmas, God With Us," all of which were deemed inappropriate.

Next the Feds felt it urgent to check the bank's Internet site and scrubbed it of offensive things like the aforementioned "Bible verse of the day."

The Federal Reserve examiners maintained that the "symbols violated the discouragement clause of Regulation B of the bank regulations, which says, "... *the use of words, symbols, models and other forms of communication ... express, imply or suggest a discriminatory preference or policy of exclusion*."

A true policy of exclusion would have been a sign that read,

"We don't accept money from Atheists, Agnostics, or Muslims."

Last time I checked money is green and has no religious or other preference.

While the Fed is Johnny on the spot in stamping out Judeo-Christian symbolism, apparently they haven't examined public schools and universities around the nation granting Muslim requests for "prayer times, prayer rooms and ritual foot baths?"

The University of Michigan at Dearborn built foot baths for Muslim students to wash their feet before prayer. An elementary school in San Diego created an extra recess period for Muslim pupils to pray. At George Mason University... 'meditation space' laid out Muslim prayer rugs and separated men and women."

Non-Muslim students are asked to "observe Muslim rules in the prayer area, such as keeping men on one side and women on the other and removing shoes."

This begs the question, "*Is separating men, and women and making Christiansand Jewsremove their shoes in a public university to respect Islamic prayer space not an example of discriminatory preference or policy of exclusion?*"

As of 2007, there were 17 universities that had footbaths under construction including, Boston University, George Washington University and Temple University. At that time, nine universities designated Muslim prayer rooms including Stanford, Emory and the University of Virginia.

I don't know about you but footbaths in a publicly funded university certainly give the "appearance of discrimination," unless of course non-Muslim students have the freedom to cool their Budweisers in the foot baths when Muslims' feet are not being washed.

Ben Gamla Charter Hebrew charter school in Broward County, Florida is being watched, "*to make sure everything is conducted as required.* "Yet tax payer funded charter school grades K-8, Tarek ibn Ziyad Academy (TIZA) in Inner Grove Heights, Minnesota shares space with a mosque and the Muslim American Society of Minnesota whose mission is, "establishing Islam in Minnesota."

The students pray, eat halal food in the cafeteria, and practice Muslim holy day washing. They attend prayer assemblies, Qu'ran readings and mandatory Islamic Studies at the end of the day.

Although executive director, Asad Zaman maintains TIZA is not a "religious school," the public, taxpayer-funded school is now being "held up as a national model for a new kind of charter school." Apparently the new model is one where separation of church and state still stands, but separation of *mosque and school* doesn't.

Meanwhile, in Florida Christian teachers were handed down a legal order that prohibited them *"communicating with a deity... bowing the head... or folding hands."*

Muslims are free to indulge in ritualistic washings within the four walls of taxpayer-funded institutions, while Christian employees in Florida schools were, *"driven... to hide in closets to pray to avoid contempt charges."* In fact, if parents mention church or faith, or emails contain the dreaded Bible verses or say, "God bless you," teachers are forbidden to respond.

The strict anti-Christianity guidelines are in response to Pace High School Principal Frank Lay and Robert Freeman Athletic Director who gave a "15 second blessing for a lunch meal for 29 adults with no students present." Both men were prosecuted on criminal contempt charges and if convicted would have faced "six months in jail and $5,000 fines each."

Bible study in private home in San Diego fined, but Muslim prayer time in public San Diego elementary schools encouraged.

Liberal lunacy is making practicing Christianity a criminal act while Muslim students are being accommodated in every way. Why hasn't the Right come forward and alerted the American public to the discriminatory practices taking place where the faith of our forefathers is being squashed and Islam exalted? When are Conservatives and Republicans going to speak up? Maybe when we are forced to remove shoes in chambers and segregated into male and female groups to respect Muslim traditions over our own?

Every time the word "Christ" is taken out of Christmas and another footbath installed at the expense of Christians and Jews, a battle on behalf of Christianity is lost and Islam wins.

Representative Keith Ellison (D-MN) is teed off at Peter King (R-NY) for proposing an investigation into radical Muslims in America, which by the way Attorney General Eric Holder recently said pose a threat. Holder warns *"there is the alarming rise in the number of Americans who are more than willing to attack and kill their fellow citizens."*

Rep Ellison disagrees with Peter King because to investigate individuals who potentially could attack, maim or kill large numbers of Americans is unfair because in Utopia, "To vilify this group, is scary." So Ellison wants you to believe that being blown up in a terrorist attack is less scary than vilifying the perpetrators of the attack.

Ellison believes we should "enlist Muslims" to safeguard this country. I guess Ellison's memory is short regarding the Muslim military man in this man's military, who shot and killed many of his own troops in Afghanistan not long ago. Or perhaps Ellison has forgotten about the Muslim who shot up Ft. Hood? Oh yeah, there was this small incident of Muslims hijacking planes and flying them into our buildings.

When the enemy is in our midst, it's no wonder Muslims rights are trumping Judeo-Christian rights. How sexy brilliant is that?

***

Liberalism can be dangerous to your health, though Liberals want to make Conservatives the bad guys. One of the talking points used to pass the health care reform bill was the number 45,000. This is supposedly the number of Americans who die each year due to a lack of health insurance. Republicans were even labeled "terrorists" by the Left for the lack of health-care, as Keith Olbermann of MSNBC did on January 5 about our allegedly murderous private health-care system:

"What would you do, sir, if terrorists were killing 45,000 people every year in this country? Well, the current health care system, the insurance companies, and those who support them are doing just that....Because they die individually of disease and not disaster, [radio host] Neal Boortz and those who ape him in office and out, approve their deaths, all 45,000 of them - a year - in America. Remind me again, who are the terrorists?"

Yet far more Americans are killed each year by Liberalism.

For example in 1975, Congress took bold action to the 1973 Oil Embargo by enacting the Corporate Average Fuel Economy (CAFE) Program. The goal of the program was to lower the dependence American drivers had on foreign oil. It worked, because thousands of motorists have had their need for foreign oil reduced because of this legislation. Those motorists are dead.

A 1999 USA TODAY analysis of crash data and estimates from the National Highway Traffic Safety Administration and the Insurance Institute for Highway Safety found that, in the years since CAFE standards were mandated under the Energy Policy and Conservation Act of 1975, about 46,000 people have died in crashes that they would have survived if they had been traveling in bigger, heavier cars.

Liberals want us to believe that 45,000 people dying from a lack of health insurance is enough reason to enact massive health care reform, but at the same time they not only refuse to consider lowering the CAFE standard, they wanted to make them stricter, which would result in more deaths.

It's estimated that 2,000 people will die this year because of CAFE standards. Liberals are not concerned about these, as they justifiable losses in order to save the planet from the ravages of man-made global climate change—a proven farce.

Two thousand people a year is small in comparison to how Liberals began killing next. This time they used homophobia, as we were to learn: *"Sex doesn't cause AIDS– a virus does."*

AIDS was first identified in the United States in 1981. Since then, "an estimated 1,051,875 people have been diagnosed with AIDS in America." Close to 600,000 of them have died.

In 1983, there were only 1,500 cases of AIDS diagnosed in America, but the rate of infection was doubling every month. The gay rights community was engaged in a campaign of intimidation against those who would label the disease "sexually transmitted." The Stonewall Gay Democratic Club in San Francisco was one of the more powerful political groups in the Bay Area, and promoted the slogan, "Sex doesn't cause AIDS – a virus does."

According to David Horowitz, in his book *"Radical Son,"* the group was afraid that when 95 percent of the cases in San Francisco were among gay men, any correlation of the disease with promiscuous homosexual activity would "create a political backlash."

Gay rights activists in government compounded the problem.

Pat Norman was the Director of the Office of Lesbian and Gay Health in San Francisco's health department. She was also the chair of the Coordinating Committee of Gay and Lesbian Services, which compared the screening of blood donors as "reminiscent of miscegenation blood laws that divided black blood from white." They even compared it to the internment of Japanese during World War II.

During all this, the gay bath houses continued to operate. Some men there would have unprotected sex with up to ten other men a night. Liberals were concerned about the political backlash of the facts. It was easier to blame Reagan for committing genocide against the gay community by not funding AIDS research, than it was to close the bath houses and screen blood.

How many cases would have been prevented if Liberals had told the truth is impossible to calculate. However, we do know that there are more than a million Americans living with the disease today. More than 14,000 of them will probably die this year.

We're supposed to ignore than over half of all people with HIV are gay men because facts are homophobic. Seems to me that letting an entire demographic die off because we're too PC to acknowledge a problem would be a lot more anti-gay of a stance.

Homosexuals were killing each other, and the same is true for the black community, as illegitimacy is killing black people. Let me explain.

Today, close to 70 percent of black children are illegitimate. It wasn't always like this, as *Jewish World Review* points out. In 1880 Philadelphia, 75 percent of black families had two parents. New York, circa 1925, showed an illegitimacy rate among black families to be around 15 percent. By 1940, the rate was still only 19 percent. When the Liberals decided to take action in the '60's, the illegitimacy rate rose to 22 percent. This intervention has had dire consequences in the black community, and now is at epidemic proportions.

The lack of a father in a child's life has a profound effect on the child. According to an article by Glenn Sacks, having a father in the house "*was five times more important in predicting teen drug use than any other sociological factor, including income and race.*"

Also, a *Journal of Research in Crime and Delinquency* study concluded:

"...fatherlessness is so predictive of juvenile crime that, as long as there was a father in the home, children of poor and wealthy families had similar juvenile crime rates."

Today, black males make up almost half of America's prison population. Of all the murders in 2007, 43 percent were black. Close to 93 percent of the time, blacks are killed by other blacks.

Forty years of lies have done what 400 years of slavery could not do. It has destroyed the black family. Thomas Sowell said, *"The black family — which survived slavery, discrimination, poverty, wars and depressions — began to come apart as the federal government moved in with its well-financed programs to 'help.'"*

How many blacks have died because of the lack of fathers in a child's life? How many blacks have died because of government's "help?" That's a stat we may never know. But what we do know is there is no worst kind of enemy than Liberalism.

***

[1] Treating Americans like three-year olds

[2] SNAP counts people receiving food subsidies

[3] Lesbian-Gay-Bi-Sexual-Transgender

[4] Unless a black was light-skinned enough to pass for white, which happened much throughout history.

[5] Actually we've had more than one black Commander in Chief, most notable prior to Obama was Eisenhower who was 25% black.

[6] Colin Powell was the first black Chairman of the Joint Chiefs of Staff, the highest ranking non-civilian military officer.

[7] Public Display of Affection

[8] Being black is a religion of sorts

[9] Muslims would have even killed the Candy Man!

[10] The KKK

[11] 187 is the police code for a homicide

[12] Pimp term for a disobedient woman

[13] My father would say a man should honor his WOMEN!

[14] Eph 5:25-27

8

TAKE A SISSY TO THE BALLET, BUT NOT A FIGHT

When I was around nine, my grandmother and I went to a PTA meeting. I'm not sure what the big deal was that made her decide to attend, because it was a hassle for us to drive to town, especially in the evenings. But there we were, in the midst of hundreds of parents, most of whom had not brought their kids. I'm not sure why my brother Kirk wasn't there, but he was always good at getting out of things.

As the meeting started, the coordinator said a few words about why the people were gathered. And as with all such meetings from my childhood, the coordinator said we would play the Star Spangled banner to kick things off.

He asked if anybody could play piano, and to my surprise nobody raised their hand. A huge problem for me.

I had been taking piano lessons all of two months, and my grandparents had bought an upright piano—a vintage model that we rarely kept tuned. For my grandmother, it was the time to showcase my talents. So as the coordinator was scanning the room for a pianist, my grandmother was mumbling to me to raise my hand.

I protested to her that I didn't know how to play well enough to be featured, and her response was to nudge me out of my chair, an act which caused a quarter of the audience to look our way.

I took what was a long walk to the piano positioned in front of God and everybody. That piano looked like every demon I had faced up to that point in my short life, 88 black and white teeth snarling at me, daring me to get near them. It was truly life in a slow motion dolly shot. I had what seemed like the entire population of the City of Brady Texas, looking at me, waiting for the black Amadeus to dazzle their ears.

I asked the coordinator if he had any sheet music—like it would have helped!—to which he smiled and replied in a Texas southern drawl, "Everybody knows the Star Spangled Banner!"

"Yeah, well then let 'everybody' come play it," I thought.

No music and no talent, perfect! I took about ten seconds to warm up, pecking out the melody with my right hand. I played the first three notes, "O o say…", and prayed that the voices would drown out what could only be described as the collision of a train with a piano. But I played. I played like my life depended on it, which it sort of did. I played as if I had played the Star Spangled Banner that way a million times, catching the right note often enough to actually make me chuckle inwardly. That crazy old lady!

Ordeal over, I arose from the piano seat and went back to my seat, thoroughly humiliated. I can't express the combination of the overwhelming sense of embarrassment and fearlessness that moment created in me. I would grow up to fear very little, except the wrath of God. My grandmother had unwittingly created a warrior!

***

Beneath the righteous indignation of most Liberals resides a scoundrel's heart. Mostly frauds who wear one mask in public, Liberals have many others tucked away and at the ready. Even their family and friends don't really know them, and if they do, it's only in the circles in which they run together.

In other words, if you know a Liberal from a cooking class, that is how they behave only at cooking class. If you see them out at a bar, don't expect to meet the same person. I actually had a Liberal tell me, "We [he and his wife] have different friends for different circumstances."

Just so you get my meaning, understand that Conservatives have friends who are different, but they are always our friends. Liberals would not dare intermingle the wrong friends, as this could be embarrassing for a Liberal.

This same philosophy with friends is how Liberals deal with issues. So as Michelle Obama gallivanted across the globe like a jet-setting fashionista, she was content to allow the poor to struggle to pay their mortgages. If it weren't for the grass roots media, Michelle's little multi-million dollar jaunt would have even received little if any scrutiny.

When the details of her trip were discovered[1], the White House said that it was an official trip to visit with the Spanish royal family. People all over America can't even dream of a vacation, yet Liberals were blaming the mortgage crisis on the Republicans, and warning Americans not to believe what we witnessed Michelle Obama doing. The Obama's do care.

As Garrison Keillor[2] bragged, "I am Liberal and Liberalism is the politics of kindness."

Spoken like a true Liberal elitist who has never visited a black neighborhood. Liberalism is also the politics of moral relativity, so be sure to have a dictionary that redefines kindness on the fly. How kind it was for millionaire Al Gore who in 1998 scraped together $353.00 to donate to charity. Don't spend it all in one place, America.

But we are supposed to be convinced that Gore has the best interest of Mother Earth in mind as he swindles mega millions from people all over the world with the farce of manmade global climate change.

Like Gore, the Obamas care too. They care about themselves. With the money they have spent on vacations since coming to power, the Obamas could have taken entire communities on vacation. Their dinner in New York City, likely to celebrate Government Motors declaring bankruptcy that week was enough to feed thousands of America's homeless.

The guy who spent more money campaigning than anybody in history (even adjusted for inflation) had the nerve to accuse Republicans of shady funding of campaigns. But it was not only the amount of money Obama raised, but the questionable sources of the funding. Even Democrats were incredulous when Obama tried accusing Republicans of cheating on fundraising, and they abandoned Obama as fast as an indicted Mafioso turning state's evidence.

The Democrats turned right around and held a fundraiser: For campaign finance reform. As it turned out, during the campaign season leading up to Eviction 2010, Democrats were actually donating to Republicans' campaigns. Things got so bad that Obama was asked to stay away from many campaigns, and was replaced by the other first black president, Bill Clinton.

Desperate, Obama accused Republicans of "trying to keep black people from voting!" Yep, the same guy who tossed out the voter intimidation case of the New Black Panther Party, one of whose leaders talked openly about "killing Liberals' babies," is accusing Republicans of the same tactics. I don't quite understand Obama's complaint, because he was the guy who legalized voter intimidation.

So how to the Liberals get away with these types of things. Bush couldn't have done the things I mentioned without taking serious heat. Bush never took Laura on a lavish date on taxpayer money,[3] and he spent the majority of his vacations at his ranch in Crawford, TX working the ranch, and not on mega million dollar taxpayer-funded boondoggles.

But the Obamas do pretty much whatever they want, while the Republicans can't get their hypocrisy to echo off the sounding board.

With the momentum building for Eviction 2010, the imminent November shellacking-to-come for Obama, soon-to-be House Speaker Boehner had barely finished his comments regarding the Republican's Pledge to America, and I already had a bad taste in my mouth. Republicans were serving lite tea, and presenting it like it was a bottle of 1787 Chateau Lafite Bordeaux.

The Pledge to America was little more than a retread of Newt Gingrich's Contract with America. If you are a stickler, we have gone from a contract, something that at least implies a binding agreement, to a pledge, something that is worth only what the owner is willing to commit.

And what exactly are Republicans willing to commit—to pledge—to the American people, or more specifically the Tea Party people? They pledged to continue to fight for something we already had.

In capitulating to get Obama extend the Bush tax cuts, Republicans were strutting around DC like the barnyard cocks of the walk conceding another

13 months of unemployment insurance. Bravo for the Republicans for getting taxpaying American our money back and allowing Democrats a practically infinite entitlement. Republicans got played.

Obama had gotten his shellacking. He told the NY Times that he may have made a "tactical error." Sure, and Hurricane Katrina was a "rain shower."

I'd say underestimating the will of the people is a bit more than a tactical error. Sexy brilliance did define "shovel-ready", as he gave 60+ House Democrats and 6 Democrat Senators the shovels to dig their own political graves.

I suggested at the time that Republican and Conservatives should gloat about the November 2010 election. The Tea Party movement was vindicated. Up to that point, politicians' expectations of the Tea Party movement reminded me of the two buzzards talking, and one says, "Can't kill nothing, and won't nothing die!" The grass roots disproved the idea that memories fade in election cycles, and that a year is many lifetimes in politics. Politics had changed for the foreseeable future, as the proletariat had been awakened.

Liberals had put Obama and the entire Democrat Party between a rock and a bigger rock! The Obama youth brigade was demoralized. The Left of center appeared to have been spooked by the ghost of Reagan, and were running to the right faster than a white woman in Compton. All this was happening and the Republicans were negotiating!

Democrats were supposedly up in arms over the provision that would not allow taxes to be raised on those making $250K. It was mostly hype, however. The Dems were just posturing, selling the age old message that the rich are evil, when they don't really believe it. But the message sells well, and allows the Democrats to appear to be for the common man. Republicans are evil capitalists, Democrats humanitarians.

Unemployment used to be 26 weeks, and Republicans allowed 13 months to be added by Democrats to this "entitlement." An additional 56 weeks. At 99 weeks we were at almost four times the original duration of unemployment, now we've added 56 weeks, more than double that original amount.

Unemployment benefits are a clever way to redistribute wealth. The Liberals got another quarter mile, and are still working towards that mile. If you don't believe me, ask yourself this question: Has there been any discussion of a limit on unemployment benefits? If there ever is, I'd like to know the absolute maximum timeframe that Liberals have in mind. Don't hold your breath waiting on that answer, because the fact is there is no limit on unemployment for Liberals. Liberals believe in lifetime benefits, particularly if undeserved. They award themselves fat pensions that pay them for life. Government workers and unions, getting paid to do nothing with no reduction in lifestyle. Unemployment benefits are a payoff to the poor to keep voting Democrat, because the poor know that most Republicans won't allow you to continually get free money.

As usual the Republicans missed an opportunity to step on Obama's skinny neck, and brightly illuminate the reason for the need to extend unemployment for two Christmases: Obama's policies can't create jobs; in fact, Obama's policies kill jobs!

Obama promised 4.1M jobs, when he campaigned, yet there is no mention of this. He then promised to create 95K new jobs every month in 2010, yet he did bupkus.

Instead of reminding Americans about Obama's inability to accomplish anything, and his complete incompetence, the Republicans caved on unemployment. The millions of people whose unemployment was to be cut off needed to be reminded of Obama's incompetence, and not sold on the idea that Republicans are heartless. Republicans are job creators. The tax cuts are a proven way to create jobs and help the economy.

This Republican move was strictly symbolic. Strategy 101. Business as usual for a group that still hasn't learned how to fight. A two-year extension of the Bush tax cuts was a reprieve, little more than a stay of execution; not a full pardon. We will have to revisit this issue again in two years, and the Republicans will feel like bullies yet again, because roles will be reversed. Obama will look like he's trying to keep the middle-class tax cuts, and Republicans will be fighting for the wealth.

In the meantime, businesses will see this as two-years to batten down the hatches, not to invest. After all, there is a socialist in the White House, and the way the Republicans fight, he might be there four more years.

Since nobody else seems willing to ask this, I will. When did the rich stop being Americans? Do they have rights or are they to be bandied about like ping pong balls for political expediency? There is nothing wrong with being rich, and poor people don't make good employers.

Most kids I know aspire to be this, so do you hate kids?![4] Most poor people I know want to be some version of "rich," do you hate poor people?

It's counter-intuitive to hate the rich, because most of us strive to be rich. Why does the government want us to hate our potential selves?

And when discussing "those who make over $250K," Democrats are quick to discuss "millionaires." Making $250K does not make you a millionaire. And even if it did, who is the government to put a limit on your productivity, your aspirations, or your dreams?

Senator Claire McCaskill (D-MO) said on Fox News commented, [pp] "...the millionaires 'second million' should be taxed heavier." Why? Because in order to be a millionaire, you must be evil, right?

The Republicans should have forced Obama to let the Bush tax cuts expire, thus increasing taxes on everybody. The unemployed would have had to deal with their lack of funds and lack of jobs, and they would know exactly where to put the blame, and Conservative would have been even more upset with him. But the Republicans were afraid of being demonized, and seen as supporting the rich. Wimps!

The rich deserve to be supported. Outside of government jobs, it is the rich who employ people and finance the government. It is time that Republicans stop allowing the rich to be treated as second-class citizens. I don't think they will, and selling the idea of being rich over poor has to be the easiest message of all to sell, even easier than making everybody and everything racist.

The Republicans' lack of backbone makes Obama Santa Clause for the next two years. He simply funded reparations to the poor, payoffs for the remainder of his campaign season. Most of the unemployed now qualify to be wards of the government. And if they don't mind waiting in long lines, along with unemployment benefits, they can now get housing assistance, a "food" credit card, a cell phone, and a host of other benefits. Welcome to Uncle Sugar Land, where Obama is King.

The added benefit for most of the poor is they can go on the hustle. A hustle is a little "somethin' somethin'" that the government doesn't have to know anything about. Cash deals or bartering. The government encourages this behavior, because you can only go so far with a hustle. Once you're on the hustle, the government has you right where they want you; voting Democrat. Merry Socialistmas, 2011 and 2012!

***

If you think the election of a half-black president in 2008 was historical, consider the history America made in the election of 2010 or what Conservatives called Eviction 2010.

Laura Ingraham touched on it in an interview with Carly Fiorina, where Ingraham called 2010 "The Year of the Woman" for Republicans. I can't totally agree with Ingraham on this, because I think this election was much more than the year of the woman. It was a Republican Renaissance.

Along with the many Republican women running all around the country in congressional and gubernatorial races, there were 15 remaining black Republicans running for the House (one more if you include the Virgin Islands). There existed the potential to get more black Republicans elected to Congress since Reconstruction, though only two made it.

There were also nine Latinos House candidates, and one Latino Senate candidate, Marco Rubio who was elected to the Senate. Finally, there were two Asians running on the Republican ticket.

In New Mexico, Susana Martinez, the first Hispanic woman to win a major party gubernatorial nomination, won her race. In Nevada, Brian Sandoval, a former U.S. District Court judge, is the new governor of that state.

Republicans in recent years bolstered their minority ranks by electing Louisiana's Bobby Jindal as the first Indian-American governor in 2007, and in 2008 New Orleans' Anh "Joseph" Cao as the first Vietnamese-American member of Congress.

It must perplex the Democrats that in the post-racial, "all things being equal society" both women and minorities are finding their safe landing zone in the Republican Party.

What should be most disturbing to Democrats is that black Conservative candidates were for the most part not running in gerrymandered districts with heavy black populations. The same was not true for the Democrats, as 37 of the 39 members of the Congressional Black Caucus (CBC) are running in majority black districts.[5]

Despite this very racist trend in the Democrat Party, don't expect the state-run media to hold Democrats to task. They have been corralling black people into "black neighborhoods," then assigning black Democrat politicians to control black people.

The obvious message by Democrats is they will allow black "leaders" to hold dominion over other black people in black neighborhoods, but these black politicians shouldn't even think about venturing out to white neighborhoods. This is true of most Latino Democrats as well. If you are a minority, the Democrats expect you to know your place.

The Congressional Black Caucus actually campaigned against Allen West, the black candidate in Florida, and campaigned for his opponent...a white man. Where is the NAACP to denounce the CBC for not supporting a decorated black military man and great American patriot?

It appears that Colonel Allen West had the right color, but the wrong political party affiliation in order to get either the Congressional Black Caucus to endorse him or the NAACP to cry "racism" against the CBC, all of whom are members of the NAACP. And don't expect La Raza to support any of the Republican Latino candidates.

Not getting the full support of the GOP across the board disappointed a few of these minority and women Conservative candidates; however they were not dismayed. Minority Republicans support the history of the Republican Party, and know that it will be they who put the GOP back on the path to Constitutional Conservatism.

This Republican Renaissance was a throwback to politics the way the Founding Fathers intended it. Most of these Conservative candidates had entered politics for the first time in their lives, and were not institutional politicians. Institutional politicians call their seats by name, e.g. Ted Kennedy's seat, Joe Biden's old seat, Barack Obama's senate seat. These candidates know that these are the people's seats.

This group of black Conservatives rejected the party "machine," opting instead for the support of the grass roots—the people. If elected, they wouldn't owe the Republican Party any favors, nor do they owe any lobbyists or big money PACS. They would be free to legislate without prejudice.

The Republican Party machine did not support many of these black Congressional candidates, but not due to racism. The Republican Party didn't support a lot of candidates, including whites. But shame on the Republican Party for not recognizing the importance of electing this new brand of politician, particularly those who could put the Left on their heels. Sexy brilliance on by the Republicans, still as lost as last year's Easter eggs.

Luckily, Americans are beginning to understand that the Left uses racism for their nefarious deeds, which is simply to make Americans more dependent on government. This is why so many blacks, Latinos, Asians, and women are entering politics as Republicans.

***

Not long ago, and certainly prior to Eviction 2010, Obama was all smiles when he complained of the Tea Party movement, "You would think they should be saying thank you!" That's how the worst kinds of criminals think, especially those who are sexy brilliant.

In November of 2010, Obama got his "Thank you," when Tea Partiers slapped that aloof look off his face, if only for a short time. Before we get too far ahead of ourselves, let's remember that after our exuberance over ruining the filibuster in the Senate with the election of Scott Brown, we still got out-lawyered.[6] Despite overwhelming opposition, Obama and team passed ObamaCare or what America's seniors can refer to as DeathCare for them.

We've proven that Obama can be beaten. However, I won't allow Conservatives to become complacent. It is not the punch you see that knocks you out, it's the one you don't see. And this group of sissies is strategizing on how to throw phantom punches, better known as "sucker" punches.

If we were talking real fighting, no true Conservative would be scared of Obama or the other Liberal sissies. Sissies punch like Obama throws a baseball. But when it comes to fighting legal battles, sissies fight like Revenge of the Nerds, and they can get downright ugly.

If you know the enemy and know yourself you need not fear the results of a hundred battles. - Sun Tzu

One secret to understanding Obama and his ilk is to know that they do not care about being right on an issue. Being right has nothing to do with the game. The real game is the Left's ability to impose their will, no matter the issue.

You don't want healthcare? The Left doesn't care. You get healthcare, whether you like it or not. Liberals know what's best for you, and what's best for you is the Liberal elites lining their pockets with your money.

The Republicans did all they could to stop DeathCare; they just didn't know the enemy. Everyone bet on the Scott Brown effect; meanwhile Obama's henchmen changed the battle plan. Though the Massachusetts loss was painful, the Democrats shifted strategy, knowing that the Republicans would not see past that short-lived victory. Then came the sucker punch. Pow.

How demoralizing for Republican who thought they had derailed ObamaCare with the Scott Brown victory, only to get knocked out a few weeks later. This is because Republican leaders of today are the smartest dumb guys in politics. They have single-threaded strategies.

So ObamaCare was forced on America by the worst kind of criminal. Right now we are blaming Obama. Soon we will be convinced that Obama-Care was what we wanted. Then eventually, when it doesn't work, it will become the Republicans fault for forcing ObamaCare upon us.

***

Perhaps Obama is right. Maybe we do need to thank him. After all he seemed to expose what the government has been doing to us more than any president. Originally we thought politicians just wanted our money. But we learned from Obama that they want control.

We have been consumed with government watching us, that we should have been watching them. Frankly we took our eye of the ball years ago, perhaps decades. While we were napping, government has been slowly implementing the mechanisms to control us.

For example, today the government can and does keep track of real time credit card purchases by citizens. It's like having a GPS signal on your entire life. You've seen how the police use credit card purchases to track down criminals, and most of us are all for this. However when you consider just how obtrusive government can be, it does make you think, "What's next?" As Wired.com points out, government may decide to interfere with your purchases …in real time. What could totalitarians do with this capability? How about ration your gasoline?

There was legislation to put a tracking device on cars, so that the government could tax you for your mileage driven. With LoJack, that is certainly easy to do. And if the government knows where you drive and how much, they could easily deny your purchase of certain vehicles or suggest you buy the more fuel-efficient vehicles manufactured by GM.

Obama suggested that we lower our thermostats, but what if the government didn't have to ask. Smart meters certainly allow the government a peek into your electricity usage. With all the green energy initiatives, it is not beyond the pale to believe that the Fed will require everyone to have solar and wind power for their homes soon. Those who do not may have their usage regulated. The technology is there with all the "smart" appliances that have been developed.

What about during rolling brownout times, can the government 'redistribute' electricity to the poor, because they need it more than those evil rich. To be sure the cutoff doesn't happen next time, all you have to do is head down to your voter registration office, re-register and vote Democrat in future elections. They have the records.

The government will soon know exactly how many appliances you own and how much you use them, as soon as you remove them from the boxes and plug into the grid.[7] Consider the "luxury penalty" a big screen TV might cause you. If your TV is too big, the government might order you to switch it off. You would get a warning on the specific TV(s) in question, before the government switches it off for you, their way of giving you choice.

Maybe the government doesn't like what channels you watch, or they notice that you watch Glenn Beck on the Fox News Channel every day at 4P, so they government decides to do systems check at 4P every day, or that's the 'peak usage' and thus the most opportune time for the government to regulate the grid.

Government has been using data to study economic patterns for years. They have predictive behavior models that study scenarios, when certain triggers are pulled. Futurists work with computer scientists to develop solutions to these scenarios. Government is always tweaking these models, so they know what to look for. One example is inside of the 2000 page Obama-Care bill, the government put a stipulation to track the precious metals purchases of Americans. What does monitoring the purchase of gold have to do with health care? Nothing, of course. But tracking gold has everything to do with a government who wants to track the people it deems radicals.

Those who own gold have a hedge against inflation, and may never need the government. They can go off the grid, essentially live an untraceable life. Gold gives you the possibility of not being tracked, and that upsets the model.

The government wants to know where you shop and what you buy. You might be shopping at Wal-Mart, where unions aren't established. The government may wish to sway you on where you buy that new Volt. In the case of the car dealers, the Fed may shut down those who donated too much to Republicans.[8]

Where are the Republicans in all of this? They're not standing up on the TSA's admitted violation of the 4th Amendment, and this is supposed to be the new, Constitution-obsessed era in the Republican Party. They have to know what's been happening, so why don't they fight harder. It does make you wonder just how much Republicans are part of the problem.

***

Government has grown way too big and way too powerful, so much so that it must constantly feed. And like an artificial intelligence computer, government has finally learned how to feed itself.

Federal agencies are created by crisis. Dozens of new departments were created by ObamaCare, all to supposedly save 45,000 people annually. My bet is if you cut the size of government, you will have the money to get those

45,000 people the medical care they need, while we look for a system that doesn't involve the Fed.

But Republicans didn't put a massive cut in the Fed in their Q1 plan, just cutting taxes. I agree with cutting taxes; however the only way to take taxes off the table is to cut the size of government continually.

Republicans should be discussing alternative tax systems, and scaling back America's biggest extortion organization. Is any Republican willing to step out on that flimsy fruit-filled limb, and begin addressing our antiquated "regressive" tax system with the Fair Tax? Obama added to America's torment as he hired 16,000 new tax collectors to enforce DeathCare.

I do give the Republicans credit for their initiative to scrap DeathCare. However that doesn't end the extortion of the IRS, as the Fair Tax would render those 16,000 and many thousand others working in the Department of Revenue, boat anchors.

In the much ballyhooed Pledge to American, the Republicans said that they will make sure that legislation is reviewed by Congress. Nice. Legislation will get reviewed. This reminds me of when Emanuel Cleaver (D-KS) after a meeting with Obama, reported back to his constituents that he [pp] "got Obama to try to add jobs in Kansas City."

Considering that the Liberals won't even read legislation before shoving it up the hind quarters of us Sodomites, I'd say that is a win—if you're a sissy Republican. Thanks for leaving gas money on the dresser.

The Republicans have pledged to cut spending, but without a lot of real specifics except that they will freeze the growth of government. That's like a 400lb man saying he will freeze eating. It's just not possible. Even if it was possible to "freeze" the size of government, big deal. How about Republicans pledge to cut the size of government, not by dieting but by liposuction? In case the Republicans are not sure where to lipo, I have the solution: Everywhere.

There is not a single government agency that doesn't look like Rosie O'Donnell's silhouette. The Department of Energy, established in 1979 by the former worst president in history Jimmy Carter was formed with the goal to "lessen America's dependence on foreign oil." This department received $26B this year, taking the total spent on "the goal" to over half a trillion dollars since inception, and America is no less dependent on foreign oil.

The Department of Energy boasts 16,000 bureaucrats ($1,625,000 per bureaucrat) not to mention the estimated 100,000 contractors needed to support the agency. For our money, America has a few ugly wind farms, and a lot of methane gas spewing from bureaucrats. Do Republicans think this agency is a sacred cow?

Another department engendered during the Carter Abomination is the Department of Education. Since the ED was formed, America has actually gotten dumber, and I'm not just referring to the electing of Obama.

The ED has 5000 employees, and oversees a budget from $56B to $68B (the numbers given on their website) depending on which report you read, demonstrating that they can have a budget differential of $12B and not even realize it.

Pick either number, as they are both huge. And what does America get for its money, many municipalities where half the kids are dropouts. Imagine running a business where half your product was thrown away? Yet these "educators" seem content with 50% of their product not making it; or making it, if you're a "cup is half full" type.

Even with this dismal report, Republicans are not trying to dismantle the ED, as Reagan attempted. Nor are they squashing the useless Department of Energy, the Department of Agriculture, Interior, and all others government money incinerators.

Instead Republicans are for the most part ignoring these over-bloated, blood-sucking leeches that live by sucking the blood of the American tax-payers... and quite a few Chinese.

Unlike the constituency of the past, Republicans will find the grass roots people of today are like the American military of WWII. Tea Party folks are willing to storm the beaches and take the fight to the enemy. All the platitudes, political double-speak, and otherwise gobbledy-goop will not work to bamboozle us.

Republicans need to throw away the Gingrich playbook and evolve. It will be a long time before the stage is set as it has been by a movement as powerful as the Tea Party. The Pledge to America is blasé to say the least, and symptomatic of what is wrong with Republicans... old guard and lacking creativity.

Republicans should understand that the 70 percent of the Tea Party is Republican. We are sick and tired of seeing Republicans giving us more of the same. What Tea Partiers won't stand for is lite tea.

***

As with Ted Kennedy, it took God himself to "retire" Senator Robert Byrd (D-WV) from the Senate. That power must be an intoxicant, because Byrd simply would not leave. Byrd is described as a fearless fighter for the Constitution, and the state-run media outlets say things like, "Byrd had a short stay in the Klan."

He is quoted in 2005 as saying of joining the Klan, [pp], "*I know now I was wrong... I apologize a thousand times.*"

To prove to you how crazy Liberals are, consider that Byrd joined the Klan in the early 1940's. He recruited 150 of his friends into the Klan. As late as 1946 or so Byrd was still using platitudes in describing the work of the Klan, though he claims he was stopped paying his dues after only a year. I had friends who stopped paying for cable, but he was still getting cable.

But even if you believe Byrd's lies, then explain to me why Byrd was still trying to deny the civil rights of blacks in 1964 when he filibustered the 1964 Civil Rights Act. Republicans sponsored that legislation, whereby blacks would actually be treated as true citizens of America. I don't recall Byrd apologizing for that.

Byrd apparently overlooked his Party's stance against the Republican-sponsored anti-lynching laws. Byrd just couldn't fathom the idea of taking away the Democrats' favorite sport of "*Eeny meeny miny mo, catch a nigger by the toe?*"

Byrd's ending? "*If he hollers, don't let him go... string that nigger up!*"

Byrd didn't regret being in the Klan; Byrd regretted having to admit that he was in the Klan. And Byrd wasn't just IN the Klan, he WAS the Klan.

Klan leadership recognized Byrd's ability to recruit, and admired his leadership. Being a stellar member in the Klan helped Byrd achieve and retain his high ranking in the Senate.

What does Byrd has to be sorry about, given that the Klan provided his meteoric rise within the "Party of the Klan"—the Democrats. Byrd should have just accepted what "fate" dealt him, and not apologized for being what he was—a cross-burning racist his whole miserable life.

Byrd was not alone in his regrets, however. In case you wonder why Jimmy Carter works so hard building houses for the poor, you should know that he is making up for all the Negros he oppressed.

Though Carter now better known for his guilt assuaging work with Habitat for Humanity and disparaging the country over which he presided over as president; let's just call a cracker a cracker. Carter should be known for the discrimination that he practiced, like when Carter felt that building a black school next to a white school in Sumter County Georgia was not such a great idea. In capitulation to his fellow Democrat racists on the Sumter County School Board, Jimmy didn't want black children to get too close white school children.

But Carter didn't limit his segregationist ways to just schools, as he said in Time Magazine in 1976:

I'm not going to use the federal government's authority deliberately to circumvent the natural inclination of people to live in ethnically homogeneous neighborhoods...I have nothing against a community that's made up of people who are Polish or Czechoslovakian or French-Canadian or blacks who are trying to maintain the ethnic purity of their neighborhoods.

Carter is the father of "the black neighborhood," as far as I'm concerned.

Carter later apologized for his actions, and that's all it took for Progressive Democrats to expunge his racist record.

Hugo Black—another racist Democrat and member of the Klan—has been elevated to the status of icon by Progressive Democrats. And as with all racist Democrat icons, Progressive Democrats say that Black "joined the Klan only to further his political career."

We have yet another member of the Klan who did no harm to blacks, but joined only for political expediency. It does leave me curious as to exactly which members of the Klan were lynching blacks and white Republicans? I guess that's where the white hoods come in handy. In case any Klansmen run for office later in life, they can always shrug and say, "Hey, it wasn't me! I was the guy serving punch in the back of the room."

For the few Progressive Democrats who know or admit that FDR appointed the flamboyant Klansman Black to the Supreme Court, they usually say, "As a member of the Supreme Court, Black later fought for the rights of blacks." Really? How much fighting should Black have done to undo his representation of a Klansman who killed a clergyman sent to protect black people?

Black's Supreme Court record on race amounts to little more than token gestures on correcting his most heinous record on race, a record of abject oppression and intimidation of blacks and the Republicans who attempted to help blacks.

None of this will matter to Leftist revisionists, who will move mountains and empty oceans to wipe away the racist past of the Democrats, in an effort to make heroes out of racists, to create sexy brilliance where there is none.

Progressive Democrat racist scoundrels who replaced lynching of blacks at the hands of whites, with drive-by shootings of blacks at the hands of other blacks.

Black, Carter, Byrd and many other white racist Democrat scoundrels traded their Klan garb for business suits, and their strategies against blacks grew smoother with age, like 25-year old Scotch.

But they now have black politicians who are even more heinous than they, and more than willing to take their place. The white racist Democrat scoundrels pale in comparison to their replacements, members of the Congressional Black Caucus—pardon the pun. And like their white racist brethren, the CBC practices oppression of blacks, and they are forgiven as well.

***

There was much hoopla over Felipe Calderon's speech to Congress, and his chastising of America for Arizona having to gall to actually protect its citizen from the scourge of illegal immigration. The atrocities didn't end there, however.

The second atrocity was committed by the Democrats in Congress who actually clapped, then gave Calderon a standing ovation. I can almost understand Obama's incessant bowing and praise of Chinese leaders, since they're holding so many IOUs with his signature on them. But what do the Mexicans have on us that we should pretend that they're the moral authority? Mexico doesn't give welfare checks and free medical care to Americans who come there illegally. If Congress thinks that Arizona's immigration bill is so inhumane, they should have been throwing tomatoes at Calderon for his own country's treatment of illegal immigrants.

For most Conservatives, that was the real atrocity, besides the idea that some third-rate, rinky-dink president would have the nerve to lecture us. However there was a third atrocity that went mostly unnoticed, and that was the Republicans' reaction.

Many would say that the Republicans were right not to react, and these same people were comforted that Republicans sat on their hands and remained quiet. Well they could not be more wrong.

By not saying anything, Republicans allowed, yet again, the narrative of the Left to win out. Republicans looked like voiceless, viagraless, sexy brilliant eunuchs, while Pelosi and the rest of the Liberal incorrigibles sold the idea to the world that the US believes our sovereignty not worth fighting for. This was despite Americans' overwhelming opposition to illegal immigration.

Liberal Democrats don't have to care what Americans think, because Republicans fight like sissies. Instead of sitting there in quiet "defiance," the passive aggressive pansies that make up the current crop of Republicans should have pulled a Joe Wilson, shouting to the rafters in unison: "ES UN MENTIROSO...NINO! Translation: "YOU LIE...BOY!"

How dare Calderon come to our country and lecture us on illegal immigration. Mexico doesn't allow illegal immigration?! How dare he lecture us on "racial profiling," when (1) Arizona's law had nothing to do with racial profile, and (2) Mexico's laws allow for racial profiling?

The Republicans should have shut Calderon down during his speech with their outrage. And if that didn't work, they should have walked out in unison. Not shouting or leaving is proof positive of the lack of warriors in the Republican Party.

If the fire burns in your belly against illegal immigration, there is no amount of decorum that should allow you to let "el jefe"[9] of Mexico—or any other country for that matter—lecture you, especially when he is wrong. "ES UN MENTIROSO...NINO!"

Calderon and the rest of Mexico should respect the laws of the United States, even if they don't respect the many traitors who currently govern this country. Calderon shows his respect by exporting drugs, gang violence, and human trafficking from a country that he can't run well enough for anybody to want to stay. If his people don't want to stay, certainly nobody wants to visit, according to Latin Business Chronicle.

Mexican tourism has fallen off big time, even in the resort areas. Don't even consider going to a border town, where murder rates are in the hundreds per month, equaling all major U.S. cities combined in some Mexican border towns. Kidnappings at the rate of 200 per month, more than all the kidnappings in the U.S. combined. Talk about the Wild Wild West.

What would Calderon had said, had Arizona adopted Mexico's policy of illegal immigration? You know, the policy that arrests illegal immigrants and puts them away for two years. The policy that allows for citizens' arrests of illegal immigrants. The policy that allows for racial profiling? That same policy says you must bring tangible talent to Mexico to be considered for legal immigration or you can't get in?

Would the Democrat traitors in Congress have clapped for that policy? Would the Republican sissies have sat on their hands? It seems nobody challenged Calderon on his sexy brilliance.

***

[1] Cost of $375K; a tenth of that just for the plane rides; brought 40 guests; all at taxpayer expense

[2] Writer for The New Yorker and Salon.com {Liberal rag} and humorist, as you can tell.

[3] Good Morning America eagerly reported Laura's expensive dinner, but didn't bother mentioning that it was paid for by a private group, not the taxpayers.

[4] Using Liberal logic to emphasize my point.

[5] Contrary to what Liberals would have you believe, it's not racist white people who are most likely to "vote their race". It's black Democrats.

[6] ObamaCare still passed, despite Brown breaking up the filibuster-proof Senate.

[7] Reminiscent of the movie, The Matrix.

[8] 900 car dealerships were closed for no other logical reason, but most were owned by registered Republicans

[9] Spanish for leader

9

EMANCIPATION II – THIS TIME EVEN WHITE FOLKS GET FREED

Like Spartacus, I began life inauspiciously. A commoner and technically a slave. I was born into a system that had already set the stage for me to be a victim, and the system expected me to accommodate that future.

The offspring of a drug dependent father who was a continual resident of the penal system, and a mother who died young, I wasn't supposed to even consider the American Dream.

Because of my mother's death, I was raised by my grandparents—a condition too many children of all ethnicities endure due to unfortunate parental circumstances; however in my case, it was truly a gift from God.

With that break, like Spartacus I managed to escape my first enslavement. The exposure I got to the life of the wealthy when my grandparents moved to a small Central Texas to work as caretakers for a very wealthy family would prove to enhance my training as a warrior. It was at that point I was taught to visualize the lies I would later be sold.

My catharsis didn't happen overnight. It took years for me to strengthen my resolve in the battles I was to face later in life. So I honed my fighting skills with the spirit of Spartacus at my side. And like Spartacus, I am now leading a slave revolt.

***

As the Eviction 2010 loomed, Obama went back to mama's milk, the black youth, having rapper B.o.B emcee his Gen44 party. That event and an article by a friend of mine, Aaron Proctor got me and my protégé KJ Adan thinking about the Tea Party, the Gadsden flag, and rap music in a different light.

In the article, Proctor wondered why a teacher would indoctrinate her students to think that the Gadsden Flag was a white power symbol, and of course a symbol of the Tea Party movement. I've attended more Tea Parties than the white chick who wrote the article, and I have yet to meet a racist. Years ago I had a run-in at a bar with three neo-Nazis, and they didn't have any tattoos of the Gadsden Flag on their bodies—at least where I could see. So why would a unionized white woman want to put the Gadsden Flag on "front street?"

As I pondered how to respond to this, I concluded that one of America's nouveau riche provide the best answer to this, as one such group speaks on this subject often and eloquently: Black rappers.

Black rappers aren't Conservative, right?! Wrong.

Black rappers may front some tired political nonsense off the mic; however when performing for the media—on the mic—their lyrics scream fiscal Conservative values. In fact, nobody on the planet is more capitalist than a successful rapper, or wannabe capitalist than a not so successful rapper. It may surprise you to learn that rappers are passionate capitalists and pro-freedom.

2 Live Crew was the first rap group to show their support of the First Amendment. When their song "Me so Horny, Me love You Long Time" was an embattled anthem of Leftist morality, 2 Live Crew fought tooth and nail for their First Amendment rights. They won, and freedom of speech was upheld for artists of varying degrees for years to come.

Further rap is rife with free market, capitalist values, as explained by 50 Cent in his rhyme In Da Club:

"My flow, my show, brought me the dough...that bought me all my fancy things. My crib, my cars, my pools, my jewels."

Note the effective use of "my." Fiddy is clear: It was not the government who brought him his stuff. It was Fiddy who did this for himself. Not only is Fiddy proud of what he's earned, he wants to keep it and doesn't cotton to ridiculous Liberal jealousy, as further expresses In Da Club:

"You mad? I thought that you'd be happy I made it. I'm that cat by the bar toastin' to the good life. You that fakin' [bleep] nigga tryin' to pull me back, right?"

And Fiddy isn't the only rapper preaching Capitalism. How about the ultimate "I'm not a businessman, I'm a business man," Jay Z? Worth nearly $1 billion, Jay Z reeks of Capitalism and free market values. And from Diamonds of Sierra Leone (remix) with Kanye West, Jay Z exposes that he was a fan on the "trickle-down" theory of Reaganomics:

"And even if I die, he's in my will somewhere, so he can just kick back and chill somewhere. Oh yeah, he don't even have to write rhymes. The dynasty, like my money, lasts three lifetimes."

Public Enemy espouses Conservative values, or one of their more notable members Flava Flav certainly does. In "I Can't Do Nuthin' For Ya Man," Flav clearly doesn't care for the welfare state, at least when it comes to his money:

"I can't do nuthin' for ya, man. You want six dollars for what? I can't do nuthin' for ya man. Yo, man, kiss my butt. I can't do nuthin' for you man. I'm busy tryin' to do for me."

When Public Enemy discourages the gimme gimme lifestyle of the welfare state, nobody can say rap is a Liberal art form.

Del the Funkee Homosapien says in his rap, "Memory Loss":

"I got my own complications. The government shoot us rations. Plantations is manned labor for five bucks for hourly intervals…Don't think I'm livin' that dream, when the IRS repossess most of your cream."

It's a shame that most Conservatives have no idea how to market the message that is already in the black communities, a message that is permeating all segments of youth in America. That message is the Conservative message.

Liberals are also quick to take a symbol of the Right, in this case the Gadsden Flag, and make it about racism. Fiscally speaking, rap is in line with

Tea Party ideals and the Gadsden Flag should be visibly tattooed on most rappers' chiseled biceps.

Liberals prefer that black kids and poor kids simply dream of the "gangsta" lifestyle that much of rap promotes, and not focus on the less obvious message, that working hard for what you get; what you earn is yours. That's a lesson government should heed.

Don't expect rappers to begin performing at Tea Parties anytime soon, notable exception being my friend and protégé David Saucedo—a Conservative rapper, based in Waco, TX.

"Govament taking all yo dimes, grandma dyin' before her time, 'cuz the government wants to control her care, then challenge the citizens who would care to…make some noise, Tea Party people!"

Rap clearly encourages reward for hard work and keeping what you earn. Rap simply restates what black people have said in rhyme of lore: "Gimme got his neck broke, messin' with the kin folk!"

So let's get America's rappers a "Don't tread on me" t-shirt and get them to a Tea Party. They'll be among their people. It would be sexy brilliant if Republicans would listen to others among us who believe we can deliver that message.

***

The Republicans were fresh off the Scott Brown win, and they had already begun to crumble. After what had been deemed Obama's loss, he gave the State of the Union speech, finally reaching out to Republicans requesting a meeting. It had only taken a year. Republicans were all wee-wee'd up.

The Republican response to Obama's State of the Union speech, though adequate, lacked passion, and the people's comments were "It was better than Jingals' response, when he gave it."

Obama called this meeting not to get inputs from the Republicans, but to act like he wanted inputs from the Republicans. Obama took a page from The Art of War and attempted to dismiss his loss, and use his opponent's win against them. If Obama really wanted this meeting to occur for the right reasons, he would have done it within his first week of his presidency, not a year after. The Great Uniter essentially told Republicans to go stick their thumbs up their butts, while he legislated left of Lenin. Thankfully the grassroots stepped in to protect the Republicans or Republicans would have rolled over like trained seals. Our job is not finished.

Obama cares about two things: (1) His hide and (2) the destruction of America as we have all known it. Republicans acted as if this were some magical meeting with the messiah. Career politicians, and easily beguiled and hedging their bets... just in case Obama regains his popularity.

Most had already forgotten Scott Brown and were already preparing to "reach across the aisle," but not to choke a Regressive. Well I say, you take the Limbaugh approach[1], and make sure Obama's policies don't work. Because any slight revival is good for Obama, not America. Improvement would only further Obama's Communist agenda.

Obama had just gotten his boney butt kicked in MA by a freaking nude model, and Republicans were lined up to spoon with him. Republicans were dusting off the same old tired ineffective tactics that have been tried over and over, all to impress an America who had already grown weary of Obama and his band of thieves, as well as the lack of true differences between the Parties.

What better time than then was it for Republicans to say, "See, I told you Democrats are this frickin' crazy!" America was tired of professional bureaucrats who have been in government way too long, and who believe the people's seats are their seats.

Due to Republican failings, God had to end Kennedy's reign over MA, and the grassroots had to smoke Dodd. Scott Brown's election was a warning for Liberals too stupid to know the smell of cut grass.

I believe most Americans are like me; tired of backing a group of losers. Losers negotiate, winners gloat. Winners talk in 3rd-person, like boxers who have just kicked the crap out of the loser, long since dispatched to his dressing room or better yet the hospital. No paparazzi for the loser, unless he dies.

Meanwhile the loser's girlfriend stands ringside ready to go home with the winner!

There is a saying, that compromise makes a good umbrella, but a poor roof. The Republicans should not consider compromise with Obama for anything, unless he finds some sanity. He won't.

You don't win in a Liberal enclave like MA and negotiate from a position of compromise. Republicans should have dealth with Obama then and now like political heavyweight champions, showcasing their new championship belt that has at its center Obama's small, well-kicked testicles.

Good speeches do not a successful administration make, as November of 2010 would later prove. Obama still had one foot in the grave and the other on a banana peel. All he needed was a little push. America had rejected Obama's policies, and resoundingly so. The policies that needed to come forward should have been Conservative … period!

Instead, Obama got ObamaCare passed. He had learned nothing after his meeting with the Republicans. Republicans would find out that Obama's words are as empty as a Liberal's skull. Obama needs continual humbling, and the time had come for Republicans to shift tactics; engage in the fight that the grassroots waged over the past couple of years. In case Republicans aren't aware … we're winning!

***

After missing the chance to rub it in the Liberals' faces with Scott Brown, though I'm not sure we can put that victory completely in the "win" column, we geared up for the November mid-terms. Liberals had been warned to take us seriously, and they did. Their only problem was they offered nothing new. The same old meme, e.g. Republicans are racists, the Tea Party is racists, Conservatives are evil. Needless to say, none of it worked, and the Liberals got trounced.

Though this election was a resounding defeat of white Liberals and the policies of Obama, members of the Congressional Black [Progressive and Socialist] Caucus went essentially unscathed. Black people continued to support these government-funded extortionists, despite the destruction these black overseers have wreaked in black neighborhoods. Blacks seem annoyed at the idea that Obama lost ground in the last two years, and the Right was said to be taking the country back.

The Right would argue that they are taking the country back from the socialist policies that have weakened the country, back to the Constitution. Blacks argue differently, saying that Conservatives want to take black people back to slavery, the excuse used by black Democrats to allow ineffective and criminal leaders to be their caretakers. Black Democrats know that the Congressional Black Caucus will continue to fight for handouts, which black Democrats now consider "entitlements." Payback for slavery that no living black has experienced.

What better payback for old slavery than the new and improved version of slavery. At least back in the day slaves knew their Massas personally, and slaves could spit in his food or pee in his drink to get some form of retribution for bad treatment. Today Massa is the government, who lures you in with promises of money for nothing, only to prostitute you, and dare you to run away.

And who would want to run away when everything is an entitlement. Gucci purses, 60" flat screen TVs in their taxpayer-funded, government-gifted homes are all entitlements. For black Democrats the government is supposed to provide food, shelter, clothing, cars (tricked out, of course), cable TV and PlayStations (the in-home babysitters), childcare, healthcare, and of course a check. The only thing left for black Democrats to do is to strategize for what to ask next.

What the government does not have to provide to black Democrats are safe schools, crime-free neighborhoods, adequate education, or jobs. The government also doesn't have to provide real hope.[2]

Thus you have the one stipulation black Democrat leaders impose on their minions, as it is mandated from the higher ups in the Democrat Party: Ask for just enough to get by, but not enough to get over. And that's exactly what blacks get.

Black Democrats are socially conservative, but fiscally communist. That reliance on government has made black Democrats the weakest group of people in America, with no sense of pride. Black Democrat pride has been bought, not by the highest bidder, but by the only bidder—the Democrats.

Based on the results of this election, black Democrat politicians operate "business as usual." In fact, their intent is to double-down on their far Left agenda, evidenced by Keith Ellison's (D-MN)[3] bid to lead the Congressional Progressive Caucus, a group that bragged that they only lost three congressional seats (of their 80 members) in the carnage of Eviction 2010.

Progressives were emboldened by their limited election losses, which is why Obama found himself getting from between the rock and the hard place only to morph into Sisyphus.[4] He knew that America soundly rejected his Progressive policies. Nevertheless, he had to continue to push for these policies, since that is what his most ardent supporters—blacks with their hands out—would demand.

Democrat centrists however will be veering right, like a NASCAR race in Bizarro World. Most had already begun the dramatic move away from Obama's policies, and Obama knew to expect more of the same for the remainder of his 'residency.' Eventually Obama may be forced to abandon his base, as we have already seen evidence of in early 2011. He will leave kicking and screaming, but now that the tarnish under the gold-plate has been revealed, there is no more fascination.

Will Republicans seize on this opportunity and begin to shift black thought to empowerment?" After all, Conservative values are the clear path to black empowerment. Should be an easy sell, right?

Republicans don't have the answer, of this I am sure. I am not really sure if they are even willing to try to reach the black vote. Lord knows I have tried to get them to pay attention to my team's programs,[5] programs that directly impact minority communities both in message and in accountability. Unfortunately, Republicans are all talk, and have been for decades.

It might interest people to know that in a 2008 national opinion poll conducted by the Joint Center for Politics and Economics, 31.3% of black Americans self-identify as conservative and 24.4% as moderate (43.6% self-identify as liberal, .7% DNA).

21% of blacks are in favor of less government. Getting 21% of the black vote would be monumental, however there are those who say, the Republicans really don't need the black vote. They just need to have the Conservative message can resonate with the rest of America, as Reagan did. Have you seen anybody close to Reagan in the Republican ranks?

Notwithstanding, when Republicans win, the cancer of Liberalism is only in remission, it's not excised. In 2008 that cancer came out of remission and infected other cells. Those cells formed into the guy who occupies the oval office, a guy who has no business leading this great country.[6]

Republicans seem to expect black Democrats to just "get it," dismissing years of indoctrination that must be overcome in the black community. As if blacks will suddenly slap the hand that feeds them. Black Democrats often ask, "What has a Republican done for me?" Even if they ignore than the Republicans freed the slaves, carried the first black Congressmen and Senators to power, and overcame vetoes to in every piece of Civil Rights Era legislation to help end systematic racism, they should at least fire back, "What have Democrats done to you?"

For all the talk about how entitlement programs have led to an unsustainable entitlement mentality in the black community, Republicans don't seem to be open change the thinking. Government handouts are no different from drug addiction, and there are a great many programs that work as "social Methadone" to help people kick the habit. Republicans are just as afraid to set up rehab as Democrats.

In addition, the November 2010 election did nothing to change that thinking within the black community, and likely just reinforced the Liberal narrative that white Republicans rejected Obama because he is black. The rejection of Obama could not possibly have anything to do with rising unemployment due to his policies that have demonstratively continued to plaque the black community, and America at large, and the fact that everything he touches turns to Fool's Gold.

I heard one radio show host ask Conservatives not to say, "We are taking the country back," as it could lead to racial tension. Well I say we are taking the country back, and I don't care who gets offended, or what tension is created.

I hope we go back to the 1950's when blacks were considered the most honest, honorable, hard-working people in America. I want to go back to the time, when the black family was the symbol of all that was good about America—functional, though not without its problems.

The 1950s black family raised its children and didn't allow the media or any other outside influences to raise them. They ate as a family, and stressed character and education. They were accountable to each other, and to the communities in which they lived.

Take this country back! Don't allow the fraudulent specter of racism make Conservatives act like losers. Start confronting the racism that exists on the Left. Liberal black leaders condone absentee "baby daddies" and single mothers, and black minions obliged them with their vote, simply because these politicians are black. They are also disingenuous racists, and the worst kind of criminals.

I don't care if black Democrats finally stop supporting the crooks that represent them, though I certainly hope they will. I just care that the rest of America stops enabling black Democrats' victim mentality, and force the same level of American exceptionalism in the black community that we expect in others.

I long for the day, when the mention of something black makes one think of greatness, not inferiority. Let's take the country back to that.

***

But taking the country back is just one "action item." A black guy in his mid-20's named Mike called into a radio show that I was listening to, and he commented that "black people don't hear things the same way whites do." I gathered that what Mike was saying is that black people apparently "hear black."

He opined that blacks don't hear the statement "Take me back to the good ol' days" the same way as whites. Blacks are not nostalgic at all about "the good ol' days", and believe this to be "code" for taking blacks back to the bondage of slavery.

To illustrate his point, Mike said that when he was in the second-grade, he and his classmates had listened to Reagan one evening, and Reagan commented that America should go back to its "glorious past." The next day at school all the black kids were crying, then asked their teacher, "Is Reagan was going to make black people slaves again?"

Neither Mike nor his classmates had ever experienced slavery, so he seemed to go a long way back to consider the good ol' days. And why blame Reagan?

My upbringing was different. I guess I never learned to "hear black." So when I hear of going back to the good ol' days, I think of being a carefree kid and having the loving support of my family. I would get out of school, take the bus home (about 15 miles), where my grandfather was usually waiting to take me and my brother fishing. We would return early evening to clean the fish, and then the handoff occurred to my grandmother who fried the fish in Crisco.

Meal fully prepared, we ate together, saying Grace before the meal. Afterwards, we would usually play dominoes, the TV on in the background for added distraction. After dominoes, we might watch a TV show, or I did my homework.

The next morning my cycle of carefree life began anew with the two mile drive to the gate, where the bus picked me up, and I was off to school.

Education was stressed, so you didn't skip out on school, though I did once. I was as nervous as Janeane Garofalo's gynecologist. I was right to worry, because I was eventually found out, as were my three co-conspirators. Even though all we did was go to the park to "hang out," I got in big trouble, grounded in fact. It seemed the whole town knew about our devious plan. I never skipped school again.

We took road trips as a family, usually going to visit relatives. We always stopped to buy chicken and cokes before ascending on them. Our arrival almost always had the feel of a mini family reunion. Lots of big smiles, hugs, and eventually cards and/or dominoes. We caught up on happenings, and got up to date on the latest gossip, family or otherwise.

Day two of any visit was usually greeted with music and as with most black gatherings, we were there for fellowship "and a barbeque broke out."

Ribs, watermelon, corn-on-the-cob, potato salad, and BBQ beans were mainstays, and orange, red and grape sodas quenched our thirsts. At some point friends and acquaintances joined in, and a pickup football or basketball game might ensue.

If the group was big enough, then somebody would "sport" their car stereo, popping the trunk. The party was official, base-beats loud enough to pop welds.

This scene would repeat itself many times during my childhood. All great memories of the good ol' days. But for many blacks the music stopped, as times changed. I remember when it happened in my family like it was yesterday.

I was around sixteen, and one of my inebriated cousins misheard a statement made by one of our uncles. In her chemically-dependent, mind-altered state she accused our uncle of trying to rip off her father. He hadn't.

Regardless, she threatened to get her pistol, and the hardware from other family members came out of the woodwork. Pistols were being brandished like afro picks. Family members took sides, without even knowing the reason for the conflict.

Amazingly, no shots were fired, but a lot of drunken truths were exposed. The family gatherings had ended. Just like that. In an instant, decades of tradition over. Perhaps this was when I should have begun "hearing black?"

I do still remember the good times, before the black community changed so dramatically. There were no Republican boogeymen around speaking in unintelligible code language, when part of the destruction of my family occurred. There were just a handful of chemically-inspired Democrat-worshipping black folks, "hearing things differently."

I thought to myself when thinking of that young black man's comment, that if you want to create a group of people who are victims, don't teach them about their "glorious past." Just teach them that they are victims, just not victims of themselves, nor are they victims of the real criminals.

Black kids are not being educated about the glorious past of our families and our culture. We just believe that the destruction of the black family is what it is. We don't even think to equate it to Democrat policies that offered blacks the "easy" button.

Because of tepid responses to questions of racism, Republicans miss wonderful opportunities to educate misguided black youngsters to the racism of Democrats. Republicans also miss opportunities to empower other Conservatives, Conservatives who are so thoroughly tired of being called racists.

Black people hear things differently, because Republicans allow them to hear and interpret differently, then essentially revise things as the black community sees fit, usually with the help of a complicit racist system run by the Liberal media and Democrats.

Republicans should embrace discussions of slavery, because these discussions allow Republicans to set the record straight and take blacks back to the good ol' days in proper context. More importantly these discussions allow parallels of Democrats racist tactics of the past to their tactics of today. This parallel showcases how blacks have replaced the old, very real plantation, and dependence on Massa, with the very real plantation of dependence on government.

Republicans should invite all blacks back to the good ol' days, so they can understand the Republicans' commitment to blacks. When that happens, I suggest to you that all of America will begin hearing things the same way... the sexy brilliant American way.

***

If true sexy brilliance is to occur, then it will occur because we are able to tap into the soul of America. If American women are the heart of America, black women are certainly its soul.

Aside from running the household for many white women back in the mid-1900's, black women were the confidantes of the ladies of the house for whom many black women worked as servants, caretakers, nannies, and maids. In these roles black women were privy to and entrusted with the most critical information of the families they served. The white women of yesteryear told our mothers and grandmothers their deepest darkest secrets, things they may not share with anyone, not even their own mothers. Black women were in many cases these women's closest friends and staunchest allies.

I watched this type of relationship develop between my grandmother and Betty Moorman, the matriarch of the family for whom my grandmother worked. That relationship was most evident when Betty's grand-daughter Ramona was killed in a tragic accident on the ranch where I grew up—the ranch that Betty owned.

I recall my grandmother made the phone call to Betty to explain that the welds had failed on the seats mounted on one of the hunting vehicles. Ramona and her boyfriend seated outside, riding essentially on the hood of the vehicle had been run over. The young man was killed instantly, Ramona died shortly thereafter.

Betty flew in on her private jet to the small airstrip outside of Brady, where a sheriff's vehicle waited to bring her to the ranch. I was told that my grandmother held Betty in her arms, comforting her, when Betty whispered to my grandmother, "I don't know what I would do without you. You're my best friend." Those scenarios played out in many homes all across America back then.

Black women of yore taught respect in their homes. Children were raised to understand that the world is watching, so you must behave. We were constantly reminded of those who came before us, like Jesse Owens, Joe Louis, Jackie Robinson, Wilma Rudolph, Althea Gibson, and many other black "firsts." Our decorum was patterned after such black gentlemen and ladies. It started with how one greeted one's elders.

Black women taught black children to show deference to elders no matter their color by calling them Sir or Ma'am. To do so to whites was not to kowtow, but to show them that no matter how they treated us, we will always take the high ground, though many white children called black men and women, boy or girl...or worse.

I recall the first time I heard one of my white friends—age eleven—curse his father for telling him to hurry up. I was amazed that his father hadn't "knocked him into next week,"[7] because I could picture the back of my grandmother's hand approaching my face like a slow-motion dollyshot had I said what my friend said. I assure you that I would have only been able to picture it in my mind's eye, because it would have happened too quickly for me to see the shot with my naked and suddenly swollen eye.

Many black women of that generation raised two families...theirs and the children of the families for whom they worked. Because of this, black women raised many of the white leaders of today, male and female. Black women taught young white children lessons of life, things that white parents were unable to teach them. There was something about white children seeing black women's work ethic that made them listen to our women.

Black women kept their families nuclear. In 1950, 78 percent of black families had two parents (married couple), and only 18 percent were single parent (female householder, no husband present) homes. By 1991, only 48 percent of black families were dual-parent homes, while 46 percent were single mother homes. In the decade since 1991, both statistics have gotten dramatically worse.

Back then black women raised men, not boys. Sons had responsibilities and were accountable, and mothers cautioned against unchaste women. Men picked women who reminded them of their mothers, and with rare exception men knew where all their children were. Men supported their families until the day they died.

Black women of that era taught independence and scoffed at the idea of welfare. They raised young ladies, not promiscuous girls. Education was stressed, and blacks in prison were the exception, not the rule.

Liberals will argue that lives of blacks since the 1950's have improved dramatically, and financially life certainly has improved for blacks. However it had nothing to do with Liberal Democrats; it was due to the policies of Republicans. With Republican policies in place, blacks were headed for what could only be described as a Black Renaissance. The 1950's black person was trusted, and believe it or not, one of the most respected people of the time.

Had blacks not bought into the policies of the Democrats, like FDR and LBJ, I contend that blacks would have proportionate representation in business ownership, home ownership, getting our fair share—and it would be without government handouts or interference, and based on merit.

Had the Democrats not implemented the Raw Deal and the InGrate Society,[8] blacks would not have the worst statistics for high-school dropout rates, college entrance rates, and college graduation rates—all categories in which blacks lead negatively.

The demise of the black community came the same way one puts on weight; one ounce at a time. Democrats accomplished it the same way they have done things for decades, in baby steps. Despite the best efforts of black women, blacks have been lab rats for years in Democrats' social experimentation.

The experiment failed in helping blacks, but then helping blacks was never the intent—the Democrat agenda of tricking generations of blacks was the real intent. Democrats didn't trick all blacks, however. A few of us escaped through holes in the net. Which is why, when I think about America, I get warm and fuzzy feelings about my Democrat-voting, Republican-thinking grandmother. Her legacy indeed represents the soul of America.

***

Somewhere along the line, America has lost its soul. Much of the destruction of the family can be pinned on the rise of radical feminism and their determination to erase gender roles. While Liberals celebrate progress like the commonality in seeing female executives, legislators, and even Supreme Court Justices, that progress has come at the expense of the glue that once held our society together.

The Senate had made it through the interminable first day of confirmation hearings for Elena Kagan, with YouTube highlights of the event second only to Obama's speeches for inducing coma-like trances. The most exciting part of the hearings was not what was being said, but what was being rumored about of Kagan's lesbianism—the legitimacy and significance of such claims denied by Liberal pundits and the Obama administration alike. "Don't Ask, Don't Tell," was the phrase of the day.

Nevertheless, while the Right was in an uproar about Kagan's radical views, like limiting free speech, expanding the authority of the federal government, and banning of the military recruiters from college campuses, it seems that the Left was helpless to keep from wetting themselves in anticipation of confirming the fourth female Supreme Court Justice.

The radical feminazis at the National Organization for Women (NOW) proudly boasted that they would "listen carefully to her answers to determine if she will be a strong guardian of the rights of women."

Even if NOW managed to stay awake long enough to make this determination, their definition of the "rights of women" referred only to the rights of women to change their gender, marry other women, and murder their unborn babies...oh I almost forgot, they want to close that $0.07 per hour wage gap that is so plaguing working women of America.

Not even a century after women were granted the right to vote, the right to freedom has fallen off the radar. NOW and the women who support them need to drop the lighters and bras, and pick up a history book to find out what true feminism is really about, and perhaps learn about women like Harriet Tubman.

If Kagan is to be revered as a strong guardian of the rights of women, then let's put her on the penny and call it a day. In comparison, Harriet Tubman should have her picture the $1000 bill.

Not content to reap the rewards of having escaped enslavement, Tubman returned to help free her family—and hundreds of other slaves.

Kagan's claim to fame? In 2003 she referred to the "Don't Ask, Don't Tell" policy as, "a profound wrong—a moral injustice of the first order." Apparently, being required to show restraint in discussing one's sexuality and romantic dalliances while serving in the military is the modern-day equivalent to being forced to spend a lifetime as someone's property!

Feminists so often refer to housewives as "voluntary slaves" to their husbands and families. Not only do these feminazis have no idea what it takes to be real women, women who extol the virtues of motherhood and family, they have no concept of what it meant to be a slave.

Harriet Tubman maintained her commitment to the abolition of slavery in spite of a $40,000 bounty on her head. Imagine what bravery Kagan would exercise, if there were an inflation-adjusted $5M bounty on her head? Hillary? Jane? Gloria? Madonna? {crickets}

As for these modern-day saviors of womankind, Kagan played softball, Hillary rode the coattails of Bill and she did accept the Margaret Sanger award for exterminating blacks and other mongrel races, Jane burned a bra, Gloria talked big then married a rich man, and Madonna, well she flew over 1,000,000 adoptable black kids to adopt black kids from another continent.

Let's give credit where it's due however. Because of the women's movement STDs are way up, rivaled only by abortions. And teenage girls are much more in touch with their sexuality, as today's 30-year-old grandmother[9] and 44-year old great-grandmother[10] can attest. Generational welfare is eyeballing the horizon, and single mothers are a veritable conveyor belt for filling America's prisons.

Perhaps it's cynical to criticize Kagan on the basis of her acts of heroism being inferior to what Tubman did. Kagan having stood up to the perceived discrimination of the military against homosexuals will go down in the annals of history with D-Day, and The Battle of Midway.

Tubman chose a different route, as she drew arms during the Civil War to become the first woman to lead a military expedition. Let me see, first woman to serve in the military, first black woman to serve in the military, first woman to fight in the military, provided the runway for women's suffrage.

In spite of all of Kagan's impassioned arguments against "Don't Ask, Don't Tell", it seems doubtful that centuries after her death she will have a national holiday named for her. As for Tubman, a full decade before Martin Luther King, Jr. Day was declared, both the House and Senate unanimously passed a resolution designating March 10th—Tubman's birthday—Harriet Tubman Day. That resolution was authorized by George H. W. Bush on Mar 9, 1990, and not at the request of NOW.

It's not even about a case of the left's amnesia of Harriet Tubman's accomplishments. It's a reflection on the short-sightedness of supposedly forward-thinking feminists who see such nobility in Elena Kagan that they would deem her worthy of our nation's highest court. NOW worships Kagan as though her positions, argued for and not fought for, make her a feminist for the ages. The Left refuses to acknowledge the monumental mistake made in choosing our 44th President based on racism, and uses the same warped process to select a Supreme Court Justice.

If feminism is about fundamental equality, a remarkable woman like Harriet Tubman should be the poster child for the movement. The Left's refusal to acknowledge her as such is proof that they value their own radical ideology over the true advancement of freedom for all women. I guess instead of fighting for the soul of America and freeing and people from bondage, Harriet Tubman should have fought for the rights of the LGBT.

Don't expect that to be a lesson in America's history books, but you can expect Kagan to bring sexy brilliance to the Supreme Court.

***

[1] Limbaugh said that he hoped Obama would fail, because Obama's policies are destructive to America.

[2] In the absence of real hope, false hope is fine.

[3] Ellison is one of two Muslims now in Congress, the other being Andre Carson (D-IN)

[4] Pushing the rock up the mountain.

[5] Forever Families helps find inner city kids their forever families as whole sibling units, "Connectors" helps kids grades 4-8 by linking parents, child, and school through a mentor. (See back of book for additional details)

[6] Obama admitted he was not capable of being president, the only smart thing I have ever heard him say.

[7] A favorite saying of my grandmother, when I misbehaved. She never accomplished this, though I was knocked from a Monday to a Wednesday a few times.

[8] My names for The New Deal and The Great Society

[9] Leticia Magee

[10] Delores Davis

10

THE FUNNY SIDE OF RACISM

I arrived in Brady in the 2nd grade. As I mentioned in my book *The BIG Black Lie*, my brother and I went to the "white kids" school, based on where we lived. We were the only two black kids at China Elementary. The other black kids went to South Ward.

I quickly established myself as a good student, and I enjoyed school. As time went on, I would also learn that I was a gifted sprinter. I was very fast. I ran against anybody and everybody, and often outran older kids. I am black, so my running ability should come as no surprise to anybody.

By the 4th grade nobody in the school would race me. If the discussion of running was mentioned, the white kids would just concede the race to me, no running necessary. It was like saying, "*Who would win a fight between Sugar Ray Leonard and Barbara Streisand?*

That same year a new kid named Dale Cole moved to town. Dale and I were instant friends and immediate rivals academically. We battled it out on grades in every class, each of us winning some and losing some. A-plus students both, and as ornery as they come.

One day while we were at recess, Dale said that he thought he could outrun me. What? It was one thing for us to compete in grades, but no white boy was going to outrun me!

To a person, our peers thought Dale had gone mad. Everybody told Dale that he needed to rethink what he had said, and that racing me would get him nothing but embarrassment. There was no talking Dale out of the race, so the race was on.

Dale and I lined up at the side of the school building with a huge entourage. Tomme Friar would be the starter, and Joel Robinette would judge the winner at the other end.

Ready, set, GO! We took off.

It was evident right away that Dale would be no pushover. Ten yards, and that little white dude was in the hunt. Twenty yards and Dale was still there, legs moving like pistons! Thirty yards, still with me. *Holy cow! RUN!* Forty yards, my white friend looked like a white flash! A photo finish.

Joel didn't have to say it. I knew Dale had won, though barely. It didn't matter; I was reeling, as nobody had ever come close to beating me who my age, and Dale had beaten me.

"Let's do it again," I challenged. Dale graciously accepted, likely feeling both vindicated and sympathetic simultaneously.

People around us were still in the shock of Dale having even kept it close, as most weren't sure of the outright winner. I was sure, however. Even if Dale just kept the race close, I lost. But the fact is I had just plain lost.

We raced again and I won, barely. That's when it hit me.

Despite two white parents, and three white brothers…Dale was really *black*!

***

Lord knows that the Fed would have declared Dale black, because the irony of racial profiling in America is that the Federal government is the biggest racial profiler of all. In fact, the Fed is also the biggest, baddest, race-baiter and poverty pimp, even more when Democrats are in power.

If you are counting people, why do you need to know their ethnicity? Unfortunately, the census doesn't have a check box for "Nunyadamnbusiness" on that census form.

The U.S. Census Bureau has thoughtfully provided a Question and Answer center on their website that showcases racial profiling, as they provide a lame excuse for their cleverly disguised yet heinous intent:

Race is key to implementing any number of federal programs and it is critical for the basic research behind numerous policy decisions. States require race data to meet legislative redistricting requirements.

The truth is the Fed must be able to track its Negros, so they can make sure to assign an overseer. That overseer will be one of the black sellouts who is a member of the Congressional Black Caucus. The system is set up so this overseer is easily and repeatedly elected.

Nazis thought "race" was important in implementing their evil plan against the Jews (and other mongrel races). Despite the fact that Nazis got their ideas from none other than Hillary Clinton's idol Margaret Sanger, who wanted to kill black people, our government sees no harm in drawing lines of distinction based on race.

If you are waiting for the Left to showcase their outrage over Americans having to check a box that immediately allows people to draw a conclusion, well don't hold your breath, Blue Boy.

Check "African American" and Bill Maher racially profiles you. Maher thinks black people all live the thug life, and carry weapons that we brandish from under our untucked shirts. Oh, that's right: Maher is supposedly a comedian, so he can impugn black people with no repercussions. It also helps that he is an atheist, non-practicing Jew who is reported to have said he would "schtupe" black women, but has no intention of marrying one.

As I wrote earlier in Chapter 10, Biden believes black men rape our "baby mamas", and never wear a condom. At least Biden does exclude "articulate and clean" blacks from the previously described debauchery.

Check "African American," and Bill Clinton believes you should be getting him coffee. Harry Reid would need to know what area of Africa from which you hail, as Harry has a color test. Once you pass that test, Harry would need to check your dialect and diction. Because as we all know Harry Reid accepts only light-skinned Negros with no Negro dialect.

Your everyday-run-of-the-mill Liberal of course thinks differently for Americans who check the "African-American" box. Given all the social engineering that their ilk has provided to the black community, these Guilters feel nothing but pride for what they have accomplished in the "African-American" community.

Guilters believe that African-Americans represent the core of America's welfare recipients, and have sub-par educations. For Guilters, African-Americans need help, as most have dropped out of high school, and the few who managed to get out of college are products of Affirmative Action. Those few are grateful for the "hand out" plans that allow them to compete with superior whites.

Guilters have their "token African-American friend" they occasionally bring to the cocktail party to feel like they are "giving back to the community."

If you're up for some fun, ask a Guilter, *"Why do I need a special program just for me? Why do I need more protections than anyone else?"* They will stand there befuddled. If they dare speak, it will remind you of the kid you knew who stuttered badly in the 4th grade. I chuckle as these Guilters try to talk in the vernacular, and remind blacks that they have "street cred" simply because they listened to De La Soul in high school, or they still recall a few of the words from Sugar Hill Gang's *Rapper's Delight.*

When they discover that a black person is gainfully employed, graduated from college on scholarship (without Affirmative Action), and that there are black men who can handle our own business, they give that conciliatory "pat pat," and express *"Wow, you have overcome so much. You are amazing. I applaud you,"* but thinking, *"He's like my cat at home, who sorted out how to open the bathroom door all by itself. He's a character."*

The pat pat is how Guilters show affection to things they feel obligated to care for, like their stupid pets. Instead of feeding the cat $10.00/lb organic Vegan cat food, providing a scratching post a pretty collar and a special bed and organic litter, they should just let the cat outside. In a couple of days the cat would scratch off the collar, become self-sufficient, and would ignore the calls for Fluffernutter.

Racial profiling allows the Fed to put people conveniently in cages or categories, dogs here, cats over there. Distemper and rabies shots, tags and microchips, and minorities are ready to be managed, controlled. Blacks are assigned their masters, and the masters are warned to stay in control of their black pets, lest the masters get fined, or in the case of the black politicians, lose their funding. Keep blacks on the plantations, black neighborhoods in echo chambers, watching BET and listening to Tom Joiner.

The Left pretends they are counting blacks to provide services, to ensure fairness, to represent blacks as a group, in order to provide equality for all. The flip side of this equality is segregation, subjugation, and alienation.

It annoys me to be treated like a breed; a husky or a Pomeranian, a Siamese or a tabby, the Fed determining your temperament and breed needs. Not the life for me. So with respect to the racial profiling of the census and all other government forms, I offer this:

Race: *Human.* Nationality: *American.*

***

You be flat illin', if you were to think that in the time of Obama, the DEA would partake in racial profiling. But that is exactly what they are doing with the hiring of people who speak Ebonics. Fashizzle, my Nizzle!

The biggest racial profiler is at it again, this time the Fed is profiling for Ebonics speakers for the DEA. Apparently, the DEA needs to eavesdrop in da hood. This being the case, doesn't this mean that the DEA has been eavesdropping disproportionately in white neighborhoods? There's a new sheriff in town and he's a Negro.

In 1997 the Linguistic Society of America passed a resolution calling Ebonics a form of communication that deserves recognition and study. Characterizations of Ebonics as 'slang,' 'mutant,' 'lazy,' 'defective,' 'ungrammatical' or 'broken English' are incorrect and demeaning.

A language formerly considered lazy a few decades ago is now *en vogue.* To emphasize this, the government needs to hire people too lazy to learn proper English to monitor those too lazy to partake in the legal version American Dream.

In the 1800's Ebonics was spoken by slaves to keep Massa from knowing what the slaves were doing, nefarious things like trying to survive slavery and attempting to learn. Ironically, the re-enslavement of America has slaves repeating history with respect to language, except blacks speak Ebonics for very different reasons these days.

Ebonics speakers are needed, as Democrat policies have led to drug *use* in black communities, thus more drug *sales* in black communities, produces more drug *crimes* in same. These crimes are perpetrated by Ebonics speakers, or so it seems.

Though CNN claims it's not just black folks' phones that are being tapped, conversations intercepted and translated, I'm not so sure. This program will be rolled out in what is described as "the agency's Southeast Region — which includes Atlanta, Georgia; Washington; New Orleans, Louisiana; Miami, Florida; and the Caribbean..."

Let's analyze these areas:

Atlanta, GA – Chocolate City
DC – Chocolate City
New Orleans – Chocolate City
Miami – Caramel Chocolate City
Caribbean – Chocolate Islands

As Jesse Jackson proclaimed while race-baiting the banking crisis, "*They are targeting the blacks and browns.*" I'm inclined to agree, as it appears this new DEA spying program has been gerrymandered. In Florida for example, these new agents are not being deployed in the very white area of *Naples*.

But you can't possibly think that Eric Holder or Obama wants to really crack down on drugs, ergo *crime* in black neighborhoods. Two brothas who would not prosecute Black Panthers?! The man who appointed Van Jones to his Czar network? Cracka *please*! Neither of these light-skinned, metrosexual brothas would run the risk of losing street cred.

This token gesture is just political posturing, and what this administration thinks will be a 'win win.' Liberal blacks who will never abandon Obama will proclaim that he is cleaning up black neighborhoods, creating jobs, providing opportunities, and so on.

However, if a Republican administration were hiring Ebonics agents, these same blacks would be crying foul, and joined in their chorus by every race-baiting Leftist organization in America. The lamestream media would report, *"Racist Republicans Target Black Capitalists with Racist Hiring"*

Leave it to Democrats to promote the use of a useless language to fight a war that can't be won with the current strategy, then to attempt to sell Ebonics as a real language.

Ebonics is creative code that takes elements of English, and synthesizes it, so it is not understood by the mainstream. Like Jazz for example, Ebonics is no longer just "black," but it belongs to all. Ebonics has a sort of poetry to it, as its use of metaphors requires one to think, sometimes deeply. Given that definition, this administration could use some creative types capable of deeper thought. Because as it stands now,

"O and his peeps pitchin' straight game, hella clownin' America. Can't nobody fade them chickenheads, cuz they stone wuck; tryin' to git all of America to catch a ride, and laying a bum beef on the Republicans. Ya feel me?!"[1]

By offering a few select jobs in this niche, the natural consequence will be that blacks will start seeing poor speaking ability as a "skill". What better way to throw blacks a bone and keep them from achieving success on their own than to convince them that failure to learn is a surefire way to get a lucrative government job?

The DEA might hire you, if you speak Ebonics. Just don't try to get hired elsewhere using it, as most people don't find Ebonics sexy brilliant.

***

Racism at the Federal level happens much more than people realize. For example, Michelle Obama compared black children's health to the age old Democrat policies of slavery and Jim Crow laws:

"We are living today in a time where we're decades beyond slavery, we are decades beyond Jim Crow, when one of the greatest risks to our children's future is their own health..."

Then Michelle Obama illuminated an often overlooked aspect of racism by me and the rest of America in this statement:

"African American children are significantly more likely to be obese than are white children. Nearly half of African American children will develop diabetes at some point in their lives. People, that's half of our children."

I think Michelle Obama has a fascination with fat kids. They are a national security threat, and now they may be working undercover to expose hidden racist agendas.

Here I thought racism was when black men intimidating white voters are not prosecuted for obvious voter intimidation, by a black Attorney General, simply because the perpetrators were black? Or that racism had occurred when a black president spoke out (without any facts) on behalf of a black professor behaving badly, and who was given preference over a white cop doing his job.[2]

Michelle Obama goes on to praise the work of the NAACP in stemming the tide of America's racist health policies in this statement:

"And if we don't do something to reverse this trend right now, our kids won't be in any shape to continue the work begun by the founders of this great organization ... "[3]

Michelle Obama neglected to honor by name the true trendsetter for the new NAACP—none other than Jesse Jackson. Jackson has been the torch bearer for the Liberal black community for decades. More recently Jackson reminded non-conforming blacks, *"You can't vote against healthcare and call yourself a black man."*

Another trailblazer, this one white, is Senator Harry Reid (D) Nevada. Reid spearheaded the pursuit of government-run healthcare, as he invoked the race card in this statement:

"When this body was on the verge of guaranteeing equal civil rights to everyone regardless of the color of their skin, some senators resorted to the same filibuster threats that we hear today."

Ironically, one of the senators to which Harry referred was the late great racist and tangential KKK member Senator Byrd (D –WVA).

As it turns out, there is a plausible explanation to this generational crisis of "racism by healthcare" that is being perpetrated on the black community, as Michelle Obama points out here:

"In fact, studies have found that African American children spend an average of nearly six hours a day watching TV — and that every extra hour of TV they watch is associated with the consumption of an additional 167 calories."

Who knew that watching TV was linked to racism? If we follow the bread crumbs we will find that not only is *watching* TV racist, but also the television *itself* is complicit in this conspiracy. A conspiracy of global proportions.

The conspiracy began with the American television manufacturers of the racially charged time of the 1950's. The torch was passed from racist American companies to racist Asian companies like Sony, LG, Samsung, Vizio— now known as Big TV.

Before we tackle Big TV, let's consider yet another racist industry and part of the conspiratorial scheme to fatten up America's poor black children. Michelle Obama explains the racism in the grocery industry:

"For many folks, those nutritious family meals are a thing of the past, because a lot of people today are living in communities without a single grocery store, so they have to take two, three buses, a taxi, walk for miles just to buy a head of lettuce for a salad or to get some fresh fruit for their kids."

The confluence of Big TV and Big Food has led to desperation by America's black children, as FLOTUS points out here:

"… So instead, they wind up grabbing fast food or something from the corner store or the mini-mart — places that have few, if any, healthy options… And we've seen how kids in our communities regularly stop by these stores on their way to school — buying themselves sodas and pop and chips for breakfast. And we've seen how they come right back to those same stores after school to buy their afternoon snack of candy and sugary drinks."

I'm just glad that Michelle Obama put the obesity of black children clearly in the hands of those who deserve the blame. In the America where Michelle Obama can finally for the first time in her adult life be proud, you cannot blame black parents or the Progressive policies for fat black kids. Doing that would make you a racist.

***

If you're wondering where America's FLOTUS got her ideas around racism, look no further than the New NAACP. The New NAACP is a far cry from the former NAACP as, the New NAACP has gone rogue, as in off the deep end.

The NAACP was angered with Hallmark for making a graduation card with a solar system theme that refers to "black holes," saying the card demeans black women.[4] If that wasn't silly enough, the NAACP then declared the Tea Party movement racist. The NAACP seems to find racism all around them, but they can't recognize their *own*. From their own website, the NAACP proclaims:

"…Fromthe ballot box to the classroom, the thousands of dedicated workers, organizers, leaders and members who make up the NAACP continue to fight for social justice for all Americans."

Perhaps we need to check the citizenship of Ken Gladney, the black Conservative who was attacked by the two SEIU thugs. As Big Government showcased in the press conference by the NAACP in St. Louis. Gladney was mocked by the NAACP spokesperson. The organization that "fights for social justice for all Americans" called Gladney an Uncle Tom. Gladney was 'right on color, but wrong on politics.'

Ironically, one of Gladney's attackers was white. So it seems that in the NAACP's Hierarchy of Worth, black Conservatives rate lower than the white thugs who would attack them.

And if that wasn't enough, there seems to be no outcry from the NAACP when the Black Panther voter intimidation case was thrown out by the InJustice Department. Apparently protecting the rights of those colored "whites" is no longer in the purview of the NAACP...the group "fighting [sic] for social justice for all Americans."

Does the NAACP condone the belief of the New Black Panthers spokesperson who said that, "*Crackersare about to be ruled by a black man!*"?

Apparently so are black GOP election officials, as they were threatened, called "race traitors," and told that there would be "hell to pay" when they left the precinct where the intimidation took place. This injustice didn't manage to make the NAACP website.

Neither did comments made by newly exonerated NBPP spokesperson, Minister King Samir Shabazz, the very same Black Panther who was intimidating people at the polling precinct in PA, when he said, "*You want freedom? You're gonna have to kill some crackers! You're gonna have to kill some of they babies.*"

In 2010 we had the NBPP threatening Tea Partiers and getting "ready to rumble." Rumble over what? The Tea Party movement stands for limited government, fiscal responsibility and accountability. The Tea Party movement is about empowerment for all, giving power back to the people; all people. Maybe that's what the NBPP and the NAACP are afraid of?

Despite not a single piece of evidence, the NAACP sells racism about the Tea Party movement to black people, like bootleg DVDs. Says the NAACP:

"*Tea party supporters also have a distorted view of racerelations, the resolution says, citing poll data that found that 25 percent believe that the Obamaadministration's policies favor blacks over whites...*"

If 25 percent believe something, doesn't that mean 75 percent don't? Nevertheless for the NAACP, black people are obviously at the mercy of the 25 percent of Tea Partiers they claim to be the racist minority.

This minority of Tea Party supporters has witnessed Obama's policy of redistribution, his reparations mentality, and they have the nerve to speak out. Here again, speaking out against policy is now racism.

The Congressional Black Caucus called the Tea Party movement racist. There were claims by the CBC that they were spat on, and call "nigger." Allegations remain unsubstantiated, though Andrew Breitbart has offered a six-figure bounty for proof. Breitbart's money is will remain as chaste as Whoopi Goldberg's e-Harmony profile.

The real truth is these unsubstantiated racist incidents brought forth by the CBC couldn't draw enough attention the so-called racism of the Tea Party movement. So the NAACP was needed to step in and hopefully escalate to Defcon One. It doesn't matter that there is no proof, because the *lie* is the proof for Liberals.

Going against the Tea Party movement is today's "Bushism." It's the cheap comedian joke, and nirvana for Liberal fundraising. It is unfortunate that a group founded in 1909 by Republicans has degenerated to the level of what the NAACP represents today. They are little more than one of the hierarchical levels of race hustlers, a Ponzi scheme for blacks on other blacks and Guilters. At worst, the NAACP is simply the new and improved KKK. Their new motto: *Blacker and Badder Than Ever.*

***

I guess if black Liberals kill all the Crackas, it will make more room for illegal immigrants. But I contend that the US policy on immigration is indeed *racist*. In the spirit of fair play to the Left, I must right this wrong on behalf of all Africans. I will elucidate the immigration policy of the US.

If you cross the border illegally into the US, you are issued a driver's license, and a social security card. These two documents will allow you participation on America's welfare system, or what is better known as The Immigrant Lotto, and you are an *instant* winner.

The illegal immigrant lotto pays off like a change machine, every time, its only delay is to reload with fresh greenbacks. Every winner gets lots of prizes better known as entitlements.

One such entitlement is a federally subsidized government home. Illegals can rent it or own it, their choice. But why not own? If you fail to pay for it, the Fed will simply keep making the payment for you. The only loser in this part of the lotto is the people who don't qualify for the Federal programs and are those who are funding it.

The next entitlement is illegal immigrants are issued a food credit card, a card that replaced food stamps. The beauty of the credit card is that it is accepted by establishments (bars) who serve food (and liquor), so illegals can now 'get their drink on[5],' without having to convert the old food stamps for cash, then buy liquor at the grocery store. A night out at taxpayer expense. Why stop there however, when you can do what they did in St. Louis (likely elsewhere) which is to buy crack with the cards.

After we feed illegals and get them their fix, they then qualify for a free education, not that immigrants should bother using it. Why even bother with education, when all a good education will get you is headaches?

By getting a good education illegals run the risk of becoming "high earners," thus opting out of the lotto. Let those high achieving, ethical Right-wing weenies go for the gold, while illegals sit on their lazy "culos" watching novellas or *The View* translated in Spanish (SAP) on that new flat screen TV they got from Rent-A-Center with taxpayer dollars.

In the education system there is the Super Lotto, however. If you are an immigrant and could miraculously get into Columbia, then Harvard. If you can fly in under the radar, who knows, you could become president. It's a 300 million-to-one chance that you will receive *that* benny, however.

What the lotto lacks in education bennies, it *more* than makes up for in healthcare. For now, the U.S. still enjoys the distinction of being the best healthcare system in the world. And as an illegal participant, you are treated to the same service as *legal* citizens, without that nagging bill. The "Get out of the Emergency Room Free" card is simply, *"No speaky English!"*

Other lotto goodies include a government subsidized GM car, a cell phone (in case the First Lady happens by), one's own lobbyists in Washington, and the right to protest one's harsh and unfair treatment by America. Finally as a bonus, illegals get to accuse their newly adopted country of imperialism against the immigrant's home country.

The 'Blame America' card: Don't leave home without it.

Add to this the right to vote illegally in America's elections, and you have what is this man's definition of *Utopia…* for *Mexicans.*

African however, should be appalled by this racist policy. Had it not been for my friend and radio producer Dave Perkins, I frankly would have missed this most racist policy of the Fed.

As Dave points out,

"...it's unfair to penalize Africans for the fact that their country is thousands of miles away, in the wrong hemisphere and across the ocean. They didn't ask to be born there. Africans should have the same right to walk across illegally into America that Mexicans have. It's only fair."

I agree. Not to mention, Africa is more than a country, it's a continent. Africa has 53 countries, not counting disputed territories, and there are many ethnicities to take into account, not just Mexicans.

Dave goes on to say,

"Therefore I am calling on Congress to create and fund a fleet of ships whose sole purpose is to sail to both African coasts and pick up anyone who wants to come to the US illegally; feed and clothe them for the voyage, and drop them off just south of Brownsville/McAllen on the eastern Mexican coast. Once there, they will be equipped with backpacks of food and Gatorade and good walking shoes, and they can simply walk across our border just like the Mexicans."

That would just be step one towards correcting this most racist policy against African illegals. And, I have not heard one iota of concern voiced in America about the translation of documents into one of the more than 2000 languages spoken in Africa, even the more prominent languages like Bantu in Angola, or Fon and Yuroba in Benin, Amharic in Ethiopia, Fang, Mbere, Punu, or Sira in Gabon, Darija in Morocco, and so on. Africans are *forced* to learn English!

Until the Democrats implement this or an equivalent solution, I will be calling them anti-African racists. Join me in this sexy brilliant idea.

***

When the government brings all those Africans over to America, they get to experience racism, Biden style. Biden's Tourette-like ramblings are legendary, and are typical of the racist Democrat mentality that I discuss regularly.

A while back when discussing AIDS in the black community, Biden wanted us to know how much he gives back. He commented on how he was, "...*going through the black sections of his town, holding rallies in parks...*" to discuss how black men should not be ashamed to get tested for AIDS.

The idea that even after Biden made this *faux pas*, "Sexy Brilliant" still selected "Sexy Stupid" as his Vice President shows you just how "smart" Obama is. Obama selecting Biden as VP is one of the reasons I invested in Harvard diploma toilet paper.[6]

What struck me is that Biden's town has "black sections" of town—obviously not where his house is. I wonder if blacks can live outside of their designated areas, like they can in Republican towns?

Biden apparently knows that blacks love parks. It's where we sell our drugs *and* our women. So by targeting the parks to do his good deeds, Biden was able to hit many black folks in one swoop. I wonder if he served BBQ chicken and red kool-aid to insure a large gathering of silly Negros.

Once gathered, Biden apparently lectured black men on how to be real men, saying, "...*it's not unmanly to wear a condom.*" My readers should know that based on my grandmother's warning and Biden's sage advice, I am never without clean underwear and have begun wearing a condom at all times...in case I get in a car wreck. I'd hate if paramedics didn't know I'm a man.

Biden's advice to black women was equally profound. Biden informed black women "...*they can say no!*"

First suffrage, now this for black women. Black women no longer have to be raped by black men, perhaps *any* man, thanks to Joe Biden. This revelation reminds me of Reid's comment that wives no longer have to be beaten by their unemployed husbands. Black women might have felt liberated, had they not understood that Biden was telling them to stop gapping their legs for just any ol' dude.

Biden explained that black folks can't help ourselves. According to him, "...*it takes the medical and the white communities' focus*" on black folks to help us out. How could any freedom-loving Democrats expect blacks to help *ourselves*? Not only did Biden insult blacks by saying that we're incapable of knowing any better, he straight-up admitted that he thinks that it's whites who have the power to change the black community. In other words,

"Don't worry about your flaws, Negroes... you can't do any better! It's up to Massa to take better care of you and whip you when you make mistakes so you learn better!"

Finally, Biden put "Barack" on front street, saying they had both been tested for AIDS. How did Biden know this back in 2007? Did they go together like "girls to the bathroom?" The idea of both these men—married for quite some time—would decide to get tested for AIDS did cause me to wonder. When you consider how much time the VP would need to spend with the Prez, and the closeness of the relationship, well I get it. I'm not gay, but "don't ask, don't tell."

Biden's "innocent" comments expose the real racism that the Democrat elite—black and white—feel toward poor blacks. Not a single black Democrat spoke out about this racist statement. This is because, most of the black elites actually agree with Biden. And for the small percentage who don't, they were not willing to call Biden what he is...the most ignorant of racists.

Biden is the most ignorant of racists, because he doesn't even know he *is* one.

But the black racists in the audience, racist against the black poor, and anybody willing to truly help them would not dare call Biden out on his obviously racist and incendiary comments. Calling Biden out could potential ruin the racism gravy train.

Sexy Stupid got a pass.

***

When Harry Reid made his now famous comment about "light-skinned" in reference to Obama's skin color, people thought Harry was Joe Biden's fraternal twin, separated at birth. Harry was just another crazy old white Democrat, and Liberals and Obama quickly forgave him. As it turns out Reid may have been as wise as Aesop, and as prophetic as Nostradamus.

For years white people have been killing themselves to become black, and finally turnabout is fair play: Black and brown people are now killing themselves to become white; uncomfortable with the skin they're in. According to the NY Times:

Dermatologists nationwide are seeing women of Hispanic and African descent, among others, with severe side effects…from the misuse of skin-lightening creams… But many others seek to lighten their entire face or large swatches of their body, a practice common in developing countries as disparate as Senegal, India and the Philippines, where it is promoted as a way to elevate one's social standing.

We have Harry Reid to thank for exposing this racist bias amongst Democrats, but we have Democrats and socialists around the world to thank for exposing the pervasiveness of it all.

Moreover, it is not as if dark-skinned women are imagining a bias, said Dr. Glenn, who is president of the American Sociological Association. "Sociological studies have shown among African-Americans and also Latinos, there's a clear connection between skin color and socioeconomic status. It's not some fantasy. There is prejudice against dark-skinned people, especially women in the so-called marriage market.

At least we know why Alan Keyes had no chance to be president, and even Sharpton and Jackson couldn't pass the color test. Dark chocolate sisters have it worse than chubbies, it would seem.

Apparently all I needed to do to improve my socio-economic status was to stay out of the sun. If I had lived a life of leisure, perhaps I could have done this. It would have limited my interaction with the rest of the world, forcing me to walk around like "bubble boy," or cocooned like those people with the rare condition where even the smallest amount of sun is carcinogenic. For all intents and purposes, getting sun is socio-economically carcinogenic for blacks making the sun somewhat of a racist. *Even the sun conspires to keep brothers down.*

Who knows what I could have achieved had I not grown up in the hot Texas sun and been adopted by Norwegians? I swear I was a very light child growing up, so much so that I actually *wanted* to be darker. I could have "passed," had it not been for my nappy hair.

I recall when my brother and I worked one summer at the ranch where we lived, and we were hired to cut trees in various clearings. That summer was Africa hot, and we worked in the peak of the heat every day, shirtless. I got so dark, that I didn't recognize myself. I peeled for the first time in my life, and panicked not knowing what was happening to me. One of my white friends, Donna Taylor had to tell me what was happening, as I thought I had a dreaded disease. On the blackness scale that summer, I was "Alan Keyes black," which is about 9 out of 10.[8]

All the girls in Jr. High noticed that I was darker, but one actually told me that my color was...*beautiful*. And I must admit, after I finished peeling, I did look healthy and frankly awesome! *Once you go blacker.*

I would never get that dark again, preferring to bounce between a 6 and a 7 versus the 9 I achieved that hot Texas summer. But little did I know the effect it would have during my potential big income producing years.

Now that I am bald, had I kept my lighter visage (about a 3), I might actually be able to pass at this stage in my life. However I have learned—the hard way—that past a certain age, the skin takes on a life of its own. After all, the skin is the biggest organ...and apparently the baddest. My skin has decided that between 6 and 7 is where I shall stay.

If I want to take my life in my own hands, I could pull a Michael Jackson and begin lightening my skin, in Mike's case going from a 6 to a 1. Not much future in that, and it has been linked to pedophilia. Woody Allen is a 1 after all!

Sammy Sosa has gone incog-negro, lighting from an 8 to a 2 on the blackness scale. Some speculate this could be to escape the whole corked bat and steroids incident. Didn't work, we still recognized him. Regardless of the reason, Sosa can do as he wishes, especially since he is rich.

I on the other hand am a slave to my skin. As a black Conservative, one would think that with all the vitriol I take from the Left that I would by now have experimented with these new creams, and I would be as white as Bebe Neuwirth.[9] Yet, here I and other black Conservatives remain, proud of our culture, living in our own skin; daring the sun to shine on us. I guess we will just ride out the rest of our lives happy in the skin we're in.

***

Black Conservatives are not the only people happy in their own skin, as many white people seem comfortable in their skin as well. I was in Las Vegas a while back, and I joked a white friend of mine, referring to "Crackers" during an interview he was doing with me on racism, and the comments by the New Black Panther leader.

My friend gave a surprised laugh, evident to all around that my comment gave him no discomfort whatsoever. Nevertheless, the blatant and open use of the term Cracker these days got me to thinking about Crackers in general. So I decided to perform a quick investigation.

In my investigation, I was surprised at how little I knew about Crackers. Like the sheer number of crackers out there. There are so many Crackers in fact, that I suggest America is made up of nothing but Crackers.

Crackers come in all colors, too. You have your white Crackers, who I call Saltines. Saltines include Germans, Russians, Slavs, many Brits and even some Spaniards. There are very white Crackers called "Gingers," who can only be of Scandinavian descent.

Well-tanned whites in America might be considered Ritz Crackers, and it is they who based on looks alone could be confused with Graham Crackers, a group that includes Arabs, Hispanics, and even some blacks. Though there is distinction between cookies and crackers for the uninitiated, however that is only for purists. There exists an Oreo Cracker, which refers only to the black Conservative.

As for Cracker origins, you would be hard-pressed to find a pure Cracker. Almost all had some flavoring, and many had nuts and seeds. I shared kosher Crackers at the home of one of my Jewish friends, so Crackers even cross religious lines. And who could forget the Communion Wafer, which we all know ain't nothin' but a Catholic Cracker.

Colleges and urban soirees have Party Crackers, whose origins I learned are from Old English Crackers, ironically served at Tea Parties. Wise Crackers come in all shapes and sizes, and they are not wise at all, but quite irritating. Firecrackers have lots of spunk, and are considered "team players." They usually climb the corporate ladder quickly, because they are hardworking and gregarious. Firecrackers can make people jealous, particularly Union Crackers (Wafers), who usually conspire to keep Firecrackers down.

Town House Crackers are little short guys who live in tree houses. Most of these Crackers are from the Keebler family, and surprisingly accepted by all. The very wealthy Town House Crackers are Club Crackers, but don't get Club Crackers confused with Crackers who just like to go clubbing. Crackers who like to go clubbing should not be confused with the LAPD, who again are just Crackers who like to club Rodney King.

Crackers don't all have to be human, as there are Animal Crackers. Bill Clinton would call Hillary a Nut Cracker, and of course there are just Nutty Crackers like Rosie O'Donnell, Janeane Garofalo, and Mel Gibson.

Liberal blacks will say that my white friend's reaction was just a testament of this being a Cracker's world. Moreover as we have learned from Shirley "I'm still really a racist" Sherrod, it's a *rich, white* Cracker's world. Liberals constantly ignore that Obama is also half Cracker—African Wheat Cracker is my guess. Whatever kind of Cracker you are, my hope is to one day go back to only caring about the content of the Cracker's character.

***

A discussion of Crackers certainly requires a good discussion about being black. One of my friends, Larry and I were discussing exactly that; specifically the definition of being black. Both of us are medium brown in color, and we both possess features associated with people of African descent. So there is little doubt that we are blacks of African descent. However blacks come in all colors and all economic backgrounds, so what really defines black?

Larry explained to me that his ancestry was African, German, and Irish, with the emphasis on African. The stronger African influence is why Larry looks black, but in no way minimizes his other two bloodlines, both of which contribute to him being caramel color and not darker. Nevertheless, even the most intense observer would not readily recognize the German or Irish in him, though it most certainly is there.

As Larry put it, "*White Europeans twice decided to hook up with one of his black female ancestors, and voila...*"

Change anything about Larry's ancestry and he ceases to exist. This makes you wonder, "Is part of one's ethnicity any more or less important to whom you are?" If Larry has even one drop of another ethnicity, he is part of that ethnicity. If you don't believe me, add one drop of urine to a glass of water then tell me what you're drinking.

The majority of the people in America are not 100 percent anything. Yet we are constantly discussing race, particularly Liberals and black Democrats. Black Democrats proffer solidarity when it benefits the collective, using skin color as the binding agent. I have asked many black people to define black for me. The idea that black people behave a certain 'way' is patently ridiculous and insulting given the "being black" unfortunately has a negative connotation.

Because I am a black Conservative, I am constantly having to prove my blackness, and I am 85 percent black,[10] yet Obama is less than 50 percent black and has to prove nothing of his "blackness."[11] Big deal he plays basketball. I *like* basketball; that ought to count for something.

Admittedly I am less interested in basketball these days, but that's mainly because I now live in a city that has no basketball team. I love track and field, especially sprints, a segment dominated by blacks. You'd think that counts for something.

I also love martial arts, though I'm not sure what ethnicity can claim ownership. Martial arts originated in India, though most people erroneously credit the Asians. These days there is a huge Brazilian influence, with the popularity of Jiu Jiutsu, so maybe they can take credit. Some historians have theorized that martial arts were born in Africa.

For the sake of discussion, let's just say that I'm not black, according to "hard core" blacks. My question to them is what's wrong with acting white?

Though I very much enjoy being black, I have seen how white people live —the rich ones that is—and I love it! If acting white means taking family vacations, or sailing in a yacht along the French Riviera, then color my black behind alabaster and call me Ivory.

Rich white people have the money to pay their bills on time, every time. And they don't put their electric bills in their kids' names. Rich white people have cars that run, really nice cars too, covered by good insurance, and not hoop-tees. When a rich white person says he will turn the matter over to his attorney, he really has an attorney to turn the issue over to.

I'd be willing to bet that many more black people would like to act white too. It certainly beats what the Left has convinced America is "the black condition". Honestly, I'm not sure what the "black condition" is. What I do know is interestingly enough, if you show me the black condition, I can show you many non-blacks living it.

White folks get welfare, enjoy basketball, eat lots of fast food, dress "ghetto," and do a lot of other things that racist and ignorant Liberals consider "acting black." Black folks can't have anything apparently as our own, including poverty.

The idea that people identify by color is as imbecilic as rallying behind height or weight. Why not find solidarity based on shoe size, God gave you that too?

I wonder if Liberals, black people, the Aryan Nation, or the Guilters who vote based on racial lines will ever get this? What they don't seem to understand is there really are no racial lines, just blurry lines.

***

Though I freed myself from the bondage I was born into, I was re-enslaved. It happened when I got my degree and began working for a living. I began to notice how politicians were using me and others like me for their.

Slowly we began to allow insane thought to become the norm. Like the idea that America is racist. That's a crazy idea. How can a country made up of every nationality, religion, and creed be racist? Are there racists in America? Certainly, but they are the exception.

In America there are many more acts of tolerance than racism, yet people seem to want to constantly define us by the minority. I have never witnessed first-hand a race riot in America, and chances are neither have you. There are certainly plenty of opportunities for race riots to occur. Millions of people visit the St. Louis arch where I live, all different nationalities, and do on, and I have yet to see a single melee.

We have sporting events all the time with a very mixed ethnic makeup and everybody generally gets along. There is the occasional riot after a team wins a huge event, like the Super Bowl or a World Series, but those are certainly not race-related. Race is typically only an issue, when politicians want our money. This is because politicians know how to manage their slaves.

When slavery was just in the private sector, a slave owner could free his slaves, but only with permission from the government. The process to free a slave was called manumission, and the laws at the time made it difficult to free a slave. It was done only under extraordinary circumstances.

Manumission allowed a slave to experience freedom, an amazing feeling for somebody who has never had it. The last thing slave-owning Democrats of the time wanted was a bunch of free blacks running around living like free men. Slave owners recognized that freed slaves were bad for the morale of other slaves, because they represented hope; the possibility of changing one's status. Who would want to be a slave, if he tasted freedom, even if only vicariously? Having freedom so dangerously close might make slaves want to leave the plantation.

That is exactly what happened. Freedmen by their mere presence caused other blacks to get the nerve to escape the confines of the plantation. And why not? The Revolutionary War slogan was "Give me liberty or give me death!" Could slaves not apply that same slogan to their plight, lest whites appear hypocritical?

Slavery today confines everybody and is not limited to blacks or the poor. Either you are being taken care of by the government—the lazy slave. Or you work through the end of August to pay your taxes, so the government can redistribute your money—the industrious slave.

Some might argue that the industrious slave is the most ignorant of the two slaves. Regardless the government needs both sets of slaves. They complement one another.

For the lazy slaves who are wards of the government, the government constantly tests what it takes to keep them from wanting to change things, or as LBJ said,

"...just enough to quiet them down, not enough to make a difference."

When this slave gets uppity, the government throws a few more dollars at them and finds the tipping point. When government gangsters need to shove a piece of unwanted legislation down the throat of taxpaying Americans, the non-working slaves must go to work.

These field hands are bused to rallies or other protests, given signs, and asked to create a rancor. The state-run media covers it as if it's the real pulse of America—a warning to the industrious slave. It is this type of logic that has ex-Speaker of the House Nancy Pelosi believing that welfare is stimulus.

That stimulus was paid for by industrious slaves, whom the government constantly tests their threshold of pain. Government will say things like, "We need to raise taxes to 70 percent!" When the industrious slave complains, the government settles on 40 percent which is 5 percent more than the government wanted anyway.

We have finally reached the pivotal point in history, where the industrious slaves are revolting. Rabble-rousers on the Right are attempting to escape slavery, and are trying to bring others with them.

It has been a long slow process that brought America to the point where Liberalism and Progressivism engrained deep-rooted opinions on everything from sexuality to environmentalism to race relations. But the past two plus years has really shown how Liberalism unchecked has the potential to ruin even the greatest country in history. Americans mindlessly dance to a dissonant and severely out of tune melody. The air is so thick that even the rational Right has lost its way and spends most of its time either punching air or standing in the fog, falsely believing they're outside the cloud of confusion.

There is a very real place in the minds of Liberals and it is call Utopia. The occupants of Utopia are Liberals and they are nuttier than squirrel feces. Liberals celebrate things that are antithetical to their own existence. It's a land where protectors are terrorists and pedophiles babysit.

Liberals search for the perfect society, never realizing that human imperfection is the impenetrable barrier to the perfection they seek. The real truth is that Liberals know that Utopia doesn't exist for real, but like Ponce de Leon they pursue the ruse. Fine Eden—just be sure to make no reference to some pesky deity.

Around 1960, Birkenstock/patchouli oil wearing liberals realized that donning suits and ties and infusing the media, pop culture, and education into politics was the best way to transform America. These institutions helped frame the debate by consistently presenting good as evil and evil as good, the motto of Utopia.

The public pays more attention to finding out who is Paris Hilton's BFF, than they do murderers, drug traffickers and illegals streaming over our borders. Requesting identification from an individual eating an ice cream cone is a bigger issue than skulls without bodies rolling like bowling balls across the Mexico border into [insert Mexico/US border state here].

Next strategy, convince the enemy—Conservatives—to turn the guns on themselves. Easy to do if the opponent is a weak-kneed whimperer who spends more time apologizing and looking guilty, than promoting policies that would ensure prosperity and freedom for all Americans. I watch almost daily as contrite Republicans stammer and stutter, explaining and defending themselves instead of recognizing the Liberal ploy and ripping the hoods off the real racists.

Republicans are Lawrence Welk in an *MTV* era, still stuck in the era of *Gunsmoke, Little House on the Prairie,* and *The Waltons,* as Liberals offer up *Jersey Shore* and *The Real Housewives.*

America's youth will eventually find their sanity, that's what happens with age. For minorities, it may take the devastation of the American way of life or at least the drying up of the money pit. Regardless of how these groups arrive in studio, the question is will Republicans have the beats?

The Conservative movement is not nearly as stodgy as we have made it seem. In fact, Conservatives are really quite hip. We just need to prove it. We also need to tell our story, in our own way, in a fresh way. Without that, the government will not offer manumission to any slave.

***

[1] The Obama administration is disingenuous with Americans with respect to race relations. Their policies are counter intuitive, yet they want people to support them. When the policies fail, Obama blames the Republicans. Understand?

[2] Obama blamed MA police in the Professor Gates incident, before Obama had a single fact.

[3] Republicans are the founders of the NAACP, yet there is no mention of "Republican" on the NAACP website.

[4] Who thinks of a woman as a "hole?"

[5] The vernacular for "get drunk."

[6] My stock is up 487% since Jan '09.

[7] I'm sure he knows this because Mrs. Biden takes advantage of her right to say no as often as she can.

[8] Miles Davis is a 10 on the blackness scale, for those who may be wondering.

[9] Bebe Neuwirth is an actress most notable as Lilith, the wife of Frasier, on the show . She is "absolute zero" on color scale.

[10] My maternal grandfather was 50% Cree, and my maternal great grandmother was 50% Navajo.

[11] He did marry Michelle, and attended a black church.

11

REFORM, RECONSTITUTE, AND RECLAIM

Nothing about government service inoculates any person against the temptation for money and power. Government is not just as corruptible as any other enterprise, but is immensely more corruptible. There is no greater power to have than the power to control people. You can literally orchestrate their lives, habits, activities, and then dig into their wallets as deep as you want. Government has the power to ruin dreams and punish those who oppose it.

Having poor people depend on you and rich people fear you is the most powerful feeling in the world, and only government can give you that feeling. Government is not just an incredible source of temptation to bad behavior which is why government employees are far more likely to break the law. In most cases they don't even believe they are breaking the law, because many feel the laws don't apply to them.

Complain all you want about evil greedy businessmen, but private-sector capitalists cannot send the IRS to audit you or send you to prison. Capitalist corporations can't send the EPA to regulate you out of business by cutting off your water supply, nor can they shut you down using the power of

OSHA, or for "national security reasons. Only government can do those things. Human history is pretty much a never-ending tragedy of what those in power do to their adversaries. Government is unquestionably the most ruthless of adversaries.

Aside from being the bully brute, Government is also the least efficient way to solve problems. Government is a bottleneck. Government interrupts the process of commerce or business, taking its cut off the front, middle, and back ends. Cash is removed from the daily flow of the economy, which slows down business and reduces opportunity and jobs. Government can thus cause more of the very problems it pretends to be trying to solve. Then it skims off half or three quarters of the money for its own expenses. While millions of private sectors jobs were lost, government grew 14% in 2009-10, proving that government did virtually nothing for the economy, but there is no argument that government did a lot of damage *to* the economy.

The proven American way is to free business and entrepreneurs to from barriers to success. Do as little harm to them as possible while governing, and consider all government policy by that standard

I do have a few suggestions as to how America can right herself—pun intended.

First Congressmen should have term limits, as term limits offer the best campaign finance reform. You'd be crazy to spend millions of dollars to serve a limited time in Congress. By eliminating the innate advantage of being a career politician, we'd make way for fresh, uncorrupted talent. Nepotism would no longer lead to the threat of dynastic families, since politicians wouldn't be able to stay in the same job their whole lives. Our country would be a lot better off if people weren't given a job just because their daddy was a Rockefeller, a Kennedy, or a Bush. Congressmen should not hold a seat for so long that the seat is named after them, like "Kennedy's seat."

To further de-incentivize making Congress a career choice rather than simply the first step in one's career path, we need to stop rewarding short-term elected officials with lifetime benefits. If *real* public servants—our police, firefighters, and military—have to risk their lives for 20 years to be offered retirement, then it makes no sense to offer up retirement benefits as reimbursement for campaigning expenses and only after a few years of service. If you know of a private industry job where you can get hired for a temporary position, lose your job, and still receive retirement benefits let me know and I'll see you there! Once this current crop of criminals are termed out, the taxpayers can recoup some of our money by never offering those platinum parachutes again.

Congressmen should no longer make more money than what they legislate as the threshold of "rich." Therefore if $115K is where the bar is set, we can save over $42 million per year just by cutting the pay of Senators and Congressmen—who will still be "rich" by their own standards. After all, if they're representing us, their lives should at least somewhat resemble ours. They should take that $115K salary and be thankful it wasn't cut in half to match the national average income.

Politicians with a net worth of more than the rate of exemption of taxes on death benefits should receive no salary or benefits. If you're worth that much, why do you need a paycheck? The current rate of $5M may have Congress re-evaluating what they consider rich, and they certainly wouldn't go back to 2001 levels of $675K for this exemption. Those arbitrary numbers alone should tell you what we are dealing with.

Congressmen and other public servants should not be able to enrich themselves, while in public office, particularly if you are a mega millionaire to begin with. What you enter Congress with is what you leave with, the only additions one's salary with reasonable investment growth. To this same point, Congress must disclose all assets, freeze all accounts, and recuse themselves from any information where there is potential for bias. Not doing so should result in dismissal from Congress, and automatic jail time.

Dianne Feinstein disclosed a net worth of $26M in 2003, and only a few years later she had an estimated worth close to $100M. This kind of gain should be investigated, and most certainly banned. John Kerry is estimated to own between $500K and $1M of AIG stock. This is unacceptable.

The man who can legislate himself wealth, John Kerry voted for the billions that went to bail out AIG, and I suspect his stock will be worth geometrically more in a few years, when he decides to sell, likely based on some inside tip. Kerry's is a prime example of why politicians get involved in supposedly private industry while employed in government: The arrangement is mutually beneficial. Just like with Democrats brought into office by unions, one hand washes the other; favors are returned, and *always* at the taxpayers' expense.

Kerry's behavior is the rule, not the exception in DC. That's how the game gets played. So I say politicians should be banned from owning ANY stock, until at least one term after their term of service ends. Congressmen should also not be able to sit on boards or have charities in their names. These groups do nothing but throw lavish parties honoring the Congressmen, allowing them to support their cronies, mistresses, and boytoys.

No more limos, private jets, or other perks. Who do these people believe they are? The average Congressman rides in a limo in a week than most people will ride in one in a lifetime. Not only do these people receive a fortune from taxpayers, the perks put them in the category of the super rich, which most of them already are. They can use their own money for those perks, not the taxpayers'.

Many of our representatives have staffs the size of small rural towns. Harry Reid is said to have as many as 100 staffers. What does Reid need with a staff that size? Congressmen should get a receptionist, an executive assistant, and a few researchers. Under no circumstances should the staff of a Congressman exceed ten people. Currently these "staffers" are a bunch of 30-something year old wannabe bureaucrats who are the authors of these insidious bills, their jobs political payback at the taxpayer expense. A typical Congressman cost the taxpayers millions of dollars, because in many instances, these same unknown bureaucrats are getting the same perks as their bosses, and I'm not talking about the American taxpayer.

While the economy gives us a record one-in-six American families receiving food stamp benefits and dealing with skyrocketing gas prices and the effects of inflation, we're shelling out billions of dollars in aid to other nations. We race to help countries like Haiti when they have a natural disaster, while American tragedies are largely ignored by the world.

America needs to balance the budget, and the budget must reflect American expenses—and nothing else. We have a maxed out credit card and maxed out banks. We can no longer pay to get the neighbor's car repaired.

Nowhere in our founding documents are we responsible for the well-being of any other country. America has helped other countries because we are a blessed nation, and this is what God would have us do. We don't help in order to improve our standing in the world; we help because it is in our nature. We have earned the right for the world to indulge our lack of help until we get our financial house in order.

As for legislation, no bill should be written that can't be explained to the average citizen. Since our citizens are the product of a dumbed-down education system, this will require Congress to have bills written by Dr. Seuss. So be it. Simpler bills will certainly make it easier for Congressmen to read bills beforehand, another of my requirements. And just like in school, Congressmen should have to pass a quiz on bills, while the world watches them live on C-Span. If a Congressman can't pass the quiz, then he can't vote on the bill.

Simply put, no more bills that have to be passed so we can find out how badly they need to be repealed. Hiding the contents of a bill from the public is bad enough, but the 111th Congress did the equivalent of screwing us with the lights off.

Private sector unions are bad enough, but public unions should be against the law. There is no doubt that Congress does not represent the taxpayer, when it comes to negotiating with unions, so it's two against one. That needs to end.

Any bills passed by Congress should apply to Congress. The threat of death panels and healthcare rationing should strike fear into the hearts of Congressmen like they do average Americans.

The new Congress is planning on a reading of the Constitution before each session, something the Tea Party movement created. The grass roots have undoubtedly established a new pulse in Washington, and groups are continuing their great work by keeping the pressure on.

***

It was the Rick Santelli rant that awakened Americans to the wickedness of government during his now famous soliloquy on Feb 19, 2009. But make no mistake about it, Obama breathed life into what is now the Tea Party movement, and his policies continue to fuel the movement's passion.

The Tea Party gave Obama his first eviction notice early in 2010, but he ignored it. Instead, as the eviction date approached, Obama tried the strategy of saying Republicans had questionable donations. Talk about the pot calling the kettle negro.[1]

Tea Party groups emerged to remind Congress that Congress won't be throwing "keggers," in the taxpayers' house and with taxpayer money. Many Tea Party groups have set up shop in DC to monitor Congress, including the Tea Party Patriots and the Tea Party Express, brainchild of Sal Russo.

The Tea Party Express helped drive the movement, as they took the party to millions of Americans over the past few years, and impacted many elections. They provided constant reminders of what we were fighting for, and were instrumental in getting a few first-time Congressmen to DC.

Tea Party Nation took the Tea Party mainstream hosting one of the first large conferences in Tennessee, and many have followed that model. Tim Phillips, President of Americans for Prosperity has built an amazing grass roots organization, and challenged the social networking of the Left with RightOnline. Mark Kibbe and Dick Armey, the founders of Freedom Works are a powerful force in the grass roots movement, providing training and grass roots support all over the nation, as does American Majority.

Black Conservatives stepped up, particularly groups like African American Conservatives (AACONS), Project 21, ZoNation, and The Conservative Messenger, to name a few. Real black leaders and bloggers and political pundits have garnered much needed recognition, like Mason Weaver, Jesse Lee Peterson, Shamara Riley, Erik Rush, Alfonzo Rachel, Marie Stroughter, and many others.

RightNetwork.com launched and now offers Conservatives a safe haven for the Conservative view on TV, the first direct challenge to Hollywood by the Right in some time. This group wants to prove that Conservatives are funny and hip, too.

The outgrowth of the Tea Party movement engendered the Tea Party Caucus, a group started by Representative and 2012 presidential candidate Michele Bachman. The Tea Party Caucus gave official recognition of the Tea Party movement, something all movements eventually need. The Tea Party hit the big time.

***

When I started this project I wanted this book to be somewhat of a bible to help Republicans find their way. The mission of my team is "To bring youth and diversity to the Conservative movement, educating with humor and satire to put racism and classism where they belong... on the Left."

I just don't see anything that convinces me that the Republicans have any idea how to accomplish this mission without me and the many others I referenced earlier. My contemporaries and I are passionate about that mission, because we don't believe youth and minorities are being taught critical thinking.

I didn't want to write a "How To" book, as it would be boring, and I don't have all the answers either. But I do know that I have good answers to many questions that I get repetitively. Like in *The BIG Black Lie*, I wanted to provide ammunition for readers to challenge their own resolve, and then challenge those who oppose my views. I am open to debate anybody on my views. The Left won't accept because there is more money and notoriety for them to not challenge their thought. Not to mention, if one was to lose a battle of reason, where would one be left?

I wrote this book also to show that though I am a registered Republican, I don't see Republicans as the sole answer, and they may not be the answer at all. To be honest, I'm not all that happy with most of the Republican "insiders," as I find them to be as tedious as Democrats. I have spoken to Republicans who could make careers, yet they succumb to their petty jealousies, and are absorbed in power.

I'm not sure where things went awry for the Republican Party, and frankly I don't care. In politics, like in Alcoholics Anonymous, the first step to recovery is admitting that you have a problem. For too long the GOP has been just as drunk off power as the Democrats, and whenever we weren't looking, they were reaching for another round of earmarks. The establishment within the GOP seems to think that the massive gains in the 2010 election signify that the problem is over. That's like an alcoholic thinking just because the bartender hasn't kicked him out, he can't be drunk.

The Tea Party got the Republicans elected, but there is no love lost. The grass roots cast a big net in the November 2010 election, and caught mostly Liberals. But the Tea Party is still fishing, and the catch of the day is RINO.

The Tea Party is not about political parties, despite what the Left says and feels. The Left should feel that way, because the Tea Party and the Left are at political dipoles for sure, ideological polar opposites. The Tea Party is about those who will honor the Constitution and the will of the people. Eviction 2010 proved that those who honor the Constitution will be fine; others should update their resumes.

The Tea Party will expect Republicans to reward those who are making the voices of the Tea Party heard, voices like Jim DeMint and Michele Bachmann. And though Republicans seem to dismiss the impact of the Republican Renaissance where minorities and women gained prominent roles in politics on the Conservative side, there is still time to play catch up.

Allen West should be a prominent figure within the Republican Party, and in Republican leadership. West earned his stripes in winning election in FL mostly with support of the grass roots. Listen to one speech by West, and you will see that he is not a politician; he is a leader. West can help Republicans change the landscape in the Republican Party and in the black community.

Men like Allen West show our youth that, as Obama would put it, *"We are the ones we've been waiting for."* West represents a black father figure, where unfortunately too many black youths have none. Black youth need Conservative role models like West.

Liberals have preyed on America's fatherless children the same way that gangs have, offering protection they don't need, and raising them to be self-destructive thugs who feel entitled to anything they can steal from others. West's success in life is entirely his own doing. Unlike the children of Liberals like Maxine Waters or Jesse Jackson, West wasn't born into the life of privilege afforded to professional race-baiters. His experiences and natural leadership make him relatable to those who have the most to gain from Conservative values. West is one of a new crop of Republicans who isn't afraid to tell it like it is, whether practicing tough love in the black community, or warning of the dangers of Islam in America.

The Tea Party brought to middle-America's attention that the debt we're piling upon future generations borders on fiscal child abuse. Even so, a majority of people who consider themselves Conservatives are still against cutting funding for entitlement programs like Social Security and Medicare.

There are plenty of cuts to be made before touching those programs. However if it does come to that, we need economic superheroes who are willing to martyr their popularity to see a return to a balanced budget. The new breed of fiscal conservatives like Governor Christie of New Jersey doesn't care if you hate him for his tough love. Christie reminds me of the mom who refuses to buy name-brand Frosted Flakes, even if it means dealing with a tantrum in the cereal aisle.

What makes politicians like these so necessary isn't just the brilliance of their minds or their Alpha personalities. The true Constitutional Conservative is unashamed of his stance on the issues, and that fearlessness is both sexy and brilliant. That bold leadership is what gives many others the strength to stand firm on their beliefs.

The Democrats stopped sending moderates to DC a long time ago, with even those from red states voting far more liberal than their constituents want them to. When the Republican Party gave up its principles and started trying to swoop up the leftover Democrats, they pushed true Conservative and Libertarians out of the party with nowhere to go. I will give the Democrats credit, as their leaders led. Leaders like Reid and Pelosi were true to their agenda, and they marched into war, regardless of the outcome. *That's what elections are for.*

Conservatives need a government of deeds, not words, and people of passion, not panderers. We need those who will act decisively for the Conservative, as if their own personal fortunes were at stake, as if their lives depended on it. What we currently have on both sides of the aisle are people whose lives don't reflect the lives of 99.9 percent of those they supposedly represent.

Politicians seem to have forgotten the great feeling that comes from giving back. When you make a direct positive impact in a person's life, it's euphoric. Politicians today are legislating from on high, and have lost touch with the victories that come from personal interactions. This is why we have so much social experimentation.

People are not an experiment, they are real. Everybody is somebody, and has something to give the world. We just need to help them find their gifts. We have essentially stolen individualism and imagination from our youth and minorities. Sit back and let the government think for you is the Liberal meme.

When Republicans consider how to get the youth or minority vote it usually comes off as disingenuous, and to a degree it is. It's not about the people, it's about the votes. Republicans aren't explaining how liberating it is to think for oneself, to accomplishing something with a hand up and not a handout.

The solution is for Republicans to commit to minority neighborhoods with acts not words. End the age old question by blacks and Latinos of "What has a Republican done for me?" Fire back, "What have Democrats done *to* you?" America is at her most exceptional, when the people are empowered. Such is our greatness. The inspiration that comes from the individual is what socialist and communist countries don't have. Individualism screams silently in China, Cuba, Iran, and so on.

Not so in America. We allow the many voices to be heard, yet the Conservative movement silenced itself in minority communities. Liberals fund ACORN, and we offer nothing to counter them. There are dozens if not hundreds of Conservative groups doing phenomenal things in minority communities, and these groups are bootstrapped for the most part with very little government funding.

The new political climate brought on by the Tea Party movement reminded Americans that we are not extremists. It's okay not to buy into the global warming scam. It's okay not to want to pay to take care of those who refuse to take care of themselves; and it's okay to expect that if your family can manage a budget, that DC should have to as well—in fact, it's normal.

When the Tea Party Caucus and Republicans in general feel the urge to compromise with the Democrats on issues, they need to remember that those who elected them do *not* compromise in our ideals.

There is no compromise with a moral code. Moral relativism convinced an entire generation that responsibility isn't a requirement of adulthood. Don't worry if you can't afford something, that's what credit cards are for. The man you like isn't exactly marriage material? Get on the pill or, better yet, just keep a Planned Parenthood clinic on speed dial in case you need to kill off an inconvenient baby. If abortion isn't really your thing, don't bother trying to find a father for the child, government will make up for your irresponsibility.

Conservatism is compassionate, but it requires passion. I am so proud to live in this time, to fight alongside so many proud and passionate Americans who recognized that we were losing the country we loved. I call us "The Second Greatest Generation," because we are battling an enemy almost as diabolical as our enemies of WWI. I conceded to the Greatest Generation, because it is because of them, we are here to fight. I believe that fighting for what we are passionate about is the true definition of *Sexy Brilliance*.

The End

[1] Obama accepted donations without requiring confirmation of the nation from which they came. Illegal donations given by foreigners exceeded $3M.

12

AFTERWORD

I get called a lot of unflattering things because I admit openly to being a Conservative Republican. Frankly I could care less. I know I'm right, and I won't be told what to say by anybody. I think that by doing so, you die a little every time.

Aside from the individual names I get called, I also get lumped in with what is known as the 'right.' But where there is 'right,' there must be 'left,' such is the universe. Good v evil, tall v short, rich v poor, and so on.

To add to the flavor of the left and right are additional adjectives to describe each. For the right, it is either the Far Right or the Religious Right. In some cases the right is called the Far Right Extreme.

Opposite of them is the Far Left. Given that the Far Right is uber religious, we must presume that the Far Left is uber agnostic, perhaps atheists. The Far Left is not known as the Unreligious Left, though I have heard them called the Lunatic Fringe or the Lunatic Left. You can draw your own conclusions from that moniker.

Nevertheless, if we consider that these two groups as indeed polar opposites, then it's worth considering a world where each side gets its way.

The Religious Right is portrayed as Bible-thumping, gun-toting, racist radicals who believe there is no separation of church and state. They believe that America was founded on Judeo-Christian values. They also want limited government, relying instead on the kindness of their fellow man.

The Religious Right believes in accountability to man, but mainly to a higher power.

Before we learned that American is not a Judeo-Christian nation, there were no school shootings. Workplace shootings were almost unheard of. I can't say for sure, but there sure seem to be a lot more serial killers out there, or certainly shows dedicated to convincing me that I'm right.

I'm my four plus decades, I have seen drug abuse increase, child abuse, spousal abuse, and divorce all increase dramatically. Our prisons are over-loaded. Criminals have gotten smarter, but our children are getting dumber.

I wrote of 30-year old grandmothers and sub-50-year old great grand-mothers. Liberals call their movement "Progressive," yet many live like Neanderthals. I'm sort of a trend guy myself, and the trend isn't looking too good for America, and America has been run socially by Liberals.

In a world run by the Left, atheism trumps belief in God. Everything you will ever be is on Earth, which for most people is a pretty pathetic existence. That alone should make most Liberals take pause. For the Left there is no afterlife, so live it up. There is no need for accountability. Do what you want, as long as it doesn't hurt anybody. If it does, who cares? Steal, kill, lie, do whatever. You have kids, molest them, then prostitute them. Sleep with your best friend's wife or husband, no problem; anything goes.

***

Conservatives are not perfect, I know I'm not. We are human, subject to the same temptations as Liberals. I suggest that the only real thing that sepa-rates most people is their moral code. The problem with Conservatives is that we live by this code, so when we fall short of the Glory of God, it's a big deal. However we cannot allow people to hold that code over our heads. Moreover, it is our duty to pass on that code to our kids and those around us.

In my first book I revealed much about myself, not all flattering. It was a catharsis of sorts to say publicly that I am no big deal. I have my issues; still do. But I work on them continually. I believe that by admitting one's frail-ties, it allows you to begin living the truth. It's God allowing you the chance to be real, as there are plenty of fakes. Once you know yourself, it's possible to give freely. One way I give back is through my work with kids.

I have been on the Advisory Board of the Adoption Exchange of St. Louis for four years. Since joining that organization in a fundraising and advisory role, I have witnessed first-hand what a good family means for America's children. It warms my heart each time we find children their "forever families," particularly since our group helps find families for entire sibling units usually. Keeping kids together is important, and that is one of our missions. My brother and I know all too well how important being adopted by our grandparents proved to be in our lives.

Essentially I want to do for dozens, perhaps hundreds of other kids what the Moorman family did for me, which is to show me a world that I would have only dreamed of. I want these kids to intern with my organization and many others organizations that I and my team support. Because the real way to give back is not through government, it's through individuals.

If you like what I do, please visit my website at www.TheBlack-Sphere.net, and hit that "Support" button.

Thank you for your support in investing in this book. If it was loaned to you, give it back and get your own autographed edition! Then tell 10 other friends to do the same.

13

EXTRAS

THE BIG BLACK LIE

Kevin's first published book, *The BIG Black Lie* is not just another Conservative political book. It's FUNNY!

Readers are treated to an eye-opening journey through the eyes of a black child who had many pressures to succumb to Democrat victimology. Jackson avoided the traps and explains how he avoided them, and how society uses race as a weapon.

Jackson exposes the widely overlooked history of Democrat racism—past and present—and challenges Conservatives and Republicans to stop addressing Democrat tactics in the same old ways. It's time to educate with satire and humor, poking fun at the Left.

The BIG Black Lie is a great book for parents, as it explains life through the eyes of a child that society would expect to fail. In *The BIG Black Lie* Kevin teaches parents how far their influence extends to their children, and it teaches children that there are no barriers to sucess. *The BIG Black Lie* provides enough laughs to be listed in the "Comedy" section of the book store or library. Readers will become empowered by *The BIG Black Lie*, and they will find it a truly enjoyable read.

***

"Kevin tells an honest heart-wrenching story that most of us can unfortunately related to. This is a must read for every person who grew up without a father and for those who were fortunate enough to grow up with a loving father." – **Rev. Wayne Perryman, Theologian, author of *Unfounded Loyalty***

"Kevin's book shows first hand that no one ever has a reason for being a perpetual victim. His raw, revealing, honest story about his father and upbringing only reaffirms that regardless of your circumstances, one can still find a foundation of values and virtues in their lives, that can assure them success in all walks of life. This should be a must read for all high schools and libraries." – **Armstrong Williams, Conservative Political Pundit, Columnist, and Radio Show Host**

To purchase Kevin's books in bulk, please contact
melissal@theblacksphere.net.

KEVIN'S BIO

Kevin Jackson is a nationally recognized rising star among young conservative thinkers and writers, political commentators, a **Fellow at the Robert J. Dole Institute of Politics**. A sought-after speaker, Kevin is a rare blend of street smarts, common sense, with the academic credentials to back it all up.

He has spoken along side of Judge Andrew Napolitano, Newt Gingrich, Andrew Breitbart, Sarah Palin, and Michelle Bachman, Herman Cain, and the list goes on. In his speeches, Kevin interweaves years of business acumen and personal experiences with the politics of the day with notable comedic flair. This is why he often appears as a guest on Fox News Channel (*Glenn Beck*, *The O'Reilly Factor*, *Your World With Neil Cavuto*), MSNBC, and is a regular guest on Fox News radio with John Gibson.

His peers call him the "valedictorian of the graduating class of political pundits," and a producer of the O'Reilly Factor said, *"Kevin will be one of the most powerful political pundit in the coming years."*

Kevin is a syndicated writer for Taki's Magazine [www.TakiMag.com], and his other written work appears regularly on *Human Events*, *The American Thinker*, *Big Government*, and others. His blog The Black Sphere is discussed almost daily in publi-

cations like *Canadian Free Press*, the *New York Times*, and many others, and his work has been and featured on Hannity (radio), The Laura Ingraham Show, as well as the Holy Grail of Conservative radio, Rush Limbaugh.

Kevin is a former Management Consultant to some of the world's largest corporations, and earned his Bachelor of Science degree in Electrical Engineering, as well as degrees in Computer Science and Mathematics from

Southern Methodist University. He owned his own Manufacturer's Representative agency in Texas and served as the Vice President of Sales and Marketing for a Dallas-based technology firm. Kevin has been part of the management team for various Management Consulting firms before leaving corporate America in 2009 to go on his current mission.

To book Kevin to speak at your next event, please contact
publicist@theblacksphere.net.

THE BLACK SPHERE UNIVERSITY
The Black Sphere University presents training sessions on race and culture, as well as political activism that is much like the Comedy Defensive Driving of politics.

Be sure to learn how to get Liberals rethinking their psychosis with the political comedy stylings of The Black Sphere training program.

Example modules are as follows:

❋ Politicians: Wits of the Nit Kind
❋ If America is so Evil, Why Does Everybody Want to Be Here?
❋ So You Think You Learned History...ROFL

Learn how to dispel the socio-political myths and have fun while doing it.

Contact theblacksphere@gmail.com for more information.

MANAGEMENT CONSULTING

Years of Sales and Management Consulting success has positioned Kevin as a true resource for companies wanting to grow. Kevin has a knack for predicting the next wave, whether it's technological, political or otherwise, so you want him on your team.

The landscape of business changes periodically, so make sure that you are seeing what lies ahead for your company. You need an experienced business professional with a firm understanding of the political climate to help you navigate minefield.

For more information, contact
theblacksphere@gmail.com.

Published by FastPencil
http://www.fastpencil.com